MEN DESIRING MEN

Kritik: German Literary Theory and Cultural Studies

Liliane Weissberg, Editor

A complete listing of the books in this series can be found at the back of this volume.

M E N
desiring
M E N

THE POETRY OF
SAME-SEX IDENTITY AND DESIRE
IN GERMAN CLASSICISM

SUSAN E. GUSTAFSON

Wayne State University Press   Detroit

Library of Congress Cataloging-in-Publication Data

Gustafson, Susan E.
    Men desiring men : the poetry of same-sex identity and desire in
German classicism / Susan E. Gustafson.
        p. cm.—(Kritik)
    Includes bibliographical references and index.
        ISBN 0-8143-3029-0 (alk. paper)
    1. German literature—18th century—History and criticism.
2. German literature—19th century—History and criticism.
3. Classicism—Germany. 4. Homosexuality, Male, in literature.
I. Title. II. Kritik (Detroit, Mich.)
PT313 .G87 2002
830.9'353—dc21   2001007849

Contents

Acknowledgments

I would like to thank the family, friends, and colleagues who have made this project a reality. Without their support this book would never have come to be. First, I want to acknowledge Betty Gustafson, Dave Gustafson, Steve Gustafson, B.J. Larson, and Tim Gustafson for their patience and interest and for being family in the very best of ways. Numerous friends have shared not only their expertise, but have also helped me to balance life and work throughout this process. For that I would like to thank Marlies Wendorf, Richard Fasse, Jean Douthwright, Eve Moore, Jonathan Rich, Bonnie Abrams-Rich, Lisa Cartwright, Tom Lightfoot, Martha Lightfoot, and Rosemary Kegl. I am thankful to Eve Moore in particular for many discussions about Goethe, the eighteenth century, and German Studies in general. I am particularly grateful to Joanne Bernardi for countless academic conversations and encouraging words. I am indebted to Tom DiPiero for innumerable discussions about theory and the eighteenth century and for his constant encouragement. I am especially thankful to Sharon Willis for her enthusiasm, her critical insights, and her limitless intellectual generosity. Thanks to Tom and Sharon for reading and commenting on various portions of this book in its earlier forms. Many of my colleagues in Modern Languages and Cultures, in Women's Studies at the University of Rochester, and in academia in general have inspired me with their own work and have offered me invaluable scholarly advice: Helmut Schneider, Richard Schade, Sander Gilman, Stephanie Hammer, Simon Richter, Gail Hart, Randall Halle, John Michael, Robert ter Horst, and Grace Seiberling. A special thanks to Alice Kuzniar, whose work and friendship have been both inspiring and formative. I am also indebted to Liliane Weissberg for her support of this project, of so many other projects, and of my career in general for so many years. I am grateful to the University of Rochester for the 1998–99 sabbatical and for the generous research support that have afforded me the invaluable time and resources to write this book. Without consistent institutional support such research would be impossible. These acknowledgments would not be complete without mention of the research assistants who have helped me over the years: James Babington, Lisa Peters, Rachael Brister, and Christen Roberts. A special thanks to Christen Roberts for helping me prepare the final manuscript for the press as the deadline loomed ahead. I would also like to thank Wayne State University Press, editors Jennifer Baise and Nancy Dziedzic, and Arthur Evans in particular for the professional production of this book and for the excellent readers they procured for it. I am especially thankful to the readers whose insightful comments assisted me in isolating those portions of the text in need of more precise formulation. I am grateful to Camden House Press for permission to reprint a portion of the article "From Werther to Amazons" in the fourth chapter and to Stanford University Press for allowing me to reprint "Male Desire in Goethe's *Götz von Berlichingen*" in modified form in chapters three and four. My greatest debts, finally, are to Gary and Xeni Gustafson. Thanks to you both for giving my life and work meaning.

chapter 1

SEARCHING FOR SIGNS OF
SAME-SEX IDENTITY AND DESIRE
IN EIGHTEENTH- AND EARLY
NINETEENTH-CENTURY EUROPE

How did men who desired men express themselves in the eighteenth and early nineteenth
centuries? Were they interested in expressing their own sentiments
and identities? Were they simply defined by the discourses of sodomy
that prevailed at the time? Did they merely accept the languages of
condemnation and excoriation so prevalent in their era? Or did they
strive to create languages affirming the naturalness and legitimacy
of their sexual sentiments or practices? Might it be that some men
who desired men consciously strove to create their own language of
self and same-sex identity and desire?[1] It is precisely these questions
that have informed my study of the political and aesthetic project
that we refer to as German Classicism. Over the years it has become
clear to me that several major male figures of the German Classical
tradition, including Goethe, Winckelmann, and Moritz, struggled
consciously and systematically to create a new language to express
their own senses of same-sex desire, identity, and community. In
their letters, aesthetic writings, and literary production, these German Classicists struggled to define, name, and express themselves as
men desiring men. These men (and many of the men they depicted
in their works) came to a sense of self through the revelation of their

desires to other men. In voicing their same-sex desires they began to conceive of themselves and their identities as inextricably connected to their desires. In essence, their same-sex desire defined them. And beyond the expression of their same-sex desires, these men endeavored to outline both the character and the genesis of their sense of identity as men who desired men. In fact, their aesthetic and literary aims were intricately joined with their desire to create a language of their own same-sex desiring selves and their same-sex identities, and to facilitate the conceptual emergence of a male self who desired men. We find, therefore, throughout their work discussions and demonstrations of the processes and techniques they developed in order to articulate their same-sex desires, identities, and the sense of community that follows from them. Above all, these men were engaged in a poetic project of self-fashioning. Their task was explicitly to articulate their own identities. As we shall see, Goethe, Winckelmann, and Moritz not only strove to express themselves in a new language of the same-sex desiring self, but they considered their project in terms of the philosophical delineation of a same-sex identified "self" in language/discourse. They realized that self and metaphor, the self in language, and self-fashioning in and through language are inextricably conjoined linguistic realities. And for that reason, the self-fashioning self, for them, is always one in and of language.

Throughout this study, I will be interested principally in tracing the development, lineage, and genealogy of this new language of same-sex self-fashioning from Winckelmann's letters, through Goethe's literary production, to Moritz's famous psychological novel *Anton Reiser*. Because Goethe's work is so systematic and because the evocation of a new language of self and same-sex desire is so prevalent in it, I will focus on his reception of Winckelmann's language of self-fashioning. In order to trace how this language survives beyond Goethe, I will turn finally to Moritz's appropriations of Goethe's expressions of men desiring men and in the epilogue to Thomas Mann's reiteration of the same tropes of poetic self-affirmation in *Death in Venice*. As we shall see, in each case these men underscored the fact that fashioning and promoting a self-affirming poetic *language* (a network of metaphors signifying a same-sex desiring self) was of paramount importance to them. Thomas Mann reiterated this German Classical fascination with the convergence of same-sex sentiment and identity in metaphor and poetry in *Death in Venice* quite succinctly when he stated that "Eros is in the word." It will be the task of this study to trace out not only how these men conceived of a same-sex Eros in the word, but also how they lent to their own sentiments linguistic and symbolic forms in an attempt to bring their own Eros into poetic and/or metaphoric expression.

Winckelmann's, Goethe's, and Moritz's languages of self–fashioning do not, of course, operate in isolation. On the one hand, they were languages of resistance within a network of languages condemning same-sex activity in the eighteenth and early nineteenth centuries. On the other hand, they were languages evolving within the contours of an emerging and formative discourse of German Classical aesthetics—an aesthetics deeply indebted to notions of "Greek love." We can only fully appreciate the significance of Winckelmann's, Goethe's, and Moritz's new poetic/aesthetic languages of male same-sex desire, identity, and community in the context of the era's prevailing discourses on same-sex activity and desire.

Situating a German Classical language of same-sex desire and identity within a broad eighteenth- and early nineteenth-century European context of identity formation and desire is inconceivable outside of current scholarly controversies over the inception of modern notions of sexual identity. Foucault's resonating insistence in his *History of Sexuality* upon the late nineteenth-century emergence of a "homosexual identity" has incited and influenced a plethora of academic studies of emerging conceptions of sexuality in the eighteenth and nineteenth centuries. His juxtaposition of new formations of sexual identity in scientific, medical, and psychoanalytic discourses at the end of the nineteenth century to the categorization of acts of sodomy in earlier centuries has come to constitute the defining parameters of inquiry for many scholars. This is particularly true for those examining the explosion of discourses in the nineteenth century and beyond.[2] At the same time, Foucauldian studies that concentrate on institutional definitions of "an homosexual identity" and "sodomitical activities" make one question whether these analyses fully address the complexities of eighteenth- and early nineteenth-century expressions of same-sex desire and identity. In other words, is the division Foucault suggests between ages of "sodomy" and those of "identity" so simple? And are same-sex desires and identities only defined within such discourses? In order to answer these questions sufficiently, it makes sense to review several major currents of thought on eighteenth-century conceptions of sodomy, "homosexuality,"[3] and same-sex desire to illuminate more precisely some of the gaps, correspondences, distinctions, and refinements that Foucault's work both encourages and glosses over. I do not propose here to provide a comprehensive review and analysis of the vast amount of research conducted to date on sexuality in the eighteenth century. I am interested in mapping out briefly some of the major currents of research on same-sex desire in the eighteenth century as they relate to the incitement of discourses and identity formations isolated by Foucault as the critical shift marking the later nineteenth century. In this manner, I hope to show how the language of self and desire that Goethe, Winckelmann, and Moritz produced challenges Foucault's assumption that something like "an homosexual identity" emerges for the first time in later nineteenth-century institutional discourses.

But before turning our attention to the network of specific discourses on sexuality and desire that we find in the eighteenth and early nineteenth centuries, it is important to note that this study diverges significantly from many Foucauldian analyses. First and foremost, I concentrate on the development of an aesthetic language of same-sex self-affirmation and self-fashioning. In contrast, Foucauldian analyses typically emphasize the ways in which discourses (languages of disciplines and institutions such as medicine and psychoanalysis) construct an object about which they speak. My objective will be to examine how men who desired men in eighteenth- and early nineteenth-century Germany spoke about themselves. Scholarship on emerging conceptions of same-sex identity and desire has focused predominantly (in following Foucault) on how social institutions define, investigate, categorize, and form an identity for a particular group of individuals (homosexuals, madmen, or criminals, for example). This study will focus on the ways in which men desiring men fashioned their own language of desire and senses of identity. While for Foucault the "homosexual identity" reserved for the later nineteenth century was an identity imposed on the self by prevailing social institutions, this study focuses on how several subjects in the eighteenth century strove to construct their own identities and to express their own desires. We will trace how they defined themselves, how they identified themselves and perceived their identities as contingent upon their same-sex desires, and how they lent themselves a particular morphology, i.e., how they saw themselves with a specific kind of childhood, history, character, and desire. These are selves who understood and fashioned themselves within the convergence of language/metaphor, same-sex desire, and explicit notions of self-fashioning. Although eighteenth-century scholarship has provided evidence of shifts in linguistic and conceptual formations in regard to same-sex desire, much less attention has been devoted to any incitements to linguistic or poetic expressions of that desire. Little attention has been devoted to re-conceptualizations of the self in the eighteenth and early nineteenth centuries as they relate to new expressions of same-sex desire or to the beginnings of same-sex identity formations.

This does not mean, of course, that the study of institutional discourses (and particularly those of sodomy and same-sex activity) is not useful for our understanding of eighteenth-century constructions of same-sex sexual activity and desire. Quite the contrary—we need to look at emerging same-sex identities and desires in multiple representations in order to fully grasp their importance and implications for emerging conceptions of same-sex desire and identity in the eighteenth and early nineteenth centuries. Indeed, any specific discourse is only fully comprehensible within the context of other, and sometimes contradictory, languages and conceptions. In order to fully understand the significance of Goethe's, Winckelmann's, and Moritz's language of self-expression and self-fashioning it is imperative to review the prevailing discourses of family, of the condemnation of same-sex sexual activity, and of the general designation of same-sex desire in the eighteenth and early nineteenth centuries. All of these discourses work to enhance, suppress, correct, and/or expand one another in a dynamic network of interaction. With this in mind, it makes sense to turn our attention first to general eighteenth-century discourses of sexuality.

As Foucault suggested in his *History of Sexuality*, the eighteenth century incited a veritable whirlwind of discourses inaugurating modern notions of (hetero-) sexuality and the family. This incitement to talk about sex began as early as the sixteenth century (*History of Sexuality*, 12) and culminated in the eighteenth century in a "discursive ferment that gathered momentum from the eighteenth century onward" (*History of Sexuality*, 18). In particular, with the institutionalization of public and private spheres and the bourgeois familial structure, discourses of sexuality and domesticity accentuated the purported necessity and naturalness of what we would call today the heterosexually based family.[4] As eighteenth-century scholarship has amply demonstrated, the family became inextricably associated with social order and was perceived as the very cornerstone of civilized society. At the same time, literature on family and familial sexuality proliferated throughout Europe. In Germany, for example, a flood of texts devoted to sexual subjects appeared. In fact, by the end of the century the *Ehestandsalmanach* (*Almanac of the Marital Estate*) listed 1,201 titles on sexual topics (Hull, 229).

Accordingly, Thomas Laqueur (*Making Sex*) has demonstrated that the predominant discourse of the eighteenth century was that surrounding the sexual difference necessary to bolster new conceptions about families and the gendered roles essential to them. The understanding of the day held that there were two stable, incommensurable, and opposite sexes that by their very "nature" determined the separate, gendered roles of men and women. Attraction between members of opposite sexes was considered thoroughly and exclusively natural because, as Rousseau had phrased it so concisely in his wildly popular *Emile*: "One sex is attracted by the other; that is the movement of nature" (*Emile*, 214). Moreover, it is precisely the innate sexual differences between men and women that determine their "moral nature" and their place in the social order (*Emile*, 357–58). Biology—that is, the assumption of stable, natural, ahistorical bodies (male and female)—came to be understood as a prescriptive determinant in the cultural order. The woman's body became the biological justification for the social status of women. One only has to remember Antoine-Léonard Thomas's *Essay on Character, Morals, and the Mind of Women in Different Centuries* (1772), in which the hysteria of woman, her wild imagination, and the violence of her impulses are attributed to that "peculiar female organ":

> Woman bears within her an organ capable of the most terrible spasms, one that controls her completely and excites phantoms of every kind in her imagination. In her hysterical frenzy, she can return to the past or leap into the future; all times can become the present to her at such moments. And it is from the organ peculiar to her sex that all her extraordinary ideas arise.[5]

The eighteenth century was intensely concerned with discursive matters we would refer to today as "heterosexual" and "domestic." Of principle concern were the domestication of women, the establishment of the modern nuclear family, and "with laying down the principles of 'normality'" (Hull, *Sexuality, State,* 258).[6] In fact, this concentration is marked at least in part by the rather pronounced lack of interest in legislation addressing nonreproductive sexual activities. In Germany a plethora of laws and revisions of ordinances focused on adultery, fornication, and premature coitus (Hull, 75–76). Similarly, in France the monarchy specifically condemned extramarital sexual acts including masturbation, bestiality, prostitution, adultery, and bigamy (Merrick, 172). Intriguingly, one finds very little evidence of prosecution and punishment for sodomitical transgressions in the eighteenth century.[7] Marriage, the nuclear family, and its fundamental importance to the prevailing social order were the most intense sites of judicial activity. As Foucault avers, the norms of sexuality were defined, delimited, and legislated in an endeavor to "expel from reality the forms of sexuality that were not amenable to the strict economy of reproduction" (*History of Sexuality,* 36).

Nonetheless, incitements to formulations of familial sexuality in eighteenth-century Europe were inextricably bound to incitements to silence and condemnation on matters of same-sex activities and extramarital desire. Eighteenth-century texts often vehemently excoriate same-sex activities while either speaking verbosely about whether these aberrations should even be named, refusing to name the activity itself, or resorting to euphemistic allusions to same-sex activity. The contradictory injunctions to the silencing and censuring of these matters stem, it seems, from the perceived nature of representations in discourse. The act of defining those sexual activities mandated, ensured, and privileged by marriage involves necessarily the naming of those activities that must remain outside its boundaries and thus "unnamed."

Kant's "Eine Vorlesung über Ethik" ("A Lecture on Ethics") is exemplary in its evocations of these competing injunctions. He begins his discussion of sexual aberrations with an unequivocal condemnation of sexual activities that lie outside the boundaries of marriage: "Jeder Gebrauch der Geschlechterneigung, außer der Bedingung der Ehe, ist ein Mißbrauch derselben, also ein *crimen carnis*" ("Every use of sexual inclination outside of the conditions of marriage, is a misuse, and as such is a *crimen carnis*," "Eine Vorlesung," 182). Of such abuses of marriage, Kant isolates in particular those conducted exclusively between partners of the same sex:

> Zweitens gehört zu den *criminibus carnis contra naturam* die Gemeinschaft des *sexus homogenii,* wenn der Gegenstand der Geschlechterneigung zwar unter den Menschen bleibt, aber verändert wird, wo die Gemeinschaft des Sexus nicht heterogen, sondern homogen ist, d.i. wenn ein Weib gegen ein Weib und ein Mann gegen einen Mann seine Neigung befriedigt. Dieses läuft wider die Zwecke der Menschheit. Denn der Zweck der Menschheit in Ansehung der Neigung ist die Erhaltung der Arten ohne Wegwerfung seiner Person; hierdurch erhalte ich aber gar nicht die Art . . . also versetze ich mich hierdurch unter das Tier und entehre die Menschheit (Kant, "Eine Vorlesung," 184).

> Secondly, the community of *sexus homogenii* belongs to the *criminibus carnis contra naturam* when the object of sexual inclination remains among human beings, but is altered, where the community of the sexus is not heterogeneous, but homogeneous, that is, when a woman satisfies her inclinations with a woman and a man with a man. This runs against the object of mankind. For the object of mankind in regard to inclination is the preservation of the species without the throwing away of one's person; in this activity however I do not preserve the species . . . and therefore place myself below the level of an animal and dishonor humanity.

As Kant understands it, the crimes of *sexus homogenii* constitute an affront to nature, a dereliction of one's natural duty to reproduce the species, and involve essentially a throwing away of one's self or, literally, the wasting of valuable sperm.[8] Indeed, for Kant, nonreproductive, same-sex sex is the most abject crime imaginable:

> Alle *crimina carnis contra naturam* erniedrigen die Menschheit unter die Tierheit, machen den Menschen der Menschheit unwürdig. Der Mensch verdient nicht, daß er eine Person ist. Dieses ist das unedelste und niedrigste, was der Mensch in Ansehung der Pflichten gegen sich selbst begehen kann . . . Dieses ist das Verächtlichste, was ein Mensch begehen kann . . . Deswegen sind auch die *Crimina carnis contra naturum* unnennbar, weil selbst dadurch, daß man sie nennt, ein Ekel verursacht wird ("Eine Vorlesung," 184).

> All *crimina carnis contra naturam* lower humanity to a level below animality and make people unworthy of humanity. That person does not deserve to be a person. This is the most ignoble and lowest thing which a person (in regard to duty) can commit against himself . . . This is the most abhorrent thing a person can commit . . . For that reason the *Crimina carnis contra naturam* are unnameable, for even the naming of it causes disgust.

Kant insists that the *crimina carnis contra naturam* are unnameable (except perhaps in Latin) not only because they constitute an attack on marriage, but also simply because giving these sexual acts linguistic form evokes feelings of disgust and abhorrence. But then Kant continues his diatribe against nonprocreative sex with a convoluted excursus on the paradoxical necessity both to name and not to name this most horrible of crimes:

> Jeder scheut sich, diese Laster zu nennen, jeder Lehrer enthält sich, selbige nicht einmal aus guter Absicht, seine Untergebenen davor zu warnen, zu nennen. Indem sie aber dennoch so häufig geschehen, so ist man hier im Gedränge und Verlegenheit, ob man sie nennen soll, um sie kennbar zu machen und dadurch zu verhindern, daß sie nicht so häufig geschehen, oder ob man sie nicht nennen sollte, um nicht dadurch Gelegenheit zu geben, daß man sie kennenlernt und sie hernach häufiger begeht. Die Ursache dieser Schamhaftigkeit ist, weil die öftere Nennung derselben so familiarisiert, daß man den Abscheu dawider verliert, und daß sie dadurch, daß man sie nennt, erträglicher werden ("Eine Vorlesung," 184–85).

> Everyone shrinks from naming this vice, every teacher refrains from naming it—even with the best intention of warning his charges

against it. Because it nevertheless occurs so often, one is here pressed and uncertain whether one should name it in order to make it recognizable and thereby prevent it from happening so often, or if one should not name it, in order not to (by that means) provide an opportunity whereby one learns about it and commits the act thereafter even more often. The cause of this shameful activity is that the more frequent naming of it familiarizes it so that one loses one's abhorrence of it and it becomes more tolerable.

Kant asserts that naming same-sex activity is unacceptable because the subject matter is disgusting. Paradoxically, he also claims that naming same-sex activity is dangerous because it dissipates its abject effect upon us. Naming same-sex desire is revolting and should cause us to turn from this crime in disgust, and yet, too much naming of the crime encourages our fascination with and possible involvement in such activities. In addition, Kant cannot decide if even mentioning the crime once might not incite the activity (i.e., that attraction rather than disgust might be evoked by even a single naming). He obsesses over the "naming" of this frequent crime[9] and is unable to decide, ultimately, what the possible effects of its linguistic formation might be.[10] In addition, Kant's own discussion of same-sex activity foregrounds the paradoxical nature of articulation. In order to delimit the "normal," the "acceptable" (here marriage and family) and to expunge all other possibilities, "those things" that lie outside its domain inevitably get "named" (and accentuated) in order ostensibly to be "squelched" and abjected once and for all. As Hull points out, the discourse on marriage in the German states in the eighteenth century inevitably gave rise to terms abjecting those who did not conform to the norms it mandated:

> The association of sexual maturity, sexual potency, solidity of character, citizenship, marriage, and social stability formed a tightly wound tautology, in which each term flowed ineluctably into the other. Indeed, the very condition of being human was defined in this constellation in which the sexual component was absolutely necessary. Hence, the common descriptions of nuns and monks as "these unfortunate middle things" ("unseeligen Mitteldinger"), "these hermaphroditic creatures" ("Zwittergeschöpfe"), or of bachelors as "sick souls." The free-thinking mayor of Königsberg, Theodor von Hippel, champion of early liberalism and female civil emancipation, made a characteristi-

cally pithy summary of this linked chain: "The word 'father' is a great word, the greatest that exists in a state (Staat). Whoever is not (a father) does not deserve the name citizen! and, even being generous, only half deserves the name human!" (Hull, 242)

What Hull describes is a cultural privileging of marriage and fatherhood that generates a language of condemnation against those others who fail to conform in their sexuality to the dominant social order. Paradoxically, it appears that one cannot put marriage into a specific discourse without juxtaposing it to those sexual realities, activities, or beings that are meant to lie outside of it. Even Kant gets caught. He cannot talk about not talking about *crimen carnis* without talking about it.

I have devoted considerable space to the preceding passages from Kant, not only to remind us of eighteenth-century excoriations of same-sex activity, but also to accentuate the interconnections between discourses of marriage in the eighteenth century and those that sought to abject extramarital sexual practices. Moreover—and this is even more important—Kant's pronouncements about marriage and same-sex sexuality emphasize his *conscious* concern with the effects of linguistic expressions. He demonstrates a disinclination to give certain kinds of sexuality symbolic forms because he realizes the tremendous cultural power significations of sexuality have. As Kant sees it, same-sex activity becomes real and proliferates once it acquires a name. He illustrates a widespread eighteenth-century assumption that the simple act of "naming" types of sexual activity insures the existence of the thing named and of the thing one hopes to silence. Because of the immense power of linguistic formations and their equally significant meaning for cultural order or disorder, Kant expresses his age's awareness of and anxiety about specific articulations of sexuality and desire. While on the one hand, as Foucault and others have suggested, the eighteenth century manifested a prodigious incitement to discourses of and on marriage, those articulations inevitably invoked "expressions of condemnation" against sexualities perceived as corroding marital privilege. Those excoriations (their abjecting function notwithstanding) in turn evoked anxiety in those persons who, like Kant, believed in the generating power of linguistic significations.

What is of particular interest to me here is both Kant's fear of certain linguistic formations and his awareness of their significance. His explication of the possible effects of naming same-sex activity demonstrates that eighteenth-century thinkers and producers of culture were not simply and naively involved in producing new articulations of sexuality. Kant represents the century's cognizance of the kind of cultural project in which it was engaged—one in which marriage was accentuated as the cultural norm and same-sex activities were to be paradoxically "named" "unnameable" to ensure their dissipation and dissolution.

And yet extramarital sexual activities were discussed in a legion of literary venues throughout the eighteenth century.[11] As eighteenth-century scholarship has amply demonstrated, titillating, yet often moralistic, diatribes, as well as libertine manifestos,[12] essays, and accounts of tribades, female husbands, cross-dressers, prostitutes, and sodomites circulated in popular forms such as pamphlets, satirical attacks, ballads, memoirs, and erotic fiction including John Cleland's *Fanny Hill*, Denis Diderot's *The Nuns*, Henry Fielding's *The Female Husband*, Johann Wolfgang von Goethe's *Elective Affinities*, Daniel Defoe's *Roxana*, Choderlos de Laclos' *Dangerous Liaisons*, William King's *The Toast*, and the Marquis de Sade's entire oeuvre, to name just a few. The eighteenth century produced a considerable body of literature addressing figures of "questionable" sexuality and gender (hermaphrodites, amazons, tribades, fops, mollies, tommies, sodomites, and eunuchs) and excursuses on transgressive sexuality and gender (libertinism, masturbation, spermatic economy, cross-dressing, passing, masquerade/sexual freedom, sodomy, and "Greek love"). Nonprocreative sexuality went, in fact, a lot less "unnamed" in the eighteenth century than Kant wished. In fact, the vast concern on the part of the eighteenth century with discourses of both marital and extramarital sexualities and desires attests clearly to the era's obsession with processes of the cultural production and containment of specific sexualities.[13]

Despite this proliferation of eighteenth-century discourses of sexual activity and genders, Foucault isolated, above all, the compulsion of earlier eras to name and categorize sodomy. He juxtaposed earlier discourses of sodomy to the explosion of discourses on sexuality and self that he highlighted in the later nineteenth century. As he saw it, desire, sexuality, and identity began to converge for the first time in the late nineteenth century in a manner that was not manifest in Europe until the medical discourses of sexologists, such as those of Carl von Westphal, Karl Heinrich Ulrichs, Auguste Ambrose Tardieu, Richard von Krafft-Ebing, Havelock Elis, Magnus Hirschfeld, and Sigmund Freud began to define "homosexuality" in terms of an "interior androgyny," the "hermaphrodism of the soul" and the "homosexual" as a "being or species" not simply or exclusively defined in terms of "sodomitical acts." Foucault summarized this now-famous conceptual and linguistic shift succinctly when he wrote:

> As defined by the ancient civil or canonical codes, sodomy was a category of forbidden acts; their perpetrator was nothing more than the juridical subject of them. The nineteenth-century homosexual became a personage, a past, a case history, and a childhood, in addition to being a type of life, a life form, and a morphology, with an indiscreet anatomy and possibly a mysterious physiology. Nothing that went into his total composition was unaffected by his sexuality. (*History of Sexuality*, 43)

What Foucault perceived as unique to the later nineteenth century is a set of discourses that began to define and delimit a specific "homosexual identity" through the representation of the individual's personage, history, type of life, etc.[14] Indeed, it is an identity that is constructed in and through nineteenth-century discourses of literature, jurisprudence, medicine, and psychoanalysis. Foucault isolated what he referred to as the discursive formation of a "homosexual identity" as the "crucial change" indicating a "massive shift" in attitudes that distinguished the later nineteenth- and twentieth-century conceptions of sexual identity from the sodomitical acts catalogued by earlier centuries (see also Weeks, *Against Nature*, 15).

The issue of same-sex *identity* formation is, of course, problematic for eighteenth-century studies of sexuality and desire. As soon as we begin to address the historical reconstruction of sexual identities several formidable questions arise: 1) Does evidence of same-sex activity in periods preceding the later nineteenth century necessarily suggest that same-sex identities are also present? And, if so, how do we determine what those identities might be? As numerous historians and theorists of sexuality have illustrated, sexuality, desire, and sexual identity are socially and historically constructed phenomena; 2) What implications can be drawn from literary representations, legal reports, and moralistic diatribes about the nature of same-sex identities and desire?; and 3) Can we assume that the lack of evidence about same-sex identities in trial records, for example, demonstrates a larger cultural lack of such identities? In other words, can we assume that the eighteenth-century evidence in legal, literary, and medical discourses concentrating on representations of sodomitical acts provides conclusive evidence of the era's disinterest in issues of same-sex identity? If accounts of acts of sodomy are the predominant ones, does that make other articulations of same-sex activity, desire, and identity less important to our understanding of the eighteenth-century cultural production of "desires" and "sexual identities"? Do we only find discourses of domination and power over same-sex desire? How might self-expressions of same-sex desire and identity arise? And finally, what is the significance of the fact that discourses of sodomy and libertinism are much less important to the eighteenth-century German tradition than to those of France and England? It is precisely these questions as they relate to new poetic and conceptual formations of sexual identity and desire that shape my study of the aesthetic production of Goethe, Winckelmann, and Moritz.

The question of same-sex identity formation arises, of course, throughout scholarship on eighteenth-century representations of sodomy in Europe. First and foremost, Foucault's simple invocation of the term "sodomy" must be understood in terms of the fluid and broadly inclusive character of the term throughout the eighteenth century. The Codex Juris Bavarici of Prince Max Joseph of 1751 defined "sodomy" legally as: "Fleischliche Vermischung mit dem Viehe, todten Cörpern, oder Leuten einerley Geschlechts, als Mann mit Mann und Weib mit Weib . . ." ("The mixing of flesh with cattle, dead bodies, or people of the same sex such as man with man and woman with woman," Derks, 141).[15] G. S. Rousseau reminds us that in the eighteenth century "sodomites" may or may not have been "homosexuals." Sodomites were a larger class of individuals who "may have committed any number of sexual and nonsexual 'crimes.'" A synonym for bugger (derived from *boulgre* or *bougre*, apparently a Bulgarian), "sodomite" was "an extreme and opprobrious form of condemnation designating religious blasphemy, political sedition, and even satanic activities including demonism, shamanism, and witchcraft" (G. S. Rousseau, "Pursuit of Homosexuality," 136).[16] Dollimore stresses an even wider scope of meanings, recalling that "sodomy" was associated before the nineteenth century with "witches, demons, werewolves, basilisks, foreigners, and (of course) papists; and it apparently signified a wide range of practices including prostitution, under-age sex, coitus interruptus, and female transvestism" (Dollimore, 238). G. S. Rousseau asserts that there was in the eighteenth century no coherent concept of the homosexual[17] "except as onanist, hermaphrodite, or mad masturbator . . . there remained no clear sense of whether homosexuality was a disorder of the mind or body, or whether it was curable" ("Pursuit of Homosexuality," 140).[18] The conceptual inclusiveness of the term "sodomy" in the eighteenth century and the wide divergences of its meaning from one social/cultural context to another preclude the notion that "sodomy" might have already represented a specific same-sex sexual identity at that time (see Edmiston, 157). Indeed, Dollimore goes even one step further in reminding us that there also seems to be no evidence of a kind of "reverse discourse" or "reverse identification" in earlier periods with the construction "sodomite":

> But *so* extreme was the sodomite's construction that most of those actually engaged in "homo/sexuality" did not identify themselves with it; not only did they not have our modern categories, but the prevailing categories were so far removed from how they saw themselves, that apparently the connection was not made. (Dollimore, 238)

What Dollimore points out is that individuals in earlier periods were not appropriating the term "sodomy" from the prevailing social discourses on it in order to designate their own same-sex identities.

With these analyses in mind, Foucault's assertion of the radical distinction between the term "sodomy" and the explosion of discourses manifest at the end of the nineteenth century is thoroughly convincing. If the term "sodomy" comprised our only evidence of expressions of same-sex activity, identity, or desire in the eighteenth century, then Foucault's analysis would be irrefutable. The question that remains to be answered, however, is whether or not the eighteenth-century interest in same-sex concerns can be represented adequately by the terminological and conceptual characteristics of the single term "sodomy." And the answer, of course, is no.

Michel Rey's analysis of Paris police records directly challenges Foucault's narrow focus on "sodomy." He demonstrates how in Paris in the eighteenth century the older term "sodomite," disappeared and was replaced by the term "pederast"—a designation that referred to a type of individual and not any specific sexual act: "Even the term sodomite disappeared. After 1738, the police use the term 'pederast' more and more often. The new term was not of religious origin. It designated a type of person without making reference to a specific act" ("Police and Sodomy," 145). Similarly, Robert Tobin (*Warm Brothers*, 30) notes that German authors began to invoke "Greek" figures such as Narcissus, Adonis, Hyacinth, and Ganymede to signify male-male desire in their literary works. Likewise, Paul Derks has outlined a tendency in German letters between 1750 and 1850 to accentuate more abstract Socratic, platonic, and pederastic inclinations over sodomitical acts. He demonstrates, as well, the coexistence in German literature of a broad range of terms designating male-male attraction, including: "Sodomiterey" (sodomy), "Knabenliebe" (love of boys), "griechische Liebe" (Greek love), "Pederästie" (Pederasty), "sokratische Liebe" (Socratic love), and "platonische Liebe" (platonic love).[19] The activity itself was sometimes referred to in Germany as "florenzen" (literally to act like someone from Florence), and the participants were signified by terms as divergent as "bougre" ("Bulgarian"), which was a term of disapprobation, and "heiliger Pederäst" (holy pederast) a term with rather more positive implications. Derks sees this terminological mini-explosion as evidence of a "Wandel" ("turn," 16) in attitudes toward "homosexuality," marking a shift away from considering "homosexual activity" exclusively within the context of "einem theologischen Sündenbegriff" ("a theological conception of sin," 16). Similarly, Randolph Trumbach has traced alternative terminologies deployed in London in the eighteenth century, such as "mollies" for men desiring men and "tommies" for women desiring women. Indeed, as Rey does in his study of Paris, Trumbach avers that in London the term "sodomite" came to refer to "an individual interested exclusively in his own gender" ("Sodomitical Subcultures," 118). According to Trumbach, in the new eighteenth-century paradigm there were actually three genders—the illegitimate third one being "the adult passive transvestite effeminate male or molly who was supposed to desire men exclusively" ("London Sapphists," 112).[20]

The work of Rey, Tobin, Derks, and Trumbach demonstrates that restricting our analysis to the term "sodomy" does not adequately take into account the proliferation of terms in eighteenth-century Europe designating same-sex activities and attraction. Each of these studies of sexuality or representations of same-sex desire provides some evidence, in the form of discursive fluctuations, of shifts in attitude toward male same-sex desire in Europe in the eighteenth century. Male same-sex desire is defined in terms of pederasty, Greek love, an Italian menace and so forth. In essence, "sodomy" was slowly displaced and/or increasingly accompanied by a wider range of terms indicating shifts in both sentiment and specificity. The proliferation of terms other than sodomy in designating male-male desire in German texts of the eighteenth century, for example, suggests the incitement to define that particular desire through terminologies that isolate specific sexual *inclinations,* thereby distinguishing them from the wide variety of sexual and nonsexual *acts* evoked by the more inclusive concept of "sodomy."

Moreover, terminological shifts in the eighteenth century coupled with evidence of nascent (male) same-sex subcultures point to specific and sometimes parodic formations of same-sex identities. Mary McIntosh, Randolph Trumbach, James Steakley, Michel Rey, D. A. Coward, Alan Bray, Theo van der Meer, and Arend H. Huussen have traced shifts in the sodomitical activities summarized in legal and prosecutorial reports, indicating the rise of distinct male sexual subcultures in large European cities such as London, Amsterdam, Paris, and Berlin. These accounts of subcultural activity— including men dressing as women, emulating feminine behaviors, enacting mock marriages, and staging birthing scenes—suggest the

possible existence of forms of group and social identity and co-
hesion marked by crossing-dressing and parodic performances.[21]
Bray stresses the tremendous shift in eighteenth-century sensibilities
from those of the seventeenth-century, pointing out that the molly
houses marked a new social identity—one with its own recognizable
terms, language, gestures, clothing, etc. He locates in the eighteenth
century the kind of shift to self-fashioning that Foucault reserved
for the later nineteenth century. For Bray the terminological shift
in England from the seventeenth century notion of "sodomy" to
the eighteenth-century concept of "molly" is crucial. "Molly," in his
view, marks a terminological revolution equivalent to that designated
by "homosexual." Bray maintains that the terms " . . . 'molly' and
'homosexual,' for example, are alike in that they both refer to such a
social identity, a kind of person, not the same identity but crucially *an*
identity nevertheless. It marked a momentous change" (103). Bray's
analysis of "an identity" manifest in the eighteenth-century "molly
clubs" is based on trial records and second-hand accounts, which
unfortunately do not provide much information about identity formations beyond the emergence of the term "molly."[22] Consequently,
he can surmise that some kind of same-sex identity was emerging,
but he does not have the requisite evidence with which to reconstruct
that identity with any specificity.

Tobin insists (and rightly) that something was happening in the
semantic field in late eighteenth-century Germany as well. He suggests that a cluster of signifiers in the German tradition, including
Hellenism, Orientalism, the cult of friendship, and the cultivation of
fashion, began forming around expressions of male same-sex desire.
Like Bray, he surmises that subcultures functioned as a focal point
for this linguistic shift:

> While many of these sodomites (or, as they might have preferred to
> be called, "warm brothers") might not have had the kind of "identity"
> that Foucault would see in the nineteenth-century homosexual—"a
> personage, a past, a case history, and a childhood . . . a type of life, a
> life form, and a morphology" (*History*, 43)—they were able to situate
> themselves in subcultures that were already prefiguring the identity of
> the modern homosexual. (*Warm Brothers*, 5)

Tobin asserts that while the eighteenth-century German tradition did not manifest "an homosexual identity" as Foucault defined it, that they were on the brink of such a formation (*Warm Brothers*, 14), even if there is no clear documentation of a "highly self-conscious homosexual subculture or identity" (*Warm Brothers*, 32).

It seems reasonable to speculate (as Bray, Tobin, and Trumbach do) that eighteenth-century male subcultures signified the emergence of (or imminent emergence of) nascent forms of male same-sex identity and discursive formations of self and sexuality. But we must also keep in mind that while linguistic articulations such as "molly" and "warm brothers" certainly indicate shifts in a culture's definitions of same-sex desire, without more contextual evidence we cannot really know what implications such terms might have had in regard to same-sex identity formations. In other words, we have new names for sodomites as recounted in legal records or by eyewitnesses spying on members of subcultures, but so far we have little first-hand information about the identities men in subcultures might have been forming for themselves around these terms. While accounts of subcultures, reports of sodomy, and literary descriptions of sexual encounters provide invaluable evidence of the emerging discourses of same-sex desire in the eighteenth century, they do not provide us with a sense of the kinds of identities and desires that individuals might have constructed for themselves. They do not provide us with a sense of how new discourses of desire and identity were being fashioned, and they do not provide us with much evidence of conscious efforts on the part of individuals and/or groups to incite new discourses of same-sex sexuality and self.

In addition, it is virtually impossible on the basis of a few terminological shifts and descriptions of same-sex activity to assume that this kind of eighteenth-century naming can be equated to that explosion of discourses that Foucault isolates at the end of the nineteenth-century. It is clear that same-sex sexuality and desire were being named in the eighteenth century throughout several discursive registers that include the languages of court and law, aesthetics, literature, philosophy, and subculture parody and performance. These discourses appear to represent shifts in sentiment toward same-sex activities and inclinations. Simultaneously, we certainly do not find in the eighteenth century the same intensity of medical and psychoanalytic scrutiny, debate, construction, and categorization of "homosexuality" that emerged in the later nineteenth century. Nonetheless, terminological transformations in the eighteenth century provide evidence of conceptual shifts away from a reductive understanding of same-sex activity as sodomitical acts and toward new forms of categorization. Some of these new terms then perhaps ultimately resurfaced during the dramatic emergence of recognizable sexual identities and medico-sexological discourses at the end of the nineteenth century. Incitements to the silencing and censuring of same-sex sexuality in the eighteenth century, buoyed by the need to preserve certain inalienable conceptions of marriage as the cornerstone of civilization, also parallel later nineteenth- and twentieth-century tendencies to pathologize homosexuality. But the crucial difference between the explosion of discourses that Foucault described for the later nineteenth century and the significatory shifts and incitements manifest thus far in eighteenth-century studies devolves upon the question of the formation of a self. And even more precisely, it revolves around the construction of the self as a sexual and desiring self in and through discourse.

Because of the significance of the self in this study of Goethe, Winckelmann, and Moritz, it is important to outline precisely the kind of self that emerged in German Classicism. I have found it useful to elucidate this self in contrast to Foucault's constructions of the self throughout his work on discourse. For the most part, Foucault's analyses of discourses concentrate on what he described in his early work as the "formation of objects" by institutional authorities (*The Archaeology of Knowledge*, 40). The important task for many Foucauldian analysts is to map out not how a self speaks about her- or himself, but how, for example, a "homosexual self or identity" is constructed by those with institutional authority such as psychiatrists, court officials, pedagogues, and doctors. Indeed, in *The Archaeology of Knowledge* Foucault insisted that he would "abandon any attempt, therefore, to see discourse as a phenomenon of expression" (55). Discourse is precisely not the linguistic production of a "thinking, knowing, and speaking subject" (55). In fact, the subject is not "the cause, origin, or starting point of the phenomenon of the written or spoken articulation of a sentence . . . it is a particular vacant place that may in fact be filled by different individuals" (95). The subject or the self, finally, is not the "speaking subject, who reveals or who conceals himself in what he says, who in speaking, exercises his sovereign freedom . . ." (122).

Foucault reiterated this elision of the speaking, self-expressing subject in his *History of Sexuality* to the extent that its concentration is again on how sexuality is being "spoken about" (17) and on institutional injunctions to speak about sex (23). Much of the scholarship on same-sex activity and desire in eighteenth-century studies has followed Foucault in this accentuation of discourses *on* the self. These studies, for example, typically rely on court accounts by eyewitnesses about mollies and warm brothers rather than on self-expressions of same-sex desire and identity. Equally important has been Foucault's brief suggestion in the *History of Sexuality* of the possibility of reverse discourses. In explaining that the later nineteenth century produced a host of discourses constructing a particular "homosexual identity," Foucault also mentions that these discourses generated reverse discourses. That is, "homosexuality began to speak in its own behalf, to demand that its legitimacy or 'naturality' be acknowledged, often in the same vocabulary, using the same categories by which it was medically disqualified" (101). Here Foucault suggests the possibility of self-expression on the part of individuals in the later nineteenth century who desired to define and identify themselves. Typically, according to Foucault, these individuals appropriated terms like "homosexuality" from the prevailing institutional discourses in attempts to describe themselves. As we have seen, scholars like Dollimore (238) have demonstrated that such reverse discourses (and in particular those that appropriate the term "sodomy") do not seem to have existed in earlier centuries. Foucault's understanding of alternative expressions by selves interested in self-definition appears limited to strategies of appropriation by later nineteenth-century selves seeking to express themselves through available terminologies. His recognition of a self with more agency slowly emerged only in his later work.

In *The Use of Pleasure* Foucault insisted on the importance of investigating a history and genealogy of the desiring subject: "In any case, it seemed to me that one could not very well analyze the formation and development of the experience of sexuality from the eighteenth century onward, without doing a historical and critical study dealing with desire and the desiring subject. In other words, without undertaking a 'genealogy'"(5). Foucault's task was to analyze "the practices by which individuals were led to focus their attention on themselves, to decipher, recognize, and acknowledge themselves as subjects of desire" (5). Here Foucault accentuated the manner in which selves are determined by cultural mandates to form themselves as ethical subjects. He envisioned "a history of the way in which individuals are urged to constitute themselves as subjects of moral conduct" (29). Such a history "would be concerned with the models proposed for setting up and developing relationships with the self, for self-reflection, self-knowledge, self-examination, for the decipherment of the self by oneself, for the transformations that one seeks to accomplish with oneself as object" (29). Within this context, Foucault allows for a certain agency of the self—as the individual becomes involved in a process of self-fashioning that is mandated in specific historical moments. Foucault does not concentrate here on a self who might construct her- or himself in opposition to a predominant discourse. The focus instead is on the self who fashions him- or herself in accord with particular, prevailing cultural injunctions. Foucault foregrounded this same type of subject in *The Care of the Self,* in which he explored the self-construction, self-fashioning, and self-controlling subject as he or she operates within discourses and models of self-cultivation (43). Again Foucault was interested in the manner in which the self "exercises sovereignty over oneself" (85) in order to construct him- or herself as an ethical subject (68). And even as Foucault occasionally stressed "the dependence and independence" of the self (238), he was ultimately concerned with the kinds of self-renunciations (239–240) such a self must make in order to become a moral self in accord with predominate cultural discourses. This is a self that has "sovereignty" over itself only to the extent that it fashions itself in accord with prevailing cultural mandates.

Finally, in his "Technologies of the Self" Foucault modified and gave more precision to his notion of the self in discourse. He asserted, first of all, that his central focus was on institutional forms of knowledge, including economics, biology, psychiatry, medicine, and penology. He admitted that he may, in fact, have concentrated too much on powers of domination in his studies of discourses (19) and further specified that a complex network of technologies (or arts of existence) inform any discourse analysis, including:

> 1) technologies of production, which permit us to produce, transform, or manipulate things; 2) technologies of sign systems, which permit us to use signs, meanings, symbols, or significations; 3) technologies of power, which determine the conduct of individuals and submit them to certain ends or domination, an objectivizing of the subject; 4) technologies of the self which permit individuals to effect by their own means or with the help of others a certain number of operations on their own bodies and souls, thoughts, conduct, and way of being, so as to transform themselves in order to attain a certain state of happiness, purity, wisdom, perfection, or immortality. (18)

Here Foucault seems to suggest greater freedom and agency of the self. And while he is still interested throughout this text in the acts of renunciation the self must make during the self-fashioning process, he does intimate that the eighteenth century marks a decisive break from the renunciation of the self and positively toward "a new self" (49). And although Foucault does not describe this new self, it appears to be a self with potentially greater capacity for self-fashioning and self-affirmation.

It is this later self, as hinted at by Foucault, that most resembles the self that emerges throughout the writings of the German Classicists—Winckelmann, Goethe, and Moritz. The self that they represent and form throughout their aesthetic production is one that is actively involved in creating new articulations and affirmations of men desiring men. The self they depict is one who *consciously* and *purposefully* decides to construct a language of, for, and about himself. The self they construct resists the popular definition of himself and strives to develop a new language of self-expression. This self does not appropriate the discourse of sodomy but struggles to create a language of his own same-sex desire and identity where none yet seems to exist. In contrast, Foucault briefly acknowledges a self with potentially more agency (in terms of constructing reverse discourses) in the *History of Sexuality,* but then only as a later nineteenth-century phenomenon. Considering the development of

Foucault's notion of the self in discourse and the limitations of his analysis of the eighteenth and early nineteenth centuries, it seems imperative to reevaluate manifestations of same-sex activity, desire, and identity in those eras. It appears reasonable, as well, to shift our focus to a "new self," to emerging conceptions of the self-fashioning self and to languages of self-expression in the eighteenth and nineteenth centuries.

Recent work by Trumbach, Rousseau, Derks, Detering, Kuzniar, Richter, Tobin, and Haggerty has begun to focus attention on other discourses (beyond sodomy) that also prevailed in the eighteenth century. Tobin, Haggerty, Kuzniar, Richter, and Aldrich in particular have shifted attention to discourses of sentiment and particularly to that of "Greek love" in the eighteenth century. Aldrich, for example, reminds us of the critical importance of Classical expressions of sexual and emotional relationships between men for succeeding generations (32). He emphasizes that: "At times when 'homosexuality' was condemned as sinful, dangerous, and unmanly, the Greek prototype provided an unparalleled and glorious image of man's desire for other men" (32). Aldrich highlights the eighteenth century, of course, as an era that relied heavily on Greek paradigms to express male-male desire. In a similar vein, Haggerty demonstrates in *Men in Love* how the eighteenth-century obsession with "Greek love" (and the cult of friendship associated with it) became a model of love between men for upper-class intellectuals and poets of eighteenth-century England.[23] And it is precisely this model that informs and structures their literary representations of men loving men. Indeed, scholarship has indicated a parallel fixation on "Greek" forms of love and friendship in the eighteenth-century German states following Winckelmann's inauguration of a "homoerotic aesthetics" of Classical art.[24] By turning his attention to the expressions of love between men in eighteenth-century literary texts by authors such as Gray, Beckford, and Walpole, Haggerty has begun to trace expressions of sentiment between men that tell us not about how sodomites were spoken about in the eighteenth century, but about how men who desired other men began to express themselves in the eighteenth century. Haggerty argues that in order to trace eighteenth-century conceptions of same-sex desire (and I would add same-sex identity[25]), we need to broaden our view of the eighteenth century to include textual expressions of sentiments between men. What these studies of the eighteenth century illustrate is the age's obsession not just with sodomitical descriptions of men sexually engaged with other men, but also with Greek models of male-male desire and love. In essence, these studies show, as Richter has argued ("Winckelmann's Progeny," 45), that in eighteenth-century Europe an elite group of artists, writers, and art historians with Classical training discovered a Greek model of expression for their own same-sex sentiments.

In Germany Winckelmann surely seems to have inaugurated—and Goethe and Moritz certainly participated in—eighteenth- and early nineteenth-century invocations of Greek models of love and friendship between men. Moreover, the language of the self that they fashioned and their aesthetic theories came to be the predominant aesthetic discourse in the German literary and aesthetic tradition extending well past the eighteenth and early nineteenth centuries. And for this reason, the aesthetic discourse of these German Classicists is of critical importance to our understanding of emerging expressions of same-sex desire and identity. Their aesthetic and literary production provides a critical counter-language to that of sodomy and the excoriation of same-sex activity and desire in the eighteenth and early nineteenth centuries. In fact, Goethe, Winckelmann, and Moritz defined their same-sex desire and their same-sex identifications in terms of their feelings for other men and rarely in reference to any sexual activity. Throughout their work desire is understood in terms of the expression of sentiments and love and as not contingent upon specific sexual acts. Indeed, as we shall see throughout this study, Goethe, Winckelmann, and Moritz characterized their same-sex desire in terms of friendship, love, attraction, and innate and natural affinities between men.[26]

What I intend to trace out in the study is not principally the concentration of Goethe, Winckelmann, and Moritz on self-expression through Greek models of friendship. I am more intrigued by their conscious attempts to create a new language of same-sex self-expression, their struggle to define and identify themselves, and their desire for a sense of community. I am interested in the ways (only one of which involved invoking Greek models) through which they strove to "put themselves into discourse," ways in which they lent their own same-sex desires and identities metaphoric forms. Indeed, the central focus of *Men Desiring Men* is on the linguistic, metaphoric, and poetic processes through which Goethe, Winckelmann, and Moritz fashion themselves and through which they perceive themselves articulating themselves as men desiring men.

And in this context, we should recall that the eighteenth century privileged literature in the expression of sentiment and in the construction of new senses of subjectivity and self (think, for example, of the bourgeois tragedy and the novel of sensibility[27]).[28] The argument for focusing on literary representations of same-sex desire and self is not contingent on the assumption of literary privilege per se,[29] but on an eighteenth-century understanding of the tremendous role of literature and of new generic innovations as culture and subject forming and transforming mechanisms. In this context it is appropriate to ask whether or not same-sex desires and identities emerged in literary productions conceived at the time to be involved in the cultural/social production of new senses of self, desire, subjectivity, and identity. In addition, we recall that the eighteenth century was an age convinced that exposure to certain kinds of literary texts transformed and molded the readers' or audiences' senses of subjectivity (remember eighteenth-century writers who warned that virtuous women could become women of vice simply by reading the wrong novel). New generic innovations also underscored the self-fashioning function of writing. Literature was understood as both a vehicle of self-expression and of self-fashioning for subjects like Werther (*Die Leiden des jungen Werthers*) and Rousseau (*Confessions*). Reading and writing in the eighteenth century were perceived in terms of the construction of senses of self and subjectivity. Given these eighteenth-century notions of the aesthetically fashioned self, the critical questions for us become: Is there evidence of literary constructions in the eighteenth century of selves who articulate same-sex desires? If so, how do those selves acquire symbolic forms? And, in fact, the critical contribution of this study is that it maps out exactly how selves who desire members of their own sex "put themselves into discourse," how they express themselves, how they perceive themselves as active creators of a new language of themselves, and how they voice new senses of their own identities.

My study of Goethe, Winckelmann, and Moritz certainly complements Haggerty's, Kuzniar's, and Tobin's analyses of the articulations of love between men as expressed in eighteenth-century English and German literature. But while they focus predominantly on the expressions of same-sex desire in English and German texts, I am principally concerned with the broader exploration of sites in Goethe's, Winckelmann's, and Moritz's oeuvre in which senses of self, same-sex desire, and same-sex identity converge. In other words, beyond the consideration of the self-expression of same-sex desire in the eighteenth century, I am interested in how eighteenth-century conceptions of self and self-fashioning converge with articulations of same-sex sentiments in German Classical aesthetics. Moreover, Goethe's literary production in particular—and this is quite amazing—is conceived and structured by him in terms of new poetic formulations of male same-sex desire, identity, and community. He clearly understood his literary production in terms of an extension of Winckelmann's struggles to articulate his desires for other men. In other words, what Goethe's aesthetic corpus offers us is a detailed, vast, recurrent, systematic model of the self-fashioning and construction of male subjects who desire and identify with other men who desire men. And like Winckelmann, Goethe struggled throughout his literary production to articulate male-male desire. As we shall see in the chapters that follow, Goethe, Winckelmann, and Moritz offer us a complex and detailed view of how they lend same-sex desire and identity new poetic formulations. What emerges in and through their aesthetic texts is an anatomy and physiology of the construction of a self, a desiring self, a self who desires other men and who identifies himself with other men who desire men. And to this extent, I would agree with Tobin's observation that *so far* no "highly self-conscious homosexual identity" has been documented in the eighteenth century (*Warm Brothers*, 32).

Documenting a highly self-conscious same-sex identity and its poetic formulation is precisely the purpose of this book. In fact, a highly developed self-conscious articulation of same-sex identity, desire, and community can be traced throughout Goethe's work—

and, indeed, structures his entire thought.[30] Identity, self, and desire converge in German Classical aesthetics in a manner that challenges Foucault's assumptions about discourses of sexuality before the later nineteenth century. Much more is being expressed here than accounts of sodomy. More is at stake here than constructing objects of discourse. Surveying the oeuvre of Goethe, Winckelmann, and Moritz discloses a late eighteenth- and early nineteenth-century morphology of same-sex desire and identity. Their work constitutes an early attempt to express male-male desire in terms of specific personages, in terms of individuals with pasts and childhoods. The man who desires other men, as captured by these German Classical writers, enjoys a particular type of life, and his very being is suffused with his sexuality. As opposed to the medical, psychoanalytic, and legal discourses of the observation and construction of a "homosexual identity," that gained ascendancy in the late nineteenth century, eighteenth- and early nineteenth-century German discourses articulate a self-fashioning of same-sex desire, identity, and community as they converge and emerge in new poetic formulations.

What I hope to accomplish in this study is a revaluation of the self-expression and self-fashioning of the same-sex-desiring man in German Classical aesthetics. We will trace here a subject formed within a conscious network of articulations—within a language this subject constructs for himself—within a language that this self creates despite the prevailing discourses of the condemnation of same-sex activity and desire in the eighteenth and early nineteenth centuries. In summary, we can trace across the aesthetic production of Goethe, Winckelmann, and Moritz their conscious efforts to illustrate and to encode new poetic and aesthetic formulations of a male same-sex desire, self, and identity. Indeed, the same-sex desiring and identifying (male) self we have not been able to locate in eighteenth-century discourses of sodomy finds a significant site of articulation in German Classical aesthetic production, where he begins to fashion his own identity, and ultimately comes to speak his own desire and self.

CHAPTER 2

GOETHE AND WINCKELMANN:
ARTICULATING SAME-SEX
IDENTITY AND DESIRE

*J*ohann Wolfgang von Goethe's literary production marks a paradigmatic emergence of a sense of self, sexual identity, and desire that is recognizably and prototypically modern. In his texts we discover consistent and recurrent paradigms of sexual desire linked to identity. Above all, Goethe's literary writings repeatedly manifest his conscious attempts to lend sexual desire and identity recognizable poetic formations in relation to each other. Goethe clearly understood his aesthetic task in terms of forming new articulations of various sexual identities and desires. Moreover, his literary work is permeated with representations of sexual identity and desire. His work is self-reflective to the extent that it continually signifies the processes of poetic expression underlying his literary production. Finally, as we shall see, Goethe conceived of his literary work specifically as an incitement to further poetic formations of sexual desire and identity. Indeed, throughout his literary production the male desiring subject struggles to name and to speak his own desiring self.

The paradigms of identity and desire to which Goethe's texts lend poetic form represent sexual inclinations as fluid and dynamic. In modern terminology, we might say that Goethe's writings accentuate various sexual identities and desires, including the "heterosexual," the "homosexual," and the "bisexual." Those designations would be, of course, only vaguely approximate. While Goethe refers to this "fluid desire" in at least one context as "elective affinities," Freud might call it "polymorphous perversity" or a "pre-oedipal bisexuality" (*Essays on Sexuality*, 90), Heinrich von Kleist may designate it with references to "amphibious beings" (Letter to Adolfine von Werdeck, July 28/29, 1801), Hirschfeld might refer to its manifestations as a kind of "Mischform" (*Die Transvestiten*, 275), Foucault might discuss it in terms of a "hermaphrodism of the soul" (*History of Sexuality*, 43) and Kristeva might insist that each individual subject has her or his own sexual desire, internal alterities, and irreconcilable psychic heterogenieties.[1] Of course, none of these significations of desires are equivalent. Each signifies vastly diverging conceptions of desire and its characteristics. But each also implies the fluidity and uncontainability of those things/feelings we call desire. The disjuncture between these various notions of sexual desire and identity illustrates both the *compulsion* to name and categorize sexual desire (an activity traceable *as a compulsion* to the Enlightenment project of classification[2]) and the impossibility of ever fully capturing a specific *essence* of desire in symbolic representations. Jeffrey Weeks isolates a similar tension surrounding our understanding of sexuality, pointing out that

> We are increasingly aware, theoretically, historically, even politically, that "sexuality" is about flux and change, that what we so readily deem as "sexual" is as much a product of language and culture as of "nature." Yet we constantly strive to fix it, stabilize it, say who we are by telling of our sex (*Against Nature*, 69).

There is, after all, no such thing as a coherent "Sex an sich" or "Begehren an sich" (sex or desire in and of itself). Desire and identity are as historically, socially, and culturally constructed as gender, sexuality, and the body. Intriguingly, in each of the examples cited above, within the context of distinguishing something like an exclusively "homosexual interior," thinkers as radically different as Hirschfeld, Freud, Foucault, and Goethe foreground that "place" or "edge" where the boundaries between specific identities and desires threaten to dissolve or to become elusive. The mere conceptualization of "distinct" sexual identities appears inevitably contingent upon the accentuation of amorphous boundaries between identities, thus resulting in the perpetual foregrounding of androgyny, hermaphrodism, cross-gendering, and amphibious beings within terminological and conceptual formations specifically addressed to the delimitation of particular sexual identities.

What I will trace out in this chapter is Goethe's contribution to questions of sexual identity and desire in terms of a general and dynamic paradigm of elective affinities—and its constituent parts—that reflects a rather postmodern sense of the destabilization of these categorizations. Goethe stands at the precipice of a (post)modern conundrum—at an edge between identity and the categorization of morphologies of identities, and at an edge where identity and "interiority" begin to emerge in the form of new discourses. But also, and especially in Goethe's case, these new "identifications" arise within a paradigm of desire that is fluid, mobile, shifting, and dynamic—evincing a volatility of desire that at least from our (post)modern perspective seems to suggest the subversion of set or exclusive sexual identities and orientations. For Goethe, however, this is not problematic. His texts express no clear anxiety about defining (or any overriding compulsion to define) same-sex desire as opposed to that between the opposite sexes.[3] While desire is fluid and dynamic, there is little sense of competing desires or of mutually exclusive ones. Within Goethe's paradigm of sexual identity and desire one discovers that while certain male same-sex identities are getting "fixed," no assumptions about the exclusivity of object choice get "made." Moreover, the tensions in the Goethean conception of desire mark quite precisely not only the constructed nature of perceptions of identity and desire, but also the position of his paradigm on the "edge" of an historical shift toward the later nineteenth-century obsession with the categorization and delimitation of desires, identities, and sexual orientations. And it is precisely the tension between identity and desire manifest in Goethe's literary work that makes it seem so modern to us. In this sense Goethe productively complicates our search for early same-sex identity formations. He does not posit set identity formations, but provides us with a poetic language in which sexual identities are in flux. In this context we might also recall Kristeva's notion of the subject and/or identity as being continually in process and on trial. This causes us to remember that "historical" and "cultural" constructions of homosexuality and/or same-sex desire are constituted within a dynamic flux of identity positions. Goethe's view of the fluid instability of identity formations is not only modern, but also stands in opposition to Foucault's more static divisions between the ages of sodomy and the ages of identity. Foucault's suggestion of a (single) homosexual identity emerging in the later nineteenth century does not capture adequately the distinctions between ages or within specific eras that inevitably manifest constructions of identity that are fluid and dynamic.

The most productive way to approach the questions of "same-sex desire" and "sexual identity" in Goethe's oeuvre is by way of tracing a "genealogy of desire" (Foucault, *Use of Pleasure*, 5) and by mapping out the "cultural poetics of desire" (Halperin, 40) whereby sexual desires are constructed and conceptualized as inextricably joined with notions of self and subjectivity[4] in Goethe's literary work. As Foucault suggests in *Use of Pleasure* (5) "one could not very well analyze the formation and development of the experience of sexuality from the eighteenth century onward without doing a historical and critical study dealing with desire and the desiring subject." Crucial to this study of the desiring subject are the practices through which individuals actively and consciously focus on, decipher, recognize, and acknowledge themselves as subjects of desire. The investigation of the desiring self in Goethe's works involves explicating the language of self-reflection, self-knowledge, self-examination, and self-fashioning that forms the foundation of his poetic production. It is Goethe's mapping out of the "desiring self" that constitutes the subject of this study. And it is precisely in this reconstruction of a morphology of the same-sex identified self that Goethe's work challenges Foucault's exclusion of earlier centuries from the process of same-sex identity formation.

To this extent my investigation of Goethe's literary production and the paradigm of sexual identity and desire manifest throughout it also stands in opposition to the analyses of the eighteenth and nineteenth century by Foucauldian scholars such as Halperin. He maintains that the invention of "homosexuality" (I would say same-sex desire and identity)

> . . . had therefore to await, in the first place, the eighteenth-century discovery and definition of sexuality as the total ensemble of physiological and psychological mechanisms governing the individual's genital functions and the concomitant identification of that ensemble with a specifically developed part of the brain and nervous system; it also had to await, in the second place, the nineteenth-century interpretation of sexuality as a singular "instinct" or "drive," a force that shapes our conscious life according to its own unassailable logic and thereby determines, at least in part, the character or personality of each one of us. (26)

Halperin concludes that before "the scientific construction" (26) of sexuality as a constitutive feature of individuals, certain kinds of sexual *acts* could be catalogued, but there was "no conceptual apparatus available for identifying a person's fixed and determinate sexual orientation, much less for assessing and classifying it" (26). Halperin maintains that it is late nineteenth-century medico-psychoanalytic discourse that first fused senses of sexuality and self together—and in particular in scientific discourses. In contrast, I will demonstrate that Goethe's oeuvre offers an alternative and yet modern *poetic* expression of self and desire (and one that is often intricately, but not exclusively, conjoined and intertwined with the scientific discourses of his day).[5] And while I would not want to suggest that Goethe's texts mark *the* inception of contemporary senses of same-sex identity, self, and desire, their modernity nonetheless signals that the issues of historically emergent forms of sexual identity and desire require an investigation of a broader set of significatory registers. What may not be apparent in eighteenth-century scientific or legal discourse may certainly be evident in other sets of discourses.[6] Moreover, a detailed investigation of Goethe's literary production illustrates specific eighteenth and early nineteenth-century self-expressions of same-sex desire and identity—a discovery that is equally, if not essentially, more significant than discourses of the categorization and description of same-sex activity, desire, and identity. For these reasons, this study of sexual identity and desire begins with an outline of how desire "gets put" into and functions in a specific set of poetic articulations in Goethe's oeuvre. Examining the manner in which self and desire converge in Goethe's poetic and scientific writings allows for a clear conceptualization of his paradigm of sexual identity and desire within its historical contours, contexts, and contingencies.

The sexual identities and desires that emerge throughout Goethe's literary production are inextricably linked to specific poetic representations. In fact, it becomes evident that Goethe was consciously engaged in producing new expressions of desire and identity and that he understood his literary work in terms of its incitement to further poetic articulations of same-sex desire and identity. I have chosen to start with an examination of four critical moments of articulation in Goethe's writings that lay out a broad theoretical framework for more specific analyses of the literary and essayistic encoding of sexual identities and desires throughout his work. In this manner we will uncover a Goethean project—one that is consciously deployed and understood in terms of "putting" specific sexual identities and desires into a poetic discourse. Indeed, the first of the moments of articulation I will address involves Goethe's attempts to spell out male same-sex identity and desire in an encomium on Winckelmann.

SPELLING WINCKELMANN

Goethe's encomium on Winckelmann, written in 1805, constitutes a remarkable moment in history of the articulation of same-sex identification and desire. He outlines in a rather systematic manner the way in which self, self-fashioning, same-sex identity, and discourse converge. Beyond descriptions of sodomy, beyond discourses of sodomy, beyond isolated accounts of homoerotic desire, beyond representations of homosocial bonding, and even beyond isolated expressions of male-male desire, this Winckelmann encomium works self-reflexively to "put" the word that is Winckelmann—that is, that which is his same-sex identity—into poetic form. What is amazing about Goethe's essay on Winckelmann is its precise and detailed excursus of the manner in which Winckelmann strove to create his own language in order to express his same-sex desires. Goethe also underscores the importance of Winckelmann's letters in which he

directly expresses his desire for young men such as Berg. It is there
that Winckelmann's struggle to articulate his same-sex desire is most
overtly manifest. But, in addition, Goethe outlines for us step-by-
step how he and the Weimar Friends of Art recognized Winckelmann's efforts and how they in turn not only furthered his project,
but also labored to give his language more precision throughout
their literary and aesthetic production. In other words, Goethe's encomium illustrates the manner in which the same-sex desire that is
Winckelmann gets spelled together by the Weimar Friends of Art—
that is, how he becomes a poetic construct (a central part of a new
discourse) and how he puts himself into discourse. Goethe's encomium offers us, in essence, a veritable "anatomy" of the creation
of a new language of male same-sex desire on the part of men desiring men.

Before turning directly to Goethe's adulation and linguistic formulation of Winckelmann in his *Skizzen zu einer Schilderung Winckelmanns* (*Sketches of a Description of Winckelmann*), it seems appropriate to remind ourselves at least briefly of Winckelmann's more
general significance. Winckelmann has long been established as a critically important figure of the eighteenth century for the history of
German aesthetics, art, and same-sex desire and sexuality. As the father of modern art history and criticism, Winckelmann promoted the
Greek ideal of artistic beauty (focusing significantly on the beauty of
Greek representations of male bodies) and contributed to the major
formulations both of the Enlightenment and Classicism in Germany.
Authors and aestheticians such as Lessing, Herder, Goethe, Moritz,
and Schiller were all his theoretical and literary disciples. Above all,
Winckelmann created a new language of aesthetics, which we can de-
scribe as a language of aesthetic same-sex eroticism (see Aldrich, De-
tering, Morrison). Of course, much recent scholarship both within
German studies and within Gay and Lesbian studies has accentuated
Winckelmann's sensual descriptions of the Apollo of Belvedere, of
Ganymede, and of Bacchus (see, for instance, Aldrich, Hans Mayer,
Morrison, Kuzniar, Detering, and Richter). In fact, Kuzniar argues
quite convincingly that "Winckelmann inaugurated a cultured, hence
permissible voicing of same-sex attraction. Even more strikingly, he
facilitated, if you will, 'The Birth of Aesthetics out of the Spirit of

Homoeroticism'" (12, see also Richter, Detering, and MacLeod). Moreover, Winckelmann, while not himself inventing the idea of "Greek love" as a euphemism for same-sex sentiments, provided his society and culture with a model worthy of admiration and imitation (Aldrich). In the Age of Goethe, it is in Winckelmann's shadow that the contours of an explicitly "homosocial" and "homoerotic" culture became apparent (Richter, "Winckelmann's Progeny," 33). Winckelmann became the focal point around which "a substantial and coherent network of friends and patrons, lovers and beloveds, models and imitators" established a Greek-oriented cult of friendship—a "homosocial culture" (Richter, "Winckelmann's Progeny," 45). Goethe certainly was not the only eighteenth-century admirer of Winckelmann. Lesser-known figures such as Mueller and Gleim also sought to make his epistolary expressions of male-male desire their own (Richter, "Winckelmann's Progeny"). But even more importantly, the male culture of Classical Germany operated inherently as a culture of the same-sex sociality and eroticism embodied by Winckelmann.

My principal interest lies not in the figure of Winckelmann per se, but in his fashioning of a new language of same-sex desire and identification. More specifically, I intend to trace Goethe's systematic attempts to put Winckelmann and the same-sex desire he represents into poetic form. I am interested in Winckelmann's aesthetic language (and its sensuousness) in its convergence with the new language of same-sex sentiment he formulated in his letters to his male friends. By shifting our attention from an exclusive focus on descriptions of art and aesthetic language to the language of Winckelmann's letters (which, by the way, were the only Winckelmann texts that Goethe took with him on his critical journey to Italy), we begin to discover that Goethe emulated not only Winckelmann's engagement with art (Morrison), but even more importantly his new sensual language, which is more evident in his private letters. And, in fact, Goethe wrote his encomium on Winckelmann within the context of publishing some of Winckelmann's letters to a male friend—a collection of letters he introduces by reminding his readers of the quintessential importance of the letters of great men. Goethe's introduction to Winckelmann's letters and his conclusion to *Winckelmann und sein Jahrhundert* (*Winckelmann and his Age*) encourage the reader to familiarize her- or himself with all of Winckelmann's letters. Goethe underscores here specifically not only the significance of Winckelmann's aesthetic writing, or of his descriptions of Greek art, but of his epistolary legacy. Indeed, Detering expresses this succinctly when he writes:

> Was Goethe in zentralen Abschnitten seines Textes unternimmt, ist nicht weniger als eine Rekonstruktion derjenigen Beziehungen zwischen Ästhetik und Homoerotik, die Winckelmann selbst in einigen Briefen und vor allem dann in der Berg-Schrift entworfen hat: die Rekonstruktion einer ihrer Absicht nach homoerotischen Ästhetik (Detering, 41–42).

> What Goethe undertakes in central sections of his text is nothing less than a reconstruction of those relationships between aesthetics and homoerotics, that Winckelmann himself drafted in some letters and above all in the Berg-writing: the reconstruction of an intentionally homoerotic aesthetics.

As Detering (41) notes further, Goethe's "Sketches on Winckelmann" constitute the first systematic attempt to analyze the relationship between Winckelmann's homoeroticism and his aesthetics. Examining the linguistic forms and patterns of Winckelmann's letters, and Goethe's analysis of them in his *Sketches of a Description of Winckelmann,* we discover that Goethe outlined Winckelmann's homoerotic aesthetics, identified with Winckelmann and his same-sex desire, and also appropriated his linguistic innovations. Moreover, Goethe modified, developed, and furthered Winckelmann's expressions of same-sex desire until they acquired bolder and bolder linguistic, symbolic, and structural forms.

Goethe certainly shared his era's fascination with and adulation of Winckelmann. In his *Italian Journey* he describes how he followed in the great art historian's footsteps and how overwhelmed he felt as he considered that everywhere he went Winckelmann had been there before him.[7] And during the course of this journey Goethe would come to the determination that Winckelmann's assessment of the noble simplicity and quiet grandeur of antique art was an achievement German Classical artists and writers should emulate and which he himself would promote vigorously upon his return to Weimar. Indeed, Goethe also agreed with Winckelmann's contention in his famous essay *Gedanken über die Nachahmung der griechischen Werke in der Malerei und Bildhauerkunst* (1755) that it was only possible to achieve greatness in and through art and/or literary production through the imitation of the ancients. Winckelmann's approach to the antiquities, his exploration of Italy, and his very language became the aesthetic templates that Goethe adopted and strove to recreate. So for Goethe the imitation of great scholarly models does not begin and end with the ancients, but also includes more contemporary predecessors and especially Winckelmann.

In 1799 Goethe would find occasion to express his adulation of Winckelmann formally. The Princess Anna Amalia requested that he publish twenty-seven (as yet unpublished) letters that Winckelmann had sent to Hieronymus Dietrich Berendis. Goethe decided that he would publish these letters in his journal, *Propyläen*. The *Propyläen* that appeared between 1798 and 1806 constituted the first systematic publications of the theses and mandates of Weimar Classicism. Most of the essays that appeared in the *Propyläen* were transcribed by Goethe's friend and collaborator, the art historian Johann Heinrich Meyer. For his part, Goethe proofed, corrected, and expanded the essays that would eventually appear in the Journal. Goethe's *Propyläen* was, then, by its very nature a thoroughly collaborative project. Goethe's writing melded with that of Meyer and of those other authors who contributed to the volumes. The *Propyläen* was, indeed, the principal literary organ of the group of men surrounding Goethe who referred to themselves as the Weimarer Kunstfreunde (the Weimar Friends of Art). The central focus of the *Propyläen* was the promotion of criticism on and about art, literature, and aesthetics. The Journal was conceived from the beginning as a collaborative project. In fact, individual articles appeared without authors' names attached to them.

In his *Tag- und Jahreshefte* of 1804, Goethe related that in order to bring together a comprehensive description of a man so extraordinary as Winckelmann he felt he had to draw together several prominent scholars. These included Meyer, Friedrich August Wolf (philosopher and philologist), and Karl Ludwig Fernow (art critic and archaeologist). Each of these men and Goethe wrote several portions of an encomium on Winckelmann entitled *Winckelmann und sein Jahrhundert* (*Winckelmann and His Age*). This collaborative collection of essays on Winckelmann consisted of seven separate sections. The first was a short introduction by Goethe explaining to his readers the critical importance of the letters written by great men to their friends and contemporaries. This was followed by the twenty-seven letters Winckelmann had written to Berendis. The third section, attributed to Meyer, was a sketch of Art History in the eighteenth century. The fourth section, written by Goethe, constitutes the core of the collection and is entitled "Skizzen zu einer Schilderung Winckelmanns" ("Sketches of a Description of Winckelmann"). It is precisely Goethe's contribution that is the boldest in its attempt to lend Winckelmann and all he represents poetic/linguistic form, a personage, a life story, and a cultural history. The fifth section, also attributed to Meyer, addressed Winckelmann as an art historian. Goethe asked Wolf to write the last major section about the schools and academies from which Winckelmann would have learned about languages and antiquities. The final section, again written by Goethe, is the conclusion, which includes a list of the almost complete collection of Winckelmann's letters available at the time.

Not only did the final encomium on Winckelmann consist of seven separate portions, but the writers also collaborated even on those portions assigned only to one of them. For example, the section attributed to Meyer and referred to as "Winckelmann as an Art Historian" was composed with Fernow, who is thought to have written the section entitled "Observations of a Friend." In its very structure, *Winckelmann und sein Jahrhundert* requires a melding of scholarly voices. The significance of these multiple voices and the participation of these various male interlocutors in a common aesthetic project will become clearer during the course of this study. At this point it suffices to say that this structure of conceptual and linguistic sharing mirrors one of Goethe's central aesthetic ideas that is intimately related to his new poetic formulations of male same-sex desire and identity. Throughout Goethe's work male same-sex desire and identity attain poetic form precisely in and through the verbal exchanges among men who share a specific/common aesthetic/affinitive language.

Goethe's publication of *Winckelmann und sein Jahrhundert*

(*Winckelmann and His Age*, 1805) formulates Winckelmann's significance for the male-identified culture of German Classicism. It comprises new articulations of a male same-sex identity and a shift in attitudes towards men who desire men. Moreover, Winckelmann's known predilection for beautiful boys is not impugned, but openly admired and idealized (compare Kuzniar, *Outing Goethe*, 10). Each of the separate parts of *Winckelmann und sein Jahrhundert* explicates the critical characteristics and achievements of Winckelmann. It is clear that the participants considered it necessary to provide a composite view of Winckelmann through summaries and analyses of art history, his work, the history of his education, his travels, his letters, and his relationships to other men. As opposed to earlier eulogies of Winckelmann (for example, Herder's), which only focused on his scholarly production, this collaborative description of him strives to lend him a childhood, a personage, a history, and a place in history, and, in Goethe's case in particular, to lend him and his same-sex desire (which are viewed as one and the same) linguistic form. Structurally, then, Winckelmann's self, letters, and linguistic struggles constitute the core of this collective encomium. Moreover, his emerging "self" is inextricably conjoined both thematically and structurally to his aesthetic and scholarly achievements. Winckelmann's core self is manifest throughout this encomium in several symbolic registers—that is, in his own aesthetic, scholarly, and epistolary representations and the multiple scholarly voices of the Weimar Friends of Art. At the same time, we must keep in mind that Goethe does not overtly depict Winckelmann's sexual inclinations but codes them in references to "Greek" forms of love and friendship. He also does not refer at any point in the essay to Winckelmann's brutal death at the hands of a possible male lover.[8] On the other hand, Goethe's reticence does not preclude his poetic formation of a same-sex identity, and it is precisely those striking formulations that are left for us to trace.

Goethe's contribution to *Winckelmann und sein Jahrhundert*, *Skizzen zu einer Schilderung Winckelmanns* is structured in a manner parallel to that of the collaborative essays as a whole. It is divided into sections with titles such as "The Antique," "The Pagan," "Friendship," "Beauty," and "Becoming Aware of Greek Art," but unlike other descriptions of Winckelmann (and including the others in *Winckelmann und sein Jahrhundert*), Goethe focuses almost exclusively on Winckelmann and his identificatory significance. He suggests throughout his essay the inextricability of that which is "Winckelmann" and that which is "art history" or "beauty" or the "desire for men." Goethe persistently reminds us that Winckelmann is his critical work and vice versa. Goethe's essay accentuates his character, his sense of self, and his linguistic struggles. For Goethe, his scholarly work, his critical texts, and his self converge in the project that is Winckelmann. As he sees it, Winckelmann's histories of art and his letters constitute a "Lebensdarstellung" ("the representation of a life," MA, 6:2, 370), "ein Leben selbst" ("a life itself," MA, 6:2, 370). Winckelmann's scholarship was, according to Goethe, "hauptsächlich deswegen merkwürdig und schätzenswert . . . weil sein Charakter sich immer dabei offenbart" ("predominately for that reason interesting and valuable because his character is always revealed in it," MA, 6:2, 375). And to this extent, Winckelmann was occupied "immer mit sich selbst . . . ohne sich eigentlich zu beobachten" ("always with himself . . . without actually observing himself," MA, 6:2, 375). Winckelmann's scholarly work and letters are always all about Winckelmann—they reveal above all his character—and it is this character, of a quintessential German intellectual and male-desiring man, that makes his criticism of inestimable value. Winckelmann represents, for Goethe, a complete man: "er hat als Mann gelebt, und ist als ein vollständiger Mann von hinnen gegangen" ("He lived as a man, and he died a complete man," MA, 6:2, 380). The purpose of Goethe's essay on Winckelmann is to outline the characteristics of this male paragon. Indeed, it is Winckelmann's aesthetic and self-forming project that Goethe insists he hopes to "fort und immer fortsetzen" ("advance forever and ever," MA, 6:2, 381). Winckelmann is the German, male-oriented intellectual that Goethe and his contemporaries adulated and emulated. As we have seen, he is one of the critical figures around which the homosocial/homoerotic culture of German Classicism revolved. Moreover, Goethe's essay strives to lend poetic form to Winckelmann's mythical identity, demonstrating how the icon "Winckelmann" attains an identity and becomes a model for the German intellectual elite. And that identity is consistently represented, as we shall see, as one of male same-sex desire and identification. In fact, what Goethe offers here is a morphology of a same-sex desiring and identified man. His essay on Winckelmann constitutes a shift from a description solely of Winckelmann's work (Herder, Ramdohr, and Morgenstern) to the construction of Winckelmann as a particular self and principally as one who desires other men. Throughout Goethe's encomium on Winckelmann, self, sexual desire, and writing (discourse) merge in and through his encomium into a morphology of the same-sex desiring man. Indeed, within layers of writings by men, the Weimar Friends of Art both construct and identify with Winckelmann.

Meyer concurs with Goethe in his outline of art history in the eighteenth century that Winckelmann's studies of ancient art introduced his age to a new world—that is, to a new and emulatable "Lebensweise" ("manner of living," MA, 6:2, 285). He emphasizes that Winckelmann became infused with the spirit of the Greek and Roman worlds (MA, 6:2, 329). Goethe takes up Meyer's observations, pushing them even further toward an acknowledgment of the critical importance of Winckelmann's same-sex desire and pointing out that his antique nature revealed itself in his need for male friendship and his love of male bodies. As Goethe sees it, Winckelmann discovered in ancient art that "das letzte Produkt der sich immer steigernden Natur, ist der schöne Mensch" ("the last product of an ever progressing and evolving nature is the beautiful person [man]," MA, 6:2, 355). Indeed, this is why, according to Goethe, we find Winckelmann so often "in Verhältnis mit schönen Jünglingen, und niemals erscheint er belebter und liebenswürdiger, als in solchen, oft nur flüchtigen Augenblicken" ("in relation with beautiful boys and he never appeared more alive and dear than in such and often only fleeting moments," MA, 6:2, 356).

Indeed, Winckelmann's letters (recall that Goethe is writing in the context of promoting the letters) provide ample evidence of his love and desire for "beautiful boys." The younger men that Goethe is referring to would certainly include Berg, Stosch, and Berendis, with whom Winckelmann corresponded and to whom he expressed his feelings of heroic friendship and love.[9] To Berendis, for example, he writes: "Ich sehn mich Dich zu sehen und zu küßen, und ersterbe Dein ewiger und eigner" ("I long to see and to kiss you and will die eternally and solely yours" Jan. 29, 1753, *Briefe*, vol. 1, 126). And to Stosch he exclaims: "Mein Herz! meine Liebe gegen Sie hat keine Grenzen, und ich werde mir eine Art Vorwurf machen, wo ich nicht bald Gelegenheit finde, ein neues öffentliches Zeugniß von derselben zu geben" ("My heart! my love for you has no limits, and I would have to reproach myself, if I did not find soon an opportunity to make a new public testimonial to it" May 27, 1767, *Briefe*, vol. 3, 264).[10]

While Winckelmann often expressed his desire for men in his letters with brief references to their friendship, his feelings of loss in their absence, the limitlessness of his love for them, his desire to kiss them, etc., these sentiments come together most clearly in his letters to Berg. Here he outlines the limitless boundaries of his desire: "Mein theuerster Freund, ich liebe Sie mehr als alle Creatur, und keine Zeit, kein Zufall, kein Alter kann diese Liebe mindern; . . ." ("My dear friend, I love you more than all other creatures, and no time and no chance, and no age can diminish this love," Feb. 10, 1764, *Briefe*, vol. 3, 17). Moreover, throughout his letters to Berg, Winckelmann explicitly conflates the notions of heroic friendship and male same-sex desire:

> In 40 Jahren meines Lebens ist dieses der zweyte Fall, in welchem ich mich befunden, und es wird vermutlich der letzte seyn. Mein werther Freund, eine gleich starke Neigung kann kein Mensch in der Welt gegen Sie tragen: denn eine völlige Übereinstimmung der Seelen ist nur allein zwischen zween möglich; alle andere Neigungen sind nur Absenker aus diesem edlen Stamme . . . Freundschaft ohne Liebe ist nur Bekanntschaft. Jene aber ist heroisch und über alles erhaben . . . eine solche Freundschaft, die bis an die äußersten Linien der Menschlichkeit gehet, bricht mit Gewalt hervor, und ist die höchste Tugend, die itzo unter den Menschenkindern unbekannt ist, und also auch das höchste Gut, . . ." (to Berg, Jan. 9, 1762, *Briefe*, vol. 2, 232–33).

In the forty years of my life this is the second time in which I have found myself (in such love) and it will likely be the last one. My dear friend no one in the world can manifest an equally strong attraction to you; for a complete harmony of souls is only possible between two, all other feelings of attraction are only lower forms of this noble family . . . Friendship without love is only acquaintance. This one however is heroic and is above all others (sublime) . . . such a friendship which spans to the outer limits of humanity, emerges with force, and is the highest virtue, that is now unknown among the children of mankind, and is therefore also the greatest good, . . .

Winckelmann attempts in this letter to describe the breadth, scope, and height of his love for Berg. And to do so, he invokes models of Greek love and heroic friendship that he perceives as forms of friendship and love more sublime than any other feelings of attraction. The heroic love—the male same-sex desire—that Winckelmann feels for Berg represents to him the highest virtue and the greatest good. Winckelmann's expression of love for Berg and his justification of his sentiments asserts not only the acceptability of male-male desire, but its elevation to the pinnacle of love relations (see also Detering, 65).

As Goethe asserted, Winckelmann could only perceive his inner self within the context of erotically charged relationships to other men: "er empfand sein eigenes Selbst nur unter der Form der Freundschaft" ("He perceived his own self only in the form of [male] friendship," MA, 6:2, 354). Winckelmann is driven by a "Freundschaftsbedürfnis" ("a need for friendship") and a form of "friendship" and "male love" that befits a man who embodies the Greek spirit. Finding himself, having a sense of self at all, requires in Winckelmann's case an identification with and desire for other men. Goethe foregrounds an indelible image of Winckelmann surrounded by loving boys, who appear, we might conjecture, to identify with and desire him. Moreover, Goethe reinvokes the irresistible scene of Winckelmann as the fulcrum of homoerotic attraction in his fantasized vision of himself and other German intellectuals welcoming Winckelmann home from Italy:

> Ihn erwartete sein Vaterland, ihm streckten seine Freunde die Arme entgegen, alle Äußerungen der Liebe, deren er so sehr bedurfte, alle Zeugnisse der öffentlichen Achtung, auf die er so viel Wert legte, warteten seiner Erscheinung, um ihn zu überhaufen."

> His fatherland awaited him, his friends stretched their arms toward him. They awaited him in order to shower him with all the expres-

sions of love which he so needed, all the proof of the public regard upon which he placed so much value" (MA, 6:2, 380).

Goethe envisions himself and his contemporaries waiting for Winckelmann's return and ready to shower upon him the expressions of love (male-male desire) that he so needs and desires. The image of the "beautiful boys" merges in Goethe's essay with that of the adoring group of male intellectuals who surround him in their loving embraces and who identify with and express their love for Winckelmann.

In Goethe's delineation Winckelmann stands at the center of same-sex identificatory emergence among the intellectual elite in eighteenth-century German letters. It is Goethe, writing about Winckelmann, who first makes the critical connection between the sexual identity that Winckelmann symbolizes, on the one hand, and its linguistic and representational formation, on the other. Detering suggests that Goethe was interested in Winckelmann's life in letters. That is, he was less concerned with how Winckelmann was in character than "wie er sich Artikuliert hat" ("how he articulated himself," Detering, 56). I think Goethe was interested in both, but particularly in the way Winckelmann constructed a language of himself and his same-sex desire. In turn, as he writes on Winckelmann, Goethe effects and outlines how Winckelmann, that is the phenomenon that Winckelmann represents (male same-sex desire), attains its first linguistic expressions. And, amazingly, Goethe's essay is principally focused on the linguistic formation of the Winckelmannian *self*—a project that Winckelmann himself intimated in a letter to Berendis in which he asserts his desire to "form himself" ("mich zu formieren," Jan. 6, 1753, *Briefe*, vol 1., 119). In *Winckelmann and His Age* Goethe insisted that Winckelmann's letters are a kind of "Selbstgespräch" (MA, 6:2, 198)—a form of monologue or, literally, one could say, a "Gespräch" ("discussion") of the "Selbst" ("self"). Like Goethe's essay, Winckelmann's letters bring the phenomenon "Winckelmann" to life. And it is a life that we ought to see in its immediacy. The purpose of reading and writing about Winckelmann, and of reading his letters, is specifically "einen solchen Charakter unmittelbar anzuschauen" ("in order to observe such a character in complete

immediacy," MA, 6:2, 401). Goethe's essay and Winckelmann's letters ought to evoke indelible images of the art historian's essential
"personage." In both forms of writing Winckelmann ought to attain
a recognizable (sexual) identity.

Throughout his essay Goethe returns obsessively to images of
Winckelmann as the initial writer of himself. He reminds us that "als
Literator" ("as a writer [literary figure]," MA, 6:2, 369), Winckelmann was "ein gemachter Mann" ("a made man," MA, 6:2, 369);
Winckelmann had developed his own style (MA, 6:2, 369). He was
constantly revising his work—that is, himself. Throughout the process of scholarly writing, "so lernte er im Entwerfen und Schreiben"
("he learned through drafting and writing," MA, 6:2, 369), and
his revisions were revisions of himself: "weil er sich immer wieder
umgeschrieben [hat]" ("because he continually re-wrote himself,"
MA, 6:2, 370). Winckelmann's writings do not just *reflect* his
"Lebensweise" ("manner of living"); through his writing he *constructs* and *revises* his own life and personage.

Despite Winckelmann's attempts to form a sense of self, Goethe
waxes eloquent over Winckelmann's nonself-reflectivity: "Er denkt
nur an sich, nicht über sich . . ." ("He thinks only of himself, not
about himself" (MA, 6:2, 375). He insists that Winckelmann, the
great aesthetician, remains oblivious to his true (sexual) nature:
"Dabei bleibt er sich durchaus ein Rätsel, und erstaunt manchmal
über seine eigene Erscheinung, besonders in Betrachtung dessen,
was er war und was er geworden ist" ("At the same time, he remains
a thorough puzzle to himself, and is sometimes surprised by his own
appearance, especially in regard to what he was and what he has become," MA, 6:2, 375). Winckelmann wrote himself and yet remained
a puzzle to himself. Meyer concurs that Winckelmann intuitively
recognized his affinity to the "Greek spirit," even if he did not always express it clearly: " . . . denn er hat, mehr als kein anderer im
Geist mit den Alten verwandt, immer das Rechte geahndet, wenn
auch nicht allemal deutlich ausgesprochen . . ." ("then he had, more
than any other spiritually connected to the ancients, always intuited
correctly, if he did not always express it clearly," MA, 6:2, 386).

In Winckelmann's letters the act of writing is as much about constructing objects of same-sex desire as it is about struggling to form

one's own self. In a letter to Stosch, for example, Winckelmann describes him as a friend "den ich mir geschaffen, erzogen, auf den ich die Kräfte meiner schönsten Jahre gewandt, und dem ich das hohe Glück einer heroischen Freundschaft, die wenigen bekannt worden, nur aber zu spät, schmecken lernen" ("who I created for myself, raised, upon whom I turned the powers of my most beautiful years, and who I taught [but perhaps too late] to enjoy the high fortune of heroic friendship, which is known only to a few" (mid-Sept. 1757, *Briefe,* vol. 1, 300). Likewise, in a letter to Füßli, Winckelmann fantasizes about himself as Füßli's epistolary creator:

> Die Welt wird mir ein Paradies und das Leben eine Wollust durch Kenntniß von Menschen ersterer Größe, wie mein Fueßli ist, und ich würde auch in großen Trübsalen wünschen zu leben, um solchen Freund von Angesicht zu Angesicht zu kennen. Unterdeßen bilde ich mir deßen Bild und werde ein Schöpfer von seiner Gestalt nach der Idee von dem was das schönste und würdigste in der Welt ist, um nach demselben meine Hände auszustrecken, und in dieser Anschaulichkeit küße ich den göttlichen Freund und ersterbe . . . (mid-April 1758, *Briefe,* vol. 1, 349).

> The world becomes a paradise for me and life becomes a delight through knowing a person of the first order such as my Füßli and I would wish to live in great afflictions in order to come to know such a friend face to face. In the meantime I imagine to myself his image and become the creator of his form according to the idea of what is most beautiful and valuable in the world—in order to reach out my hands to him, and in this vision to kiss this divine friend and to die . . .

Although Winckelmann had never seen Füßli he brought him to life in his letter in the form of Classical male beauty. The letter to Füßli provides Winckelmann with a mechanism through which he can imagine not only his desire for Füßli, but also Füßli's attractive body, and himself embracing it. Similarly, in a letter to Genzmer, Winckelmann imagines Genzmer's desire for him: "Ich bin überzeugt, daß Dein Herz mich wahrhaftig liebt. Du bist ein Freund, so wie ihn jener Weise gesucht. Durch wie viel Angenehmen locktest Du mich nicht zu Dir zu kommen? Ich schätze dieses Dein Verlangen eben so hoch, ja noch höher, als alles, was Du mir zeigen wollen" ("I am convinced that your heart truly loves me. You are a friend for whom every wise man searches. Through how many pleasures you lured me to come to you? I treasure this your desire as highly, yes even higher than everything which you want to show me," Sept. 29, 1747, *Briefe,* vol. 1, 75).[11] For Winckelmann, writing letters was clearly about constructing images of other men like himself who desired men. To this extent, Winckelmann was involved not only in self-fashioning, but also in the fashioning of other selves in a community of like identification. Winckelmann asserts in his letters that he is not isolated in his desires. For him, same-sex identity is a product of self-fashioning, which takes place within the context of envisioning others of the same identification. Like Foucault, Winckelmann realized that discourse operates both in the construction of self and other. But in contrast to Foucault, Winckelmann envisioned these linguistic operations emerging specifically and principally within the dynamic interchange between self and others of like desire and identity. Moreover, Winckelmann shared with Kant the idea—indeed, he put it into action—that same-sex desire and identity become reality and begin to spread once they acquire forms of articulation.

Winckelmann's letters clearly allow him to express and to construct both himself and other men as men who desire men. But even more significantly, certainly for our understanding of Goethe's interest in Winckelmann's letters, Winckelmann emphasizes the incitement to a discourse of desire that his letters represent. He stresses repeatedly his need to express his sentiments of love to his male friends. To Genzmer he writes: "Ich liebe Niemand außer Dir . . . Mein Auge weint vor innerster Sehnsucht gegen Dich, wenn ich itzo die Feder ansetze an Dich zu schreiben" ("I love no one but you, my eye cries with the innermost longing for you, as I now set the pen to write to you," Summer, 1747, *Briefe,* vol. 1, 73–74)[12] and "Aus der Fülle meiner Seele wollte ich mit Dir sprechen; es ist unglaublich viel, was ich Dir zu sagen habe" ("Out of the fullness of my soul I wanted to speak to you; what I have to explain to you is unbelievably vast," Sept. 29, 1747, *Briefe,* vol. 1, 75). Similarly, Winckelmann tells Berendis: "Göttlicher Freund ich muß Dich sprechen" ("Divine friend, I must speak to you," April 13, 1753, *Briefe,* vol. 1, 134), and Francke: "Wie viel wollte ich Ihnen erzählen, wie viel sollten Sie hören" ("How much I wanted to tell you, how much you should

hear," July 7, 1756, *Briefe,* vol. 1, 236), and finally to Wille: "Aus der
Fülle meiner Seele möchte ich schreiben, was ich empfinde, um Ihnen
das Herz zu zeigen, das gewaltig in mir schlägt von entzückenden
Vergnügen, die jemals ein Freund gefühlet" ("Out of the fullness of
my soul, I want to write what I am feeling, in order to show you the
heart that pounds powerfully with the most delightful pleasures that
ever a friend felt," mid-April, 1758, *Briefe,* vol. 1, 347–48). Winckelmann's letters demonstrate the critical importance of writing in the
representation of incitements to new articulations of same-sex desire
and identity. Writing to other men constitutes self-fashioning, the
fashioning of like selves, and incitement to further more specific expressions of desire. Underlying the compulsion to write is the belief
that continual writing and re-writing will eventually end in more and
more accurate articulations of the same-sex desiring man. Repeated
attempts at linguistic formation will result in new expressions that
in turn will facilitate bonds between men. In fact, as we shall see,
Winckelmann's own writing certainly illustrates his attempt to write
beyond the awkward expressions of his day to include references to
Greek friendship.

As much as Winckelmann foregrounds the function of his letters to lend his desire linguistic and conceptual form, it is clear in
his letters to Berg that he *struggles* continually throughout them to
develop a new language of male same-sex desire and particularly one
that his male objects of desire can understand (see also Detering, 63).
Indeed, Winckelmann's first letter to Berg is precisely all about his
attempts to articulate his love for the young man in ways that Berg
could envision. Because of the significance of this letter for our understanding of Winckelmann's conscious attempts to give his desire
linguistic form, I will quote it here at length:

> So wie eine zärtliche Mutter untröstlich weinet um ein geliebtes Kind,
> welches ihr ein gewaltthätiger Prinz entreißt und zum gegenwärtigen
> Tod ins Schlachtfeld stellet; eben so bejammerte ich die Trennung
> von Ihnen, mein süßer Freund, mit Thränen, die aus der Seele selbst
> fließen. Ein unbegreiflicher Zug zu Ihnen, den nicht Gestalt und
> Gewächs allein erwecket, ließ mich von dem ersten Augenblicke
> an, da ich Sie sahe, eine Spur von derjenigen Harmonie fühlen, die
> über menschliche Begriffe gehet, und von der ewigen Verbindung der

Dinge angestimmet wird. In 40 Jahren meines Lebens ist dieses der
zweite Fall, in welchem ich mich befunden, und es wird vermuthlich
der letzte seyn. Mein werther Freund, eine gleich starke Neigung
kann kein Mensch in der Welt gegen Sie tragen: denn eine völlige
Uebereinstimmung der Seelen ist nur allein zwischen zween möglich;
alle andere Neigungen sind nur Absenker aus diesem edlen Stamme.
Aber dieser göttliche Trieb ist den mehresten Menschen unbekannt,
und wird daher von vielen übelverstanden gedeutet. Die Liebe in
dem höchsten Grad ihrer Stärke muß sich nach allen möglichen
Fähigkeiten äußern:

> I thee both as a Man and Woman prize
> For a perfect love implies
> Love in all capacities.
>
> —Cowley

und diese ist der Grund, worauf die unsterbliche Freundschaften der
alten Welt, eines Theseus and Pirithous, eines Achilles und Patroclus
gebaut sind. Freundschaft ohne Liebe ist nur Bekanntschaft. Jene aber
ist heroisch und über alles erhaben . . . eine solche Freundschaft,
die bis an die äussersten Linien der Menschlichkeit gehet, bricht
mit Gewalt hervor, und ist die höchste Tugend, die itzo unter den
Menschenkindern unbekannt ist, und also auch das höchste Gut,
welches in dem Besitze derselben besteht . . . Ein einziger Monat
Ihres verlängerten Aufenthalts in Rom und mehr Musse, mit Ihnen,
mein Freund, besonders zu sprechen, würden diese Freundschaft
auf unbeweglichen Grund gesetzt haben, und alle meine Zeit wäre
Ihnen gewidmet gewesen. Demohngeachtet hätte ich mich in starken
und schriftlich unaussprechlichen Worten esklären müssen, wenn ich
nicht gemerket, daß ich Ihnen in einer ungewöhnlichen Sprache reden
würde" (June 9, 1762, *Briefe,* vol. 2, 232–33).

Just as a delicate mother cries inconsolably over a beloved child,
which a violent prince has torn from her and placed before present
death on the battlefield, just so I lamented the separation from you,
my sweet friend, with tears that flow from the soul. An inexplicable
attraction to you, that was not solely awakened by build and form,
let me feel from the very first moment that I saw you, a trace of that
harmony, which transcends human conception and is determined by
the eternal connection of things. In the forty years of my life this is
the second time (this has occurred) and is likely to be the last time.
My dear friend, no one in the world can feel as strong an attraction
to you, for a complete agreement of souls is only possible between

two; all other attractions are only of a lower level of this family. But this divine desire is unknown to most people, and is therefore misunderstood/misinterpreted by most. Love in the highest level of its power must express itself in all its possible capabilities:

> I thee both as Man and Woman prize
> For a perfect love implies
> Love in all capacities.
>
> —Cowley

and this is the foundation, upon which the immortal friendships of the old world, of a Theseus and Pirithous, of an Achilles and Patroclus are built. Friendship without love is only acquaintance. This is, however, heroic and above all others (sublime) . . . such a friendship, that spans to the outer limits of humanity, emerges with force, and is the highest virtue, which is now unknown to the children of mankind and is also the greatest good . . . A single month-long extension of your stay in Rome and more leisure with you my friend—especially to talk, would have set this friendship on an immovable foundation and all of my time would have been devoted to you. Apart from that I would have had to explain myself in strong words and words inexpressible in writing, if I had not realized that I would speak to you in an unusual language.

Throughout this letter, Winckelmann invokes the languages/discourses of love available to him and that he thinks Berg might understand in order to outline his love for him—that is, in an attempt to express his male same-sex desire. He begins with a reference to the strength of a mother's love for a precious son who has been stolen from her, forced into military service, and who faces almost certain death. He then tries to describe his physical and psychic attraction to Berg within expressions of its uniqueness within his own life's experience of love. Winckelmann assures Berg that this is only the second time in his forty years that he has felt such an intense desire for another man and that this may well be the last time. The kind of love he feels for Berg, he insists, is of the highest level, but is misunderstood, unknown to, and misinterpreted by most people. Despite his age's condemnation of same-sex desire and in direct contradistinction to Kant, Winckelmann asserts that love of this power must express itself in all of its possible capabilities. And here he invokes the poetic passage from Cowley that defines perfect love as that which manifests itself in all its capacities. Cowley's poetic discourse of love is coupled with allusions to Greek forms of male-male desire. Such heroic forms of friendship/love are, Winckelmann assures Berg, manifestations of the highest virtue and the greatest good. Winckelmann's letter to Berg represents his conscious attempt to construct a new language of love—one that might express through more familiar discourses a language of male same-sex attraction that would otherwise be restricted to the expression of "unaussprechliche Worte" ("inexpressible words") in a "ungewöhnliche Sprache" ("an unusual language"). Similarly, in another letter to Berg, Winckelmann accentuates specifically his struggle to articulate his own same-sex desire:

> Alle Namen, die ich Ihnen geben könnte, sind nicht süß genug und reichen nicht an meine Liebe, und alles, was ich Ihnen sagen könnte, ist viel zu schwach, mein Herz und meine Seele reden zu lassen. Vom Himmel kam die Freundschaft, und nicht aus menschlichen Regungen. Mit einer gewissen Ehrfurcht näherte ich mich Ihnen; daher ich bey Ihrer Abreise des höchsten Gutes beraubet zu seyn schien. Was hätte ich nicht schreiben müssen, wenn nur unter hunderten meiner Leser ein einziger dies hohe Geheimniß begreifen könnte. Mein theuerster Freund, ich liebe Sie mehr als alle Creatur, und keine Zeit, kein Zufall, kein Alter kann diese Liebe mindern . . . (Feb. 10, 1764, *Briefe*, vol. 3, 17).

> All the names which I could give you are not sweet enough and do not extend to my love and everything that I could tell you is much too weak to allow my heart and soul to speak. Our friendship came from heaven and not from human stirrings. With a certain adulation I approached you, and appeared to be robbed therefore at your departure of the greatest good. What wouldn't I have had to write, if only one of my hundreds of readers could comprehend this high secret. My dearest friend, I love you more than all other creatures, and no time and no chance and no age can diminish this love; . . .

For Winckelmann language does not contain the notions, names, and concepts that he would require in order to name his beloved Berg. Anything he could say, any language he could develop (given the bits of discourses he has at hand: mother's love, Greek love, Cowley's poetry, etc.) would be too weak to allow his soul to speak its sentiments.

Moreover, not only can Winckelmann barely find a language within which to express his desire for Berg, he cannot construct one that would be understandable to others either. It is unimaginable to him what he would have to write in order to convey his meaning to even *one* of his hundreds of readers. It is clear in Winckelmann's letters to Berg that he is centrally concerned with creating a language through which he could express his desire not only to his male lovers, but also to his readers at large. Winckelmann struggles in his letters to Berg to find ways of speaking his desire. And he is convinced that he has not yet discovered or constructed a language that would allow his soul to fully speak its same-sex sentiments. It is important to note here that the discourses Winckelmann relied on, and that Goethe and Moritz appropriated, do not reflect the terminological shifts surrounding "sodomy" during his era. Winckelmann obviously strove to fashion a language of sentiment and identity, not one that expressed a particular sexual activity. His focus was not on sodomy, but on desire and identity as the critical self-expressions he longed to define and relate. Moreover, Winckelmann's linguistic experiments seem to confirm Dollimore's contention that earlier centuries did not construct reverse discourses through which they identified themselves with the term "sodomite." However, as Winckelmann's work demonstrates, that does not mean that men of his inclination did not construct languages of same-sex identity and desire. Winckelmann surely did, but he turned to expressions of sentiment and not to terminological innovations of the day such as sodomy, Italian menaces, and holy pederasts.

In his encomium on Winckelmann, Goethe refers precisely to his incitements to a new language of male same-sex desire. While Goethe does not directly address Winckelmann's letters to Berg, he focuses on Winckelmann's inability to express himself and/or his same-sex desire.[13] Goethe describes Winckelmann's incitements to "form himself" and construct his desire and identity and a language of them in terms of his failure to provide his readers with readily decipherable "Winckelmannian words." Although Winckelmann is amazingly adept in lending his male-male desire symbolic form and is certainly conscious of his linguistic project and its limitations, both he and Goethe see his initial endeavors as incomplete. Goethe concentrates his attention in particular on Winckelmann's struggle to articulate himself and his desire through a new language of love. His emphasis on Winckelmann's heroic and yet not fully developed representations of himself points directly to the struggles that Winckelmann addressed in his letters to Berg. And Goethe highlights that linguistic struggle in his insistence that Winckelmann could barely cobble together a few self-defining syllables. According to Goethe, Winckelmann (like most men) remains to himself a semi-expressed being, something between word and image: " . . . eine vielsylbige Charade . . . wovon er selbst nur wenige Sylben zusammenbuchstabiert, indessen andre leicht das ganze Wort entziffern" ("a charade of many syllables, of which he himself only 'spelled together' a few, while others easily decoded the whole word," MA, 6:2, 375). Winckelmann is a "charade of syllables" (another German word for charade is "Silbenrätsel"—literally, a puzzle of syllables); he is a semi-formed linguistic construct who cannot attain or maintain self-reflection and/or a sense of self-identification. He commands only a few self-delimiting bits of discourse, attaining, therefore, no clear, precise sense of self-identity. In Goethe's opinion, Winckelmann never completed the decipherment and reformulation of himself as a man desiring other men. Others, however, and specifically Goethe in his essay on Winckelmann, can readily spell out and decode the "whole word" ("das ganze Wort") that is Winckelmann. The viewer of the charade of syllables deciphers, decodes, and reconstructs the terminological and conceptual formations intimated by the Winckelmannian charade. And Goethe recognizes this challenge to linguistic expression as his own. His task is to put the syllables together, the bits and pieces of discourse, which comprise Winckelmann— which constitute the same-sex desire and identification that Winckelmann signified. By himself, Winckelmann constitutes at best a draft awaiting revision. Goethe's essay attempts to push Winckelmann further into recognizable linguistic articulation. Winckelmannian identity and desire ought to assume a distinct shape through Goethe's words—a recognizable contour with which Goethe and his contemporaries can identify, emulate, and desire to desire. Winckelmann is no longer a mishmash of semi-connected syllables. He is a decoded word—a word with layers of signification—that Goethe and the Weimar Friends of Art have fashioned during the course of their encomium and reconstituted in linguistic form.

In Goethe's words Winckelmann became an age, a paragon, a morphology of male same-sex desire. He was "put into discourse" (Foucault, *History of Sexuality*, 11) and he rose to the apex of human existence in his instantiation of Greek love and friendship:

> Die leidenschaftliche Erfüllung liebevoller Pflichten, die Wonne der Unzertrennlichkeit, die Hingebung eines für den andern, die ausgesprochene Bestimmung für das ganze Leben, die notwendige Begleitung in den Tod setzen uns bei Verbindung zweier Jünglinge in Erstaunen, ja man fühlt sich beschämt, wenn uns Dichter, Geschichtsschreiber, Philosophen, Redner, mit Fabeln, Ereignissen, Gefühlen, Gesinnungen solchen Inhaltes und Gehaltes überhäufen. Zu einer Freundschaft dieser Art fühlte Winckelmann sich geboren . . . (MA, 6:2, 354).

> The passionate fulfillment of loving duties, the bliss of inseparability, the sacrifice of one for the other, the pronounced determination [identification] for all of life, the necessary accompaniment in death, leave us—in the bond between two boys—in astonishment. Yes, one feels ashamed when poets, historians, philosophers, and speakers shower us with fables, events, feelings, and convictions of such content and meaning. Winckelmann felt himself born to such friendship.

Winckelmann, in Goethe's formulation, became not just a word, but a poetic construct—a literary ideal of male-male desire. He merged with a long line of poetic, male models of Greek love, before whom Goethe and his readers stood in utter awe. Winckelmann was a quotation of the ideal Greek man—the quintessentially complete man ("ein vollständiger Mann" MA, 6:2, 380)—and as such the ideal of his Classically oriented contemporaries. Moreover, Goethe insinuates that it is poets and writers who depict great men like Winckelmann and who fashion them into identities that in turn inspire and infect the men who read about them. Winckelmann's letters provide both an image of Winckelmann and a set of tropes that signal the struggle to express the male same-sex desire that is so central to Winckelmann. The critical expression of his same-sex desire and several tropes that recur throughout German Classical writing are succinctly summarized in his letter to Berg dated June 9, 1762:

> Edler Freund! Ein unbegreiflicher Zug zu Ihnen, den nicht Gestalt und Gewächs allein erwecket, ließ mich von dem ersten Augenblick an, da ich Sie sahe, eine Spur von denjenigen Harmonie fühlen, die über menschliche Begriffe gehet . . . (June 9, 1762, *Briefe*, vol. 2, 232).

> Noble Friend! An inexplicable inclination to you that is not awakened solely by build and growth evoked in me the first moment I saw you, a trace of that harmony, which transcends human conceptualization . . . .

Within the context of asserting the impossibility of expressing a desire beyond "human conceptualization," Winckelmann reiterates his love for his friend Berg. Throughout German Classical writing and particularly in Goethe's literary production, the key tropes of this letter resurface. The "inexplicable inclination" Winckelmann has for Berg, his incomprehensible and instant desire, will reappear in Goethe's theory of the elective affinities. Winckelmann's isolation of the exact moment in which he first *saw* Berg and perceived his desire for him will resurface in Goethe's literary production in terms of visual cathexis and visual reciprocity.

In addition, Goethe's entire excursus on Winckelmann provides a specific and detailed outline of what German Classicists perceived to be the defining components of a nascent morphology of the same-sex desiring man. In other words, we can trace exactly how Goethe, Winckelmann, and the Weimar Friends of Art sought to isolate specific characteristics of—that is, the identity of—men who desired men. What did they look for or at? What profile did they create? Goethe's encomium demonstrates that they were reconstructing Winckelmann's identity in several ways. They were investigating, among other things, his childhood, his education, his travels (especially his interest in Italy and Greece), his creativity and brilliance, his love and emulation of the ancients, his awareness of Greek art, his sensitivity to beauty (and especially to beautiful male bodies), and his struggles to express his desires to other men in both his letters and in his professional writings. Winckelmann's *Lebensweise*, his manner of living, becomes the template for a new morphology of the man who desires other men. As we shall see, these components of identification will resurface throughout Goethe's literary work as he struggles to lend the desire and identity that is Winckelmann even more precise contours. What is manifestly clear here is that Goethe and the German Classicists are not only outlining Winckelmann's morphology, but also their own system of self-identification, to which they return throughout their poetic production to represent men desiring men. In fact, the quintessential characteristic of these men (as they saw it) appears to have been their compulsion to fashion them*selves* in a new language of same-sex desire and identity. And so in these ways, Winckelmann's same-sex identity is also that of Goethe, Moritz, and the Weimar Friends of Art.

While these are not the only recurrent themes and tropes revolving around expressions of same-sex identity and desire in German Classicism, they are some of the central ones. Moreover, for Goethe, literary, epistolary, and historical venues function critically in the construction of male models, male fantasies, and emulatable male identities. The fictional identities created by writers, philosophers, and art historians become the fantasies whereby and against which the reading man assesses his own identity, desire, and self-formation.

The importance of Goethe's essay on Winckelmann is at least fourfold: 1) he isolates a moment in which the word "Winckelmann" took shape; 2) his essay actually serves to "put" the phenomenon "Winckelmann" into linguistic form in a self-reflective way—that is, Goethe sees himself spelling out the "syllables" that comprise Winckelmann; 3) he demonstrates not only his own but his age's identification with Winckelmann—the Greek and male-loving man; and 4) he outlines a specific set of characteristics that identify the man who desires other men, providing him with a particular morphology. And, if that were not enough, Goethe insists as well that the "word" "Winckelmann" "erregt in uns den lebhaftesten Drang, das, was er begonnen, mit Eifer und Liebe fort und immer fortzusetzen" ("inspires in us the liveliest urge to advance with zeal and love what he has begun," MA, 6:2, 381). Winckelmann's epistolary struggles will live on in the works of his contemporaries and certainly, as we shall see, in Goethe's oeuvre. Finally, in Goethe's view, Winckelmann is a model of identification, a phenomenon of language/discourse, whose desire is the desire of his contemporaries. Goethe's project in this essay and elsewhere in his poetic writings is to "advance what he (Winckelmann) has begun." What is at issue is the way in which Winckelmann and the sexual identity he represents gets "put into discourse" (Foucault, *History of Sexuality*, 11).

Of course, Goethe is neither Foucault nor a nineteenth-century sexologist. And perhaps, for precisely this reason, his essay on Winckelmann captures an eighteenth- and early nineteenth-century conceptual shift, constituting a process whereby a specific sexual identity begins to move from a space of inarticulation into a place of linguistic formation. Moreover, the Winckelmann essay discloses the tremendous importance of the articulation of same-sex identity and desire for a much larger Goethean project. As we shall see, Goethe's literary production provides a huge corpus of textual evidence of the expression of same-sex identities. What the Winckelmann essay insinuates about sexual identity acquires much clearer contours throughout Goethe's literary production. And it is precisely this "putting of sexual identity into discourse" that has been missed by scholars assessing Winckelmann's letters and Goethe's Winckelmann encomium in the past. In fact, Hans Mayer set the trajectory for critical assessments of Goethe's essay with his comment that Goethe "attempted to block out anything that might have contradicted his version of a happy and harmonious scholar and connoisseur of art" (167). Indeed, scholars concurring with Mayer have generally cited the Winckelmann essay as evidence of Goethe's "glossing over of Winckelmann's homosexuality" (Sweet, 148),[14] of a murky "stylization" of Winckelmann (Sweet, 148), indicating perhaps even anxiety about homosexuality on Goethe's part and the collapse of his critical method (Derks, 234). But Goethe's careful elucidation of the formation of the word that is "Winckelmann" actually suggests otherwise.

It is true that Goethe's description of Winckelmann both idealizes him and to some extent veils his sexual identity. But veiling his identity is not the same as glossing it over. Nor does it indicate Goethe's inability to address the issue (compare Sweet, 148). While Goethe may be reticent in his expression of Winckelmann's same-sex identity, he nonetheless begins the process of lending it linguistic and conceptual form. *Winckelmann und sein Jahrhundert* foregrounds an incitement to the poetic expression of male same-sex desire. Moreover, Goethe's essay provides us with critical evidence about an important shift in attitudes about same-sex identity in eighteenth- and early nineteenth-century Germany. The new formulation of same-sex identity and desire in Goethe's encomium is significant precisely because it constitutes the process of the self-understanding, self-expression, and self-fashioning of men who desired men. In contrast to the explosion of discourses (legal, medical, psychoanalytical) at the end of the nineteenth century, these discourses elucidate how Winckelmann and Goethe began to formulate and identify with their own expressions of same-sex desire.

ELECTIVE AFFINITIES OR METAPHORS OF SELF AND (SAME-SEX) DESIRE

Although it is true that Goethe's encomium attempts to lend Winckelmannian sexual identity a linguistic form, the recurrent paradigm of sexual identity manifest in Goethe's works is contingent upon notions of desire as fluid and protean. While the Winckelmann essay foregrounded the issue of sexual identity, Goethe's literary paradigms of sexual desire generally revolve around a conception of multiple sexual identities that include male same-sex identification and desire, but are not restricted to it. Goethe's texts are not principally concerned with sexual acts,[15] but in the dynamics of what we might call desires, sentiments, or feelings of attraction. At the same time, the Goethean paradigm of desire and identity contributes to our understanding of a nascent coding of male-male desire. Indeed, to understand how male same-sex desire acquires poetic form in Goethe's works, we need to understand his rather complex conceptions of how desire works whether in same-sex relations or in those between members of the opposite sexes. Same-sex identity is a fundamental part of the Goethean paradigm of desire, but it does not operate in isolation. The paradigm that emerges throughout Goethe's literary production suggests a multiplicity and fluidity of desire that often destabilizes notions of exclusive sexual identities. With this in mind, I would like to turn to a second paradigmatic moment of articulation in Goethe's writings, revolving around his notion of "elective affinities." I have chosen this symbolic moment not only because of its focus on desire and identity, but also because of its almost compulsive foregrounding of the nature and function of poetic formulations in the construction of desire and identity. Here we will trace Goethe's literary project and will discover that it is constantly aware of the complexities of discourses and of their multiple and dynamic interactions.

What I have referred to as his paradigm of sexual desire and identity Goethe would likely have explained in terms of "elective affinities." His 1809 novel bearing that title, *Die Wahlverwandtschaften* (*The Elective Affinities*), contains the first thorough explication in his work of *Verwandtschaften* (affinities) and *Wahlverwandtschaften* (elective affinities), although, as we shall see, one finds this model of desire throughout Goethe's oeuvre and even in works as early as *Götz von Berlichingen* (1773)[16] and *Die Leiden des jungen Werther* (1774). Goethe's conceptualization of the "elective affinities" is central and critical for our understanding of the history of sexual identities and the place of Goethean poetry within a crucial moment of historical shift. But before looking directly at the passages that focus on the elucidation of the "elective affinities," it makes sense to consider briefly the novel's basic reception and narrative.[17]

As J. Hillis Miller has suggested, "rarely in a novel has the power of erotic desire been expressed more powerfully than in *Die Wahlverwandtschaften*."[18] And the scholarly attention it has garnered has been equally fierce. Goethe's *Wahlverwandtschaften* was dismissed from its first appearance for its salacious representation of adultery and welcomed for its defense of marriage.[19] Ever since, the reception of the novel has been dogged by the controversy over whether Goethe's notion of "Wahlverwandtschaften" is more about "Wahl" (the choice to respect marriage vows despite one's contrary inclinations) or about "Verwandtschaften" (affinities which have no respect for social conventions). Many scholars have focused on the famous fourth chapter of *Die Wahlverwandtschaften* in which the elective affinities are discussed as a key to understanding the following events and symbols of the novel itself. I will, in contrast, explore the significance of the paradigm of identity and desire suggested by the novel's discussion of "Wahlverwandtschaften" both in terms of its significance for the novel and for our understanding of how desire and identification operate throughout Goethe's literary and aesthetic production. At the same time, I am less interested in Goethe's illustration of the *elective affinities* as it applies to his novel than in its various permutations throughout his literary production. Indeed, the contours of his paradigm of the affinities, as manifested in the *Wahlverwandtschaften,* constitute only one of the possible trajectories of desire implied by Goethe's paradigm.

Die Wahlverwandtschaften tells the story of how a recently married couple, Charlotte and Eduard, decide to invite two friends, the Captain and Ottilie, to come and live with them on their estate. This experiment in communal living is not consciously intended to destabilize their marriage, but it results ultimately in a shift of desire and inclination whereby Charlotte and the Captain and Eduard and Ottilie fall in love. The scandalous "adultery" depicted in the novel consists of Eduard and Charlotte (the married couple) sleeping with each other, *but* while thinking about the other two. In accord with the eighteenth-century notions of the physiology of reproduction, which held that fantasies or emotional turmoil experienced during pregnancy were believed to alter the baby's body, Charlotte bears a son nine months later who has Ottilie's dark eyes and the Captain's facial features. In the meantime, Eduard has failed to convince Charlotte to divorce him so that he can devote himself to Ottilie and Charlotte can pursue her love for the Captain. Eduard has consequently left the estate, demanding that Ottilie not be removed from Charlotte's presence, and has thrown himself into several suicidal battles while hoping for an eventual capitulation on Charlotte's part. Given these circumstances, the Captain decides to leave the estate. Ottilie, while caring for Charlotte and Eduard's infant son, encounters Eduard on the estate grounds unexpectedly. This meeting so upsets her that she recklessly decides to return home with the child by rowing across a lake. The boat they are in tips, and the baby slips into the water and drowns.

After this tragic turn of events, Charlotte finally agrees to Eduard's request for a divorce. But Ottilie, so distraught over the child's death and her role in the dissolution of the relationship between her friends, insists that Charlotte and Eduard remain together as a married couple; under these circumstances she will never consent to a relationship with Eduard. The Captain, Eduard, Charlotte, and

Ottilie now all return to the estate and appear to resume the daily activities they had conducted before their desires led them astray. Unbeknownst to the others, however, Ottilie slowly starves herself to death. And the novel finds its denouement when Charlotte and the Captain find Eduard lying dead among several keepsakes he had collected from Ottilie. Eduard and Ottilie are then reunited in death as they are enshrined together in a chapel on the estate.

On the surface, this is the story. Of course, Goethe's novel is vastly more aesthetically complex than my short summary of its contents could possibly convey. But for now it is sufficient to note that Goethe's *Wahlverwandtschaften* is not really a story of illicit sex or acts of adultery, but of "illicit" desires and metaphorical adulteries.

Indeed, desires and metaphors or metaphors of desire are the critical problem in the *Wahlverwandtschaften*. Beyond Charlotte's belief that there is nothing more dangerous than talking too freely about divorce and proposals for five-year marriages (and thereby inciting such activity, MA, 9, 352),[20] the whole novel is constructed around a metaphor of desire as fluid, protean, ubiquitous, and ultimately uncontainable. Goethe, as we know, borrowed the notion of "elective affinities" from the chemical theories of his day. The concept of "sympathies," "affinities," and/or "Verwandtschaften" were indeed central to chemistry in Goethe's age. Bergman was the first to use the actual term "Wahlverwandtschaften" in 1774, and it was commonly used thereafter by other chemists. Goethe likely encountered these ideas principally in the work of Macquer, Bergman, and Newton.[21] In 1718 Etienne-François Geoffroy created the first table of elective affinities. It is also clear that "Verwandtschaft" was often associated in eighteenth-century Germany with "sympathetic love." In Goethe's *Clavigo* (1774) the love between Clavigo and Marie is described as an "innige Verwandtschaft unserer Seelen" ("an inner affinity of our souls"), and in Wieland's *Agathon* (1766/1767) "eine Liebe der Sympathie" ("a love of sympathy") results from "eine geheime Verwandtschaft der Seelen" ("a secret affinity of the souls").[22] And so, love and chemistry begin to converge in analogical form well before Goethe's *Wahlverwandtschaften* (1809).

Given these eighteenth- and early nineteenth-century allusions to chemistry and love, we can ask ourselves what happens to the scientific notion of "affinitas" when it becomes a metaphor for human desires in Goethe's literary work? Or perhaps even more precisely, what is the nature of such a metaphor? And what does it tell us about the intersection of self, identity, and desire? Those are exactly the questions elucidated by the discussion of the "elective affinities" in Goethe's novel. As we shall see in the following passages from *Die Wahlverwandtschaften*, self, identity, and desire begin to converge in and through the metaphor of "affinitas" and become new poetic expressions.

Once the Captain joins Eduard and Charlotte on their estate, they spend their evenings together engaged in activities such as playing music, talking, and reading. On one such evening Eduard reads aloud from an unspecified book on chemical properties. Charlotte interrupts him when he reads a term unfamiliar to her: "Verwandtschaften" ("affinities"). She surmises at first that the word must refer to things that are related—in the manner in which she is related to her cousins, for instance. Charlotte spontaneously works to understand a concept she has never encountered before by relating it to herself. Eduard corrects her, insisting that a "Gleichnisrede" (metaphor) has led her astray and confused her because in this context "affinities" reflect the characteristics of soils and minerals:

> Es ist eine Gleichnisrede, die dich verführt und verwirrt hat, sagte Eduard. Hier wird freilich nur von Erden und Mineralien gehandelt, aber der Mensch ist ein wahrer Narziß; er bespiegelt sich überall gern selbst; er legt sich als Folie der ganzen Welt unter (MA, 9, 313).

> It is a metaphor that has led you astray and confused you, said Eduard. Here admittedly only soils and minerals are dealt with, but the human being is a true narcissist; he gladly mirrors himself everywhere, establishing himself as the foil [foundation] of the whole world.

Despite the fact that Eduard "corrects" Charlotte's misapprehension of the word *Verwandtschaften*, his insinuation of its metaphoric function and his references to the narcissistic underpinnings of our understandings of the outside world actually demonstrate how typically "human" her impulse to apply the word to herself is.[23] Indeed, the

Captain clarifies that the source of the metaphor in the first place is the self:

> . . . so behandelt er [der Mensch] alles was er außer sich findet; seine Weisheit wie seine Torheit, seinen Willen wie seine Willkür leiht er den Tieren, den Pflanzen, den Elementen und den Göttern (MA, 9, 313–14).

> . . . that is how he [the human being] treats everything that he finds outside of himself, he lends to the animals, the plants, the elements and the gods his wisdom as well as his folly, his will as well as his whim.

Eduard and the Captain establish the *self* as the source of the metaphor of "affinities"—in this case affinities between the self and the outside world. Indeed, the three discussants demonstrate how the narcissistic metaphor originates with the self, gets applied to the outside world (soils and minerals) and then back to the self—as someone like Charlotte tries to determine its meaning in relation to herself. The circular process illuminates for us the manner in which the self represents itself in metaphoric forms and how those metaphoric/linguistic symbols then become the means by which the self attempts to understand itself. We might think here a bit on Lacan and his notion of the subject's entrance into language. Once the narcissistic subject (of the mirror stage, i.e., something like Goethe's "sich bespiegeln") enters the symbolic order (that of metaphor and language) she or he can only understand her- or himself within a limitless chain of signification. There is no going back to something like a "self in and of itself" (Selbst an Sich). Once in language or metaphor the subject cannot "get outside" of the Symbolic and return to a pre-Symbolic (Real). The self becomes and is a self only in symbolic representation. The metaphor in this case will always mediate back to us—the self with which we have infused it—and we are trapped within that significatory system. We can now no longer understand ourselves outside of the symbolic order—we are "caught" in the metaphor.[24] What is astounding here is Goethe's understanding that the self both generates and is caught up in discourse. The desiring self, for him, is a symbolic self in its most fundamental being.

To complicate the issue, the metaphor functions, according to

Goethe, in multiple layers of representation in what Foucault would call discourses. Charlotte insists that she only wants to understand what "affinities" means in *this* context: "wie es eigentlich hier mit den Verwandtschaften gemeint sei" ("what is meant by the affinities here," MA, 9, 314). It is clear from her comments that she wants to limit her understanding of the metaphor to the local context—i.e., chemical properties. Her interest is in how the metaphor "acts" or functions in a specific scientific discourse. Charlotte's ultimate question is about how the metaphor got "put" into the language of chemical properties, and in order to understand the metaphor she feels compelled to exclude its other possible meanings. Her delimitation of the answer she expects reveals, as well, her cognizance and expectation of the multiplicity of meanings that any given metaphor might acquire. Moreover, the previous discussion about self and metaphor makes it abundantly clear that, try as she might, Charlotte will not be able to avoid relating the metaphor to the self and more specifically to herself. Charlotte clearly tries to understand something that also intrigued Foucault: that multiple discourses form the dynamic linguistic tensions that ultimately result in metaphoric representations of the self and desire. And, indeed, the characters of Goethe's novel will continue to outline the complex nature of layers of signification.

The Captain, for example, agrees to try to explain the "affinities" to Charlotte as he learned it ten years before. He notes, however, that his understanding may no longer be in accord with the present state of the profession: "Ob man in der wissenschaftlichen Welt noch so darüber denkt, ob es zu neueren Lehren paßt, wüßte ich nicht zu sagen" ("Whether one still thinks about it in the scientific world this way, whether it will accord with the newest teachings, I cannot say," MA, 9, 314). Eduard adds that one cannot learn things for life anymore; they have to be constantly relearned: "'Es ist schlimm genug,' rief Eduard, 'daß man jetzt nichts mehr für sein ganzes Leben lernen kann . . . wir aber müssen jetzt alle fünf Jahre umlernen . . .'" ("It is bad enough,' Eduard shouted, 'that one now can no longer learn anything for one's whole life . . . we now have to relearn things every five years," MA, 9, 314). Both Eduard and the Captain complicate the issue of metaphoricity even further, by pointing out that even within a given discourse (here chemical) the metaphor's function and significance change, evolve, and shift over time. Metaphoricity itself is a protean entity. The metaphor acquires, in a sense, a life of its own within various discourses. Every five years, as Eduard suggests, one has to reevaluate the state of the metaphor. The metaphor metamorphoses in and through language. And this is crucial, because we know that the metaphor is the self—it originated in the narcissistic self—and reflects back upon it. If the metaphor changes in language so does the self. As the self gets put into and caught up in metaphor/discourse, it courses within and along signifiers like "affinities" and "elective affinities," which are constantly shifting and metamorphosing. If, as the Captain suggests, one allows one's conceptualization of metaphor and self to become outdated— one may discover a wide disjunct between one's perception of one's self and the self and metaphor that has metamorphosed all along into new symbolic formations.[25] Finally, it is critical to keep in mind that the dynamic model of self and metaphor that Goethe's *Wahlverwandtschaften* is mapping out implies that as the self courses along and across metaphors and signifiers it changes, transforms, and becomes less and less containable. Like the metaphor it constitutes and that constitutes it, the self flows within and among several discourses/languages. That is, the self is always metamorphosing in/as a discursive phenomenon.

And if that were not enough, Charlotte then insinuates an even further complication, noting that she really only wants to understand the word "affinities" in this particular text and not within the context of scientific debates and disagreements over the meaning and function of the term:

"Deshalb möchte ich nur wissen, in welchem Sinne dieser Ausdruck eben bei diesen Gegenständen gebraucht wird. Wie es wissenschaftlich damit zusammenhänge, wollen wir den Gelehrten überlassen, die übrigens, wie ich habe bemerken können, sich wohl schwerlich jemals vereinigen werden" (MA, 9, 314).

"For that reason, I only want to know in what sense this expression is being used in conjunction with these objects. How it corresponds scientifically, we can leave to the scholars, who by the way, as I have been able to ascertain, will hardly ever agree on anything."

Here Charlotte points to competing discourses, competing functions of the metaphor "affinities," within a specific body of scientific representations. Within one particular science such as chemistry, multiple and often conflicting discourses struggle to define a concept like "affinities." Even within the discipline of chemistry contradictory and competing ways of knowing and understanding assert themselves in different theories, models, and systems of explication. So one has by implication manifold and often competing layers of symbolic formations of the metaphor of "affinities" and layers upon layers of metaphoric formations of the self. Keep in mind that within each of these discourses the self is shifting, sliding, and metamorphosing. The model of metaphor and self that *Die Wahlverwandtschaften* elucidates constitutes a complex representation of multiple metaphoric formations. Moreover, Charlotte's attempts to limit their discussion of "affinities" to the signification of one word in one passage of one text reveals itself as thoroughly unrealistic. Even within this narrow scope, the metaphor of soils and minerals, is also always already a metaphor of the self that is caught in multiple layers of discourse.

What Goethe outlines here is an incredibly complex and sensitive model of competing discourses that demonstrates his phenomenal understanding of how self and metaphor merge within the context of linguistic and conceptual shifts. It is also clear that Goethe does not adhere to a philosophy of the self as a fixed identity. In addition, he is interested in the self and the self in and of metaphoric representation, but not in sexual acts, as the defining elements of identity formation. Finally, he provides an amazingly detailed explication not just about how scientific discourses construct selves (think about later nineteenth-century medical discourses), but also how multiple discourses within one discipline compete against each other.

After these parameters of the metaphoric formation of the self have been established in *Die Wahlverwandtschaften*, Eduard and the Captain shift their attention from the more general characteristics of the "affinities"—to the more intimate question of how self and other—relate and interact with one another—that is, how desire works. The Captain claims first and foremost that all natural beings have an inclination or affinity for themselves: "an allen Naturwesen, die wir gewahr werden, bemerken wir zuerst, daß sie einen Bezug auf sich selbst haben" ("We notice first of all natural beings of which we are aware, that they have an inclination to themselves," MA, 9, 314). The Captain suggests that the self is attracted to the self. That is, after all, the definition of the narcissistic self.[26] And, by analogy, one would expect that like is attracted to like. In less abstract terms, the Captain's analysis also implies the natural inclination and desire of one member of a species for another member of that same species. Indeed, Eduard goes on to explain that among substances like water, oil, and quicksilver we find that each constitutes a unity in and of itself. This unity or attraction to the self can only be sundered by force (which would suggest a less-than-natural separation from the same). But once any obstacles to unity are removed these substances return to their original unified states. And Charlotte asserts as well, "so sieht man in diesen einfachen Formen die Menschen, die man gekannt hat" ("one sees in these simple forms the people one has known," MA, 9, 315). At this point, it seems that Eduard, Charlotte, and the Captain are establishing a model of desire that is predicated on the assumption that desire first emerges, as desire for one's self and/or for an other like one's self (same-sex desire), then shifts perhaps to one of desire for the other sex, and then ultimately back to desire for one's self/the same sex. Charlotte dispels, however, any assumption on our part that anything like such a set trajectory is really being mapped out here when she says: "'Lassen Sie mich voreilen,' sagte Charlotte, 'ob ich treffe, wo Sie hinwollen. Wie jedes gegen sich selbst einen Bezug hat, so muß es auch gegen andere ein Verhältnis haben'" ("'Let me rush ahead,' said Charlotte, 'to see if I can anticipate where you are going. As each element [person] has an inclination to themselves, so must they also have a relationship to others,'" MA, 9, 315). As Charlotte's summation suggests, the most basic contingency of desire is simply an inclination toward the self and toward others.[27] She does not specify any necessary character of those others—she does not distinguish between same-sex and opposite-sex attraction. Eduard agrees with Charlotte, emphasizing that the character of the affinities will be different in accord with the differences between elements/persons: "Und das wird nach Verschiedenheit der Wesen verschieden sein" ("And that will be different in accord with the difference between beings," MA, 9, 315). In this conceptualization, desire manifests itself in "nature" as polyvalent.

Moreover, according to Goethe, in a social context desire (the affinities) demonstrates that while some elements/persons are immediately attracted to one another, in other cases no affinities are established:

> "Bald werden sie sich als Freunde und alte Bekannte begegnen, die schnell zusammentreten, sich vereinigen, ohne an einander etwas zu verändern, wie sich Wein mit Wasser vermischt. Dagegen werden andre fremd neben einander verharren und selbst durch mechanisches Mischen und Reiben sich keinesweges verbinden; wie Öl und Wasser zusammengerüttelt sich den Augenblick wieder aus einander sondert" (MA, 9, 315).

> "Soon they will meet as friends and old acquaintances, who will quickly meet, unify without changing one another, the way that wine and water mix. Contrastively, others will stand next to each other, but distant, and even mechanical mixing and rubbing will in no way bind them together; like oil and water that has been shaken together, in an instant they will separate out from one another again."

Now the conversation has turned to an overt discussion of the dynamics of desire among individuals brought together in a social mix.[28] The affinities between partners either result in their uncomplicated unification—they mix together easily like water and wine—or their lack of affinity comes to the fore and they stand distant from one another and refuse to mix, like oil and water. Not even sex—that "mechanical mixing and rubbing"—can bring together those individuals who do not desire one another. As Charlotte maintains, desire is a matter of the head and soul; we are talking, therefore, about "Geistes- und Seelenverwandte" (intellectually, psychically, and spiritually "related" persons, MA, 9, 316). And, moreover, it is precisely the characteristics of the two individuals—that is, their identities—that facilitate mutual desire:

> " . . . wenn Sie diese Ihre wunderlichen Wesen verwandt nennen, so kommen sie mir nicht sowohl als Blutsverwandte, vielmehr als Geistes- und Seelenverwandte vor. Auf eben diese Weise können unter Menschen wahrhaft bedeutende Freundschaften entstehen;

denn entgegengesetzte Eigenschaften machen eine innigere Vereinigung möglich" (MA, 9, 316).

" . . . when you call your strange beings related, they don't strike me
so much as blood-related, as related intellectually, psychically, and
spiritually. In this manner truly significant friendships can arise; for
juxtaposed characteristics [as in personal characteristics/personalities]
make an inner unification possible."

What makes these desiring individuals (whether friends or lovers)
"verwandt" ("related" and expressing affinity for one another) is
their status as psychic and spiritual soulmates. They mirror one another (just like the original self/metaphor), and desire and identity
converge. The Goethean metaphor is equally one of desire and identity. And, indeed, desire and identity are its inextricable, constituent
parts. In this analysis identity and desire are not contingent upon
bodies—or sexual *acts*—but upon psychic affinities between soulmates. That is, Goethe extends Winckelmann's language of desire
and identity in choosing sentiment over sexual acts in his attempt to
express his same-sex desire. The metaphors explicated here are not
about sex, but about desire and identity.

But desire, according to Goethe's model, does not function simply within the context of two mutually attracted individuals. Desire is a product of a much larger paradigm of social interactions.
In chemistry Eduard and the Captain insist that two substances that
are attracted to one another or repulsed by one another can be unified or divorced from one another by the addition of one or two
other elements. Indeed, the addition of new elements can cause radical transformations and reformations of affinities:

Z. B. was wir Kalkstein nennen ist eine mehr oder weniger reine
Kalkerde, innig mit einer zarten Säure verbunden, die uns in Luft-
form bekannt geworden ist. Bringt man ein Stück solchen Steines
in verdünnte Schwelsäure, so ergreift diese den Kalk und erscheint
mit ihm als Gyps; jene zarte luftige Säure hingegen entflieht. Hier
ist eine Trennung, eine neue Zusammensetzung entstanden und man
glaubt sich nun mehr berechtigt, sogar das Wort Wahlverwandtschaft
anzuwenden, weil es wirklich aussieht, als wenn ein Verhältnis dem
andern vorgezogen, eins vor dem andern vorgezogen, eins vor dem
andern erwählt würde (MA, 9, 317).

For example what we call limestone is more or less a pure calcium oxide intimately united with a thin acid which is known to us in a gaseous form. If you bring a piece of this limestone together with diluted sulphuric acid, the latter will seize onto the lime and join with it to form gypsum; that thin gaseous acid in contrast escapes. Here a separation and a new combination occurs, and one even believes oneself justified in applying the word elective affinities, because it really appears, if one relationship has been preferred to another, as if one were chosen over the other.

Now Eduard applies this metaphor of desire directly to the relationships established between himself, the Captain, and Charlotte: "Am Ende bin ich in deinen Augen der Kalk, der vom Hauptmann, als einer Schwefelsäure, ergriffen, deiner anmutigen Gesellschaft entzogen und in einen refraktären Gyps verwandelt wird" ("In the final analysis, I am in your eyes the lime, that the Captain as sulphuric acid has seized and removed from your pleasant company and transformed into a recalcitrant gypsum," MA, 9, 318). Eduard discloses the reconfiguration of their affinities. He reveals that the Captain's arrival has had the effect of driving Eduard and Charlotte apart—of creating a "chemical" and "psychic" splitting of their desire—to make room for Eduard's and the Captain's desire for each other. A separation and a new reconfiguration of desire has occurred, just as it occurs when chemical substances are combined. What is striking about Eduard's analysis is his assumption that desire is desire.[29] That is, he openly juxtaposes his desire for his wife (which has abated) with his desire for the Captain (which is now in ascendancy). He, himself, depending on the social mix, desires both women and men. And in this case, his desire for another man causes his separation from his wife. Moreover, Eduard expresses no anxiety about his desires. He accepts his attraction to the opposite sex and his same-sex desires as a matter of course. For him, sexual identity and desire can shift; they are not rigid, fixed entities. And in this Goethe's conception of desire and identity stands in contrast to later nineteenth-century and even modern ideas about the relatively fixed nature of identity formations. By this I mean that discourses as diverse as Freud's psychoanalysis and contemporary gay and lesbian identity politics often seem to imply that identities and sexual orientations are rather definable, set, and identifiable. But this is not at all Eduard's understanding of desire in *Die Wahlverwandtschaften*.

Charlotte reacts quite negatively to Eduard's application of the metaphor to their own relationships, insisting that human beings can transcend metaphors:

> Diese Gleichnisreden sind artig und unterhaltend, und wer spielt nicht gern mit Ähnlichkeiten! Aber der Mensch ist doch um so manche Stufe über jene Elemente erhöht, und wenn er hier mit schönen Worten Wahl und Wahlverwandtschaft etwas freigebig gewesen; so tut er wohl, wieder in sich selbst zurückzukehren und den Wert solcher Ausdrücke bei diesem Anlaß recht zu bedenken. Mir sind leider Fälle genug bekannt, wo eine innige unauflöschlich scheinende Verbindung zweier Wesen, durch gelegentliche Zugesellung eines Dritten, aufgehoben, und eins der erst so schön verbundenen ins lose Weite hinausgetrieben ward (MA, 9, 318).

> These metaphors are good and entertaining, and who doesn't gladly play with similarities! But human beings are elevated, indeed, so many levels above those elements. And if he has, in this case, been somewhat liberal with the beautiful words "choice" and "affinity," it would be well for him to turn back to himself and to consider seriously on this occasion the worth of such expressions. Unfortunately, enough cases are known by me in which an apparently indissoluble connection between two persons has been utterly destroyed by the accidental introduction of a third and one or the other of the once so beautifully united persons was driven off into the wide yonder.

First and foremost, Charlotte once again implies the necessity of evaluating the self in relation to the metaphor. But Charlotte also implies that there is a way to escape the metaphor. She thinks that human beings are higher creations than chemical elements and that moral or self-assessing contemplation of the function of beautiful words like "choice" and "affinities" can circumvent those cases in which a third being (individual) breaks apart a couple who were previously quite content and unified.[30]

Eduard and the Captain reject this analysis, asserting that the metaphor of affinities signifies a higher determination of inclinations and one that is completely justified by the realities of desire:

> . . . diese Fälle sind allerdings die bedeutendsten und merkwürdigsten, wo man das Anziehen, das Verwandtsein, dieses Verlassen, dieses

Vereinigen gleichsam übers Kreuz wirklich darstellen kann; wo vier, bisher je zwei zu zwei verbundene Wesen in Berührung gebracht, ihre bisherige Vereinigung verlassen und sich aufs neue verbinden. In diesem Fahrenlassen und Ergreifen, in diesem Fliehen und Suchen glaubt man wirklich eine höhere Bestimmung zu sehen; man traut solchen Wesen eine Art von Wollen und Wählen zu, und hält das Kunstwort Wahlverwandtschaften für vollkommen gerechtfertigt (MA, 9, 318).

... these cases are indeed the most significant and interesting of all; here one can actually portray the attraction, the relatedness, the repulsion, and the unification as they cross back and forth—where four substances previously joined together as two pairs are brought into contact and leave their previous unity in order to unite anew. In this process of relinquishing and seizing, in this fleeing and searching one believes one is really witnessing a higher determination; one entrusts such beings with a form of will and choice and considers the artificial term [metaphor/linguistic construct] "elective affinities" completely justified.

Moreover, the Captain continues, once one sees the pushing, pulling, separating, and recombining that are set into motion by different mixes of elements, one begins to recognize an "eternal life" of desire, which is only barely comprehensible:

Man muß diese totscheinenden und doch zur Tätigkeit innerlich immer bereiten Wesen wirkend vor seinen Augen sehen, mit Teilnahme schauen, wie sie einander suchen, sich anziehen, ergreifen, zerstören, verschlingen, aufzehren und sodann aus der innigsten Verbindung wieder in erneuter, neuer, unerwarteter Gestalt hervortreten: dann traut man ihnen erst ein ewiges Leben, ja wohl gar Sinn und Verstand zu, weil wir unsere Sinne kaum genügend fühlen, sie recht zu beobachten, und unsre Vernunft kaum hinlänglich, sie zu fassen (MA, 9, 319).

One must see these substances in action before one's own eyes—entities that appear dead, but are internally always ready to spring into action—one must observe with sympathy how they seek each other, attract each other, destroy one another, swallow each other, devour each other and then emerge out of this most intimate union in renewed, new and unexpected shapes: then one credits them with an eternal life, yes even with sense and understanding, because our senses appear scarcely adequate to observe them correctly and our understanding hardly capable of grasping them.

Once one observes the mixing of elements/persons, once the experiment occurs before our eyes, according to the Captain, we will begin to have some cognizance of the realities and vast complexities of desire. And that is precisely the project of the novel itself. It places the experiment of affinities before our eyes, beckoning us to comprehend how inexplicable, shifting, and reconfiguring desire always is. In this model desire is never "fixed" forever on one object but is a dynamic process contingent upon the interaction of several participants. If the participants change, if someone is added or subtracted from the mix, desire reconfigures itself. We can recall here Weeks's suggestion above that sexuality is not fixed or stable across time. Goethe underscores the idea that desire is not fixed at any time historical or synchronous.

Curiously, the Captain initially suggests that Charlotte will really only be able to acquire a nascent understanding of the "affinities," if she observes several experiments. Direct observation will provide her with a better sense of the workings of desire than could abstract terms such as words, names, and artificial expressions. The metaphor itself [Wahlverwandtschaften] appears to occlude the understanding of desire, and the implication seems to be that the metaphor brings together too many layers of competing meanings. One way to circumvent that kind of significatory layering might be to view experiments. The other possibility, which is the one the Captain chooses, is to revert to what he refers to as a "Zeichensprache" (a language of signs—here, literally, letters):

> . . . so kann ich wohl in der Zeichensprache mich kürzlich zusammenfassen. Denken Sie sich ein A, das mit einem B innig verbunden ist, durch viele Mittel und durch manche Gewalt nicht von ihm zu trennen; denken Sie sich ein C, das sich ebenso zu einem D verhält, bringen Sie nun die beiden Paare in Berührung: A wird sich zu D, C zu B werfen, ohne daß man sagen kann, wer das andere zuerst verlassen, wer sich mit dem andern zuerst wieder verbunden habe (MA, 9, 319).

> I can indeed briefly summarize this in a language of signs. Imagine an A intimately united with a B, and which cannot be sundered from it by most means and forces; imagine also a C that is similarly bound to a D; now bring the two pairs into contact: A will throw itself at D

and C at B without our being able to determine who was the first to leave the other, who was the first to unite with the other (partner's partner).

Eduard agrees with the Captain and maintains that the relationships and affinities signified here can best be expressed by these individual letters: "Doch können wir leicht mit Buchstaben einstweilen das Verhältnis ausdrücken, wovon hier die Rede war" ("Indeed, we can in the meantime easily express the relationship discussed here by means of letters," MA, 9, 319).

The idea seems to be that if we could throw out the vast structures of discourses and competing discourses we could return to the basic building blocks of language and metaphor and to some kind of linguistic and conceptual transparency. But then Eduard attempts to reduce the possible confusion even further, by bringing those individual letters, those bits and pieces of the metaphor, back to the self—that is, back to themselves:

> . . . bis wir alles dieses mit Augen sehen, wollen wir diese Formel als Gleichnisrede betrachten, woraus wir uns eine Lehre zum unmittelbaren Gebrauch ziehen. Du stellst das A vor, Charlotte, und ich dein B: denn eigentlich hänge ich doch nur von dir ab und folge dir wie dem A das B. Das C ist ganz deutlich der Capitain, der mich für diesmal dir einigermaßen entzieht. Nun ist es billig, daß wenn du nicht ins Unbestimmte entweichen sollst, dir für ein D gesorgt werde, und das ist ganz ohne Frage das liebenswürdige Dämchen Ottilie, gegen deren Annährung du dich nicht länger verteidigen darfst (MA, 9, 319–20).

> . . . until we have seen all of this with our own eyes, we can consider this formula a metaphor, from which we extract a lesson which we can apply directly to ourselves. You represent the A, Charlotte, and I your B; for indeed I depend entirely on you and follow you just as B follows A. The C is obviously the Captain, who at the moment is to some extent drawing me from you. Now it is only fair, that, if you do not want to disappear into thin air, a D must be provided to you, and that is without question the dear little lady, Ottilie, against whose approach you may no longer resist.

Of course, Eduard simply re-inscribes here the circle of metaphoricity—moving from self to metaphor (here, letters) and back to the self—underscoring once more that we are trapped as desiring beings in metaphor and language (remember Lacan). But at the same time, by assigning the letters to the novel's participants in desire, Eduard maps out a dynamic of desire that continually reasserts the possibility/reality of same-sex desires. Recall that when the Captain arrived, Eduard's desire gravitated from Charlotte to him. Now, if we compare the analysis that the Captain provided of the coupling of the letters A, B, C, and D with Eduard's assignment of those letters— we find the following configuration:

Eduard's schema

A = Charlotte
B = Eduard
C = the Captain
D = Ottilie

According to the Captain's analysis the following letters will combine once these four letters get mixed together:

A (Charlotte) with D (Ottilie)
B (Eduard) with C (the Captain)

The Captain's analysis combined with Eduard's assignment of the letters to specific characters foregrounds an initial paradigm of same-sex desire. The women are initially attracted to each other, as are the men. It is striking that both male-male and female-female desire come to the fore in Goethe's paradigm of identity and desire. Intriguingly, while some scholars refer to this same-sex coupling in passing, most ignore it altogether.[31] Some refer to the same-sex coupling in terms of friendship and the opposite sex couplings in terms of love, although the novel does not make those distinctions. For the most part, scholars have ignored the implications of the Captain's and Eduard's coupling of these specific letters and have concentrated on the possible bonds between men and women suggested by the discussion of the affinities and their later permutations in the novel. Several scholars have noted which possible male-female combinations do not get included in this analysis by Eduard and the Captain (see, for instance, Lindner, Miller, Schlaffer ["Namen und Buchstaben"], Zons, and Winnett). But for the most part, Goethe scholarship has been strangely silent about the same-sex desire that Eduard and the Captain outline. I think that this oversight can be explained in part by the fact that scholars have focused on the trajectories of desire as they are manifest throughout the novel, which accentuates the adulterous relationships between Eduard and Ottilie and Charlotte and the Captain. Nonetheless, explicit references to same-sex desire surface throughout these passages and the novel as a whole.[32] Goethe's conception of the "Wahlverwandtschaften" accounts equally for desire between the sexes and for same-sex attractions. But the greater significance of Goethe's paradigm of the elective affinities is precisely its *structural allowance* for the foundational establishment of the same-sex desire of both men and women. And as we shall see, it is precisely this complex model of desire (both between the sexes and among the sexes) that reemerges throughout Goethe's literary and aesthetic oeuvre. Here Goethe effects a reversal of the predominant Western myth of heterosexuality as *the* foundational desire. He stands in opposition to his age, which was obsessed with the "normative" character of family structure and domesticity (as we know from Hull, Laqueur, and Foucault, et al). At the same time, his views contradict those of the predominant discourses of the later nineteenth century and early twentieth century that insisted on the pathological nature of such "perversions/inversions." And, finally, in contrast to Freud's notion of bisexuality as an originary state of desire (see *Three Essays on Sexuality*) grown out of in the course of becoming a well-adjusted, heterosexual adult, Goethe's paradigm insists on an equally originary and natural evolution of both opposite-sex and same-sex desires.

Nonetheless, even though Eduard's and the Captain's preliminary speculations on desire appear to foreground same-sex attractions over those between the opposite sexes, Eduard later warns the Captain to protect himself from the "D" (Ottilie), for what would he (Eduard) then do without his "C" (the Captain). Well, of course, he would then have to return to his "A" (Charlotte). And then, to complicate matters even further, Eduard suggests he would be returning ultimately to his "A und O"—that is, Charlotte and Ottilie

(MA, 9, 324).[33] This is, of course, also one of the major tensions of the novel: whether Eduard will eventually divorce Charlotte and unite with Ottilie. What is accentuated here is the fluid nature of desire. Same-sex and opposite-sex desires are contingent upon specific social mixes. As persons are added to or subtracted from the melange, desire shifts to new objects. To this extent desire is conceived as contingent, like metaphors and words, upon highly substitutable components: persons and letters. Indeed, the Captain and Eduard conflate the letters with the persons underscoring the fluid and interchangeable nature of relationships of desire. The fluid nature of language or discourse (consider the difference in the meaning of the word "love" if you add the letter "g" and get "glove") mirrors the fluid nature of the subject's desire. Like letters in an alphabet or metaphors in discourses, the desires of persons shift as new persons get added to the mix. The letters Eduard and the Captain invoke underscore the fluidity and protean character of desire. Letters can combine to form an infinite number of words and concepts. Like letters, desires are fluid and in flux. Adding a letter to a word changes its meaning; adding a "letter" (new person) to the social mix may change the entire direction of desire.[34] And at any given time, an addition or subtraction of a letter or affinity can occur, altering the entire formulation. The possibilities are endless. Once letter and self converge, desire can course in infinite directions. During the course of the discussion of the "elective affinities," Charlotte, the Captain, and Eduard have elucidated the metaphor of desire along a circular path reflective of the structure of metaphoricity and discourse formation. They have moved from an explication of the self in its relation to the outside world, to an assessment of the nature of scientific discourse and metaphoric formations of the self, which then in turn reflect back upon and modify the self. They have demonstrated the convergence of self, identity, and desire, and finally they have returned to the conflation of self and desire in and through metaphoric formations. The structure of their own poetic language foregrounds the circular inclusivity of the metaphor and illustrates that (contra Charlotte) even the intellectualization of metaphoricity cannot help the desiring subject to escape the structure of symbolic representation. Eduard, Charlotte, and the Captain ultimately only understand

themselves, their identities, and their desires as metaphoric formations and in accord with the fluid structure of metaphoricity.[35]

But this also does not mean that the mapping of letters of desire
by Eduard and the Captain actually mirror in an uncomplicated way
the exact trajectory of desire. Goethe's model of sexual desire and
identity demonstrates quite clearly that elective affinities (desires)
shift in a manner that is not the subject's prerogative to control.[36]
If we consider how desire manifests itself throughout the novel,
several complicating factors come into view. First and foremost, it is
evident that desire cannot be directed by outside forces. Charlotte's
attempts before her marriage to Eduard to match him with Ottilie fail
because Eduard is totally enamored of Charlotte and barely notices
Ottilie (MA, 9, 297). On the other hand, after their marriage, neither
Charlotte nor Eduard can stem their attractions to the Captain and
Ottilie, respectively. Like their chemical counterparts, the characters
of Goethe's novel attract and repulse one another in accord with
specific interrelational mixes.

Indeed, before the Captain joins them, Eduard and Charlotte appear indivisible. Once he arrives, however, he and Eduard become
inseparable. Eduard moves out of the wing of the estate where Charlotte sleeps, accompanying the Captain to his quarters. As Eduard
explains to Charlotte:

> Es wird höchst nötig, daß ich zu dem Hauptmann auf den rechten
> Flügel hinüber ziehe. Sowohl Abends als Morgens ist erst die rechte
> Zeit zusammen zu arbeiten. Du erhältst dagegen für dich und Ottilien
> auf deiner Seite den schönsten Raum (MA, 9, 324).

> It is most necessary for me to move over to the Captain in the right
> wing. The mornings as well as the evenings are the right time to work
> together. You, in return, will get on your side the most beautiful room
> for yourself and Ottilie.

The Captain and Eduard involve themselves immediately in activities that leave them with time for Charlotte only in the evenings:
"Brachten die Freunde auf diese Weise ihre Tage zusammen zu, so
versäumte sie Abends nicht Charlotten regelmäßig zu besuchen"
("And if the friends spent their days together in this manner, they
did not neglect to visit Charlotte in the evenings," MA, 9, 311). As

Eduard and the Captain suggested in their illustration of the dynamics of their desire, the two men are immediately drawn together, and Eduard is separated from Charlotte. But their predictions about the transformations of their desires are otherwise rather erroneous.[37]

Once Ottilie joins the other three, no attraction evolves between her and Charlotte, as we would expect from the model Eduard and the Captain outlined. Ottilie functions in relationship to Charlotte as a distant stepdaughter. She manages the household for Charlotte and later serves as a nurse and guardian for Charlotte's son, but no close relationship develops between them like that between Eduard and the Captain. In fact, Ottilie's addition to the "mix" of characters results in a totally different reconfiguration of desire. Ottilie and Eduard are drawn together, as are the Captain and Charlotte. So instead of the same-sex trajectory Eduard and the Captain anticipate, the attractions between the members of the opposite sexes shift. We might wonder if Goethe accentuated these other conflicting trajectories of desire in order to "cover up" or mitigate in the course of the novel the potentially explosive implications of his initial model of desire and its same-sex foundation. If so, it seems to have worked since scholarship has typically focused on the attractions between men and women in the novel and not on the same-sex affinities it foregrounds.

At any rate, the importance of the unexpected transformations of the Goethean metaphor of desire within the context of the novel is at least twofold. First, the unpredictability of the trajectory of desire within different social mixes is accentuated. One never knows exactly how desire will reconfigure itself among various partners until the "experiment" is put into motion. Moreover, one can never predict what further shifts in desire will occur as new potential partners are added to the mix or as old partners separate off and become attached to new ones.

Secondly, and this is extremely critical for our understanding of Goethe's model of sexual desire and identity, while the metaphor of desire that Eduard and the Captain initially propose allows for the possibility of both male and female same-sex desire, the novel as a whole consistently subverts the possibility of female-female desire. Throughout the novel, the realization of female same-sex desire is persistently thwarted. The inability of women to develop bonds with one another is overtly juxtaposed to a man's need to desire other men:

> Man betrachte ein Frauenzimmer als Liebende, als Braut, als Frau, Hausfrau und Mutter, immer steht sie isoliert, immer ist sie allein, und will allein sein. Ja die Eitle selbst ist in dem Falle. Jede Frau schließt die andre aus, ihrer Natur nach: denn von Jeder wird alles gefordert, was dem ganzen Geschlechte zu leisten obliegt. Nicht so verhält es sich mit den Männern. Der Mann verlangt den Mann; er würde sich einen zweiten erschaffen, wenn es keinen gäbe: eine Frau könnte eine Ewigkeit leben, ohne daran zu denken, sich ihres Gleichen hervorzubringen (MA, 9, 450).

> One thinks of a woman as a lover, as a bride, as a wife, housewife, and mother—and she always stands isolated, she is always alone, and wants to be alone. Yes, even the vain woman fits into this scenario. Every woman shuts every other woman out—in accord with her nature. For each woman is required to do everything demanded of the whole sex. This is not the case for men. A man demands a man. He would create a second man if there were not any. A woman can live an eternity without once considering bringing forth her own kind.

According to this view, men necessarily gravitate to other men, while women always stand alone, distant, and incapable of intimate relationships with one another. This ellipsis of female-female desire in Goethe's novel as a whole is crucial because it reflects a gesture of omission that repeats itself persistently throughout his poetic production.[38] Although allowing for the structural possibility of female same-sex desire, Goethe's paradigm of the affinities clearly suppresses it, while privileging and highlighting the expression and critical reality of male same-sex desire. We recall as well that in later nineteenth-century discourses of medicine and psychoanalysis the predominant focus is on the male homosexual, and much less attention is devoted to female-female desire. Moreover, Goethe's reticence here might also reflect a certain strain of eighteenth-century thought in which female same-sex desire was perhaps even more disturbing and inexpressible than male same-sex desire (see Tobin, *Warm Brothers*, 68–69). In each case, female desire is either ignored or suppressed, and in this regard Goethe's omission of female same-sex desire certainly seems to reflect a larger cultural trend.

If we consider the Winckelmannian word and the metaphor of elective affinities, we discover in both cases that syllables and letters, the basic building blocks of signification, get "spelled together" into new, decipherable linguistic formations. And each of these elements of discourse involves the "spelling out" or articulation of the self and desire whether in the form of a word (and its decoding) or in the form of a metaphor. And, indeed, in both cases identity and desire are critical. In the case of "Winckelmann" male same-sex desire begins to acquire a linguistic form as a "charade of syllables" and solidifies into a Winckelmannian "word." The metaphor of affinities, on the other hand, accentuates the fluid and protean nature of a desire that is not limited to any specific sexual identity. Nonetheless, identity in the form of recognizing one's self in another—a recognition of one's soulmate—is significant to this metaphoric moment as well. In the Winckelmann essay of 1805 we find a minutely constructed linguistic formation of same-sex desire and identity. One word gets spelled: Winckelmann. Contrastively, *Die Wahlverwandtschaften,* written in 1809 (just four years later!), offers a highly complex model of multiple discourses, competing discourses, and an explicit illustration of the basic building blocks and tensions operating within systematic metaphoric formations of self and desire. In opposition to Kant's injunction against naming same-sex desire, each of these moments of articulation establishes same-sex desire as the most fundamental desire and one that must be expressed. Each also demonstrates how new notions of self and desire get "put into poetic discourse."

If we think of the Winckelmann essay within the context of the *Wahlverwandtschaften,* we find immediately in both texts the impulse to identify the self, to spell the self together, and to account for desire through new linguistic and conceptual formations. Like Goethe's *Farbenlehre (Theory of Colors),* the *Wahlverwandtschaften* and the Winckelmann encomium focus on isolating, constructing, and promoting "eine Sprache, eine Symbolik, die man auf ähnliche Fälle als Gleichniß, als nahverwandten Ausdruck, als unmittelbar passendes Wort anwenden und benutzen mag" ("a language, a Symbolism that one can apply to similar cases as a metaphor, as a closely related expression, as a directly fitting word," *Farbenlehre,* "Vorwort," WA, II, 1, XI).[39] In the *Farbenlehre* the metaphoric language sought is one of nature; in the Winckelmann essay and in the *Wahlverwandtschaften* it is one of sexual identity and desire.[40] And, as we shall see, it is a metaphor of identity and desire that Goethe applies to analogous cases and situations of desire throughout his literary production.

Goethe's "Symbolik" of identity and desire as it surfaces in the Winckelmann encomium might appear to run counter to the implications of the metaphor of desire mapped out in the *Wahlverwandtschaften*. At first glance, we might surmise that these two models manifest mutually exclusive trajectories. I have chosen them, however, because they represent so succinctly a critical tension between identity and desire that resurfaces throughout Goethe's oeuvre, and which, indeed, constitutes a central structuring mechanism in his literary work. A specific identity is not foregrounded in the explication of the metaphor of desire in the *Wahlverwandtschaften*. But it is at least intimated in the novel's concentration on the self and metaphoric articulations of the self and is alluded to in the reference to the identification of desiring subjects with potential soulmates. We can best understand the implications of these two representative moments in Goethe's work if we think of the Winckelmannian impulse to outline a specific sexual identity as a constituent part or subset, if you will, of the metaphor of desire illustrated in the *Wahlverwandtschaften*. Same-sex desire and identification is one of the possible psychic trajectories accentuated throughout the structure of metaphoricity and desire. What the Goethean metaphor of desire seems to preclude is the possibility of the total exclusivity of any particular desire or attachment. It insists, indeed, that while same-sex identities manifest themselves within the structure of desire, they are exclusive identities only within certain social configurations. As Ottilie remarks in her diary: "Unsere Leidenschaften sind wahre Phönixe. Wie der alte verbrennt, steigt der neue sogleich wieder aus der Asche hervor" ("Our desires are true phoenixes. As soon as the older one burns out, a new one arises out of the ashes," MA, 9, 426). More unsettling, perhaps, is that Goethe's metaphor of desire insists that the basic structure of desire, the metaphor—which the speaking being cannot escape—is one of multiple sexual identities and fluid desires. In this view, the basic structure of desire is one of various sexual identities and desires. Goethe's model distinguishes itself from modern theories of sexual desire—post-Freud—that might insist on a type of pre-oedipal polymorphous perversity in that it explicitly accentuates a fluid structure of desire for adults. In other words, the Goethean metaphor of desire subverts the notion of stages of sexual development and transformations of desire that result in the rigid codification of specific sexual identities and desires.[41] This metaphor of desire does not relegate the fluidity of desire to an infant stage that is necessarily overcome as the child develops into a "normal," "adjusted" member of the social order.[42] And, for precisely this reason, the sexual implications of Goethe's literary production cannot be reduced to debates over whether or not his works reflect some kind of quintessential "heterosexuality" or subversive "homosexuality." Studies that acknowledge only one form of desire to the exclusion of others in Goethe's oeuvre miss entirely the principal significance of the Goethean metaphor of desire and identity. In fact, Goethe's elucidation of desire in general is critically important to our understanding of the central role that male same-sex desire plays throughout his literary production. As we have seen, his aesthetic project strives specifically to lend male same-sex desire metaphoric and structural form. Indeed, Goethe's elucidation of the fluidity of desire has the ultimate effect of naturalizing male same-sex desire, of presenting it as just as "natural" (or constructed as "natural"), structurally inherent, and originary as any desire between the sexes.

WERTHER AND WILHELM: INCITING POETIC
EXPRESSIONS OF MALE SAME-SEX
IDENTITY AND DESIRE

With the implications of the Winckelmannian word and the metaphor of elective affinities in mind, we can now turn to two additional moments of articulation. The first one occurs in Goethe's *Briefe aus der Schweiz* (*Letters from Switzerland*, 1808) and the second one in *Wilhelm Meisters Wanderjahre* (*Wilhelm Meister's Travel Years*, 1829). Each of these moments of articulation reiterate the fluidity of desire, accentuate distinct moments of male-male desire, and connect male same-sex desire specifically to the very process of voicing desire (whether male-male or male-female).

The first installment of Goethe's *Briefe aus der Schweiz* consists of fictional letters sent from Werther (the hero of his famous novel, *Die Leiden des jungen Werthers* [*The Sorrows of Young Werther*]) to a male friend, which the narrator assures us were found among Werther's papers (MA, 4:1, 630). Werther's correspondence to his friend opens with a rather lengthy dismissal of his own descriptions and with expressions of his dismay at his inability to transform the images and concepts he perceives into understandable language:

> Nun steh ich und schaue diese Wunder und wie wird mir dabei? ich denke nichts, ich empfinde nichts und möchte so gern etwas dabei denken und empfinden. Diese herrliche Gegenwart regt mein Innerstes auf, fordert mich zur Tätigkeit auf, und was kann ich tun, was tue ich! Da setz' ich mich hin und schreibe und beschreibe. So geht denn hin ihr Beschreibungen! betrügt meinen Freund, macht ihn glauben, daß ich etwas tue, daß er etwas sieht und liest (MA, 4:1, 630).

> Now I stand and observe these wonders and how do I feel? I think about nothing, I feel nothing and would so like to think about and feel something. This tremendous presence excites my innermost being, challenges me to activity, and what can I do, what do I do! I sit down and write and describe. So off with you, descriptions! deceive my friend, make him believe that I am doing something and that he sees and reads something.

Werther laments ironically his inability to think or feel anything while observing the wonders of the Swiss landscape unfurling before his very eyes. But, and this is crucial, the mere act of sitting down to write, the injunction to write to his male friend seems to almost literally "pull" a language of impressions (Bilder) and expressions (Beschreibungen) from him. For Werther, as for Winckelmann (see the discussion earlier in this chapter), the act of writing becomes an incitement to formulate his desire in words. And, in fact, the Werther of Goethe's novel *Die Leiden des jungen Werthers* refers explicitly in his letters to his friend to the function of his letter writing in terms of the expression of his desire and the expansion of his soul: "Bruder, nur die Erinnerung jener Stunden macht mir wohl, selbst diese Anstrengung, jene unsägliche Gefühle zurück zu rufen, wieder auszusprechen, hebt meine Seele über sich selbst . . ." ("Brother, just the memory of those hours comforts me. Even this effort to recall those inexpressible feelings, to say them again, elevates my soul above itself . . ." MA, 1:2, 239). Accordingly, the Werther of the Swiss Letters begins immediately—despite his fears that his "writing" will be nothing but a linguistic farce—to construct a metaphor of desire quite reminiscent of the one we have already encountered in the *Wahlverwandtschaften*.

At first Werther begins to relate moments of intense desire to his male correspondent in bits and pieces, in sentences such as: "wie liebte ich Ferdinanden! wie dankte ich ihm für das Gefühl das er in mir erregte" ("how I loved Ferdinand! how I thanked him for the feeling which he invoked in me," MA, 4:1, 633). Similarly, of Eleonore he writes that she was

> eine schlanke, zarte Gestalt, eine reine Bildung, ein heiteres Auge, eine blasse Farbe . . . Bald, ja ich darf sagen gleich, gleich den ersten Abend gesellte sie sich zu mir, setzte sich neben mich . . . (MA, 4:1, 636).

> a slim, delicate form, a pure development, a cheerful eye, a pale color . . . Soon, yes I can say immediately, immediately on the first evening she came to me, setting herself next to me.

His language is choppy and repetitive, indicating a reluctance or inability on his part to express directly the desires he feels for both Ferdinand and Eleonore.[43] The desires themselves do not seem to cause him any anxiety, but the form and impact of his writings on that desire do concern him. He reflects openly in the letter about whether or not he should reveal to his friend the "experiments in desire" that he is in the process of conducting:

> Soll ich oder soll ich nicht? Ist es gut dir etwas zu verschweigen, dem ich so viel, dem ich alles sage? Soll ich dir Bedeutendes verschweigen, indessen ich dich mit so vielen Kleinigkeiten unterhalte, die gewiß niemand lesen möchte, als du, der du eine so große und wunderbare Vorliebe für mich gefaßt hast; oder soll ich etwas verschweigen, weil es dir einen falschen Begriff von mir geben könnte? Nein! du kennst mich besser, als ich mich selbst kenne, du wirst auch das, was du mir nicht zutraust, zurecht legen . . . (MA, 4:1, 638).

Should I or should I not? Is it good to conceal something from you, to whom I say so much, to whom I reveal everything? Should I conceal something important from you, while entertaining you with so many inconsequential things? conceal something from you that certainly no one other than you will read—you who have developed such a great and wonderful fondness for me? or should I conceal something because it might give you a false impression of me? No, you know me better than I know myself. You will know how to deal even with those things that you do not think me capable of.[44]

Regardless of his anxieties about his own articulations of desire and how they will be understood, as in the opening passage of his letter, the writing of letters to his male friend seems to compel Werther to continue formulating his desires. We might recall in this context that Kant argued that linguistic representations of *crimina carnis* might have a contaminating effect, that is, that the mere naming of the desire would result in its spread. Here, however, Werther does not express the desire to "contaminate" his friend with his desire but struggles rather to express himself and his desire to his friend. Indeed, he struggles over the question of whether he should try to express his desires, and ultimately decides that he *must*. So, while Kant looked at the problem of the naming of same-sex desire from the outside and hoped to contain it, Werther represents the same-sex identified subject who must struggle to express his sense of self through linguistic revelations of his desire to another man.

Werther continues by reminding his friend of his love of the arts and describes his lack of response to a beautiful representation of Danae shown to him by a friend. He attributes his lack of interest in her to his lack of experience with the human body. Werther explains that he decided that he needed to observe a naked body directly and that he convinced his friend Ferdinand to bathe in a lake while he views him:

Ich veranlaßte Ferdinanden zu baden im See; wie herrlich ist mein junger Freund gebildet! welch ein Ebenmaß aller Theile! welch ein Fülle der Form, welch ein Glanz der Jugend, welch ein Gewinn für mich, meine Einbildungskraft mit diesem vollkommenen Muster der menschlichen Natur bereichert zu haben! Nun bevölkre ich Wälder, Wiesen und Höhen mit so schönen Gestalten; ihn seh' ich als Adonis dem Eber folgen, ihn als Narciß sich in der Quelle bespiegeln! (MA, 4:1, 640).

> I induced Ferdinand to bathe in the lake. What a splendid build my young friend has! what symmetry of all the parts! what fullness of form, what a brilliance of youth, what a profit for me, for my imagination to be enriched by this complete paragon of human nature! Now I people the woods, meadows, and heights with such beautiful figures; I see him as Adonis tracking a boar, I see him as Narcissus mirroring himself in the pool!

Werther is thoroughly enthusiastic about his friend's body—its shape, its size, its completeness of form.[45] The erotic experience of observing a naked male body is intimately joined in Werther's thought to his imagination and creative impulses. Once he sees Ferdinand's ideal body, he relates how he is compelled to "people" the woods, meadows, mountains, etc., with such beautiful forms.[46] Viewing a naked male body induces Werther to create a new discourse/ language-to "fill" the world with like simulacra and multi-layered metaphors of male same-sex desire and identity. He sees Ferdinand, Adonis, and Narcissus mirrored in the lake. Male figures of self (Ferdinand), love (Adonis), and self-love (Narcissus) merge and reiterate the narcissistic underpinnings of the metaphor of desire outlined in the *Wahlverwandtschaften.* In addition, Werther sees and loves himself (and all of those male selves invoked here) in Ferdinand. Male same-sex identity is clearly foregrounded here. These new poetic formulations allow for both an expression of male-male desire and a site of identification, more specifically one in which the male self can identify itself with other men who desire men. This is a Winckelmannian moment as well, to the extent that Werther observes Ferdinand's beautiful body with the eyes of an artist (as Winckelmann viewed the beautiful bodies of Greek art through the eyes of the art historian) and expresses his male same-sex desire and identity across and through that ideal image. And yet we see here that Goethe really is taking the Winckelmannian "word" a few steps further. In Goethe's text the images of beautiful male bodies, male same-sex desire and identity, and the incitement to metaphoric formulations of that desire and identity are much more overtly expressed and tightly interwoven than in Winckelmann's letters.

And it is precisely the image of male same-sex desire and identity—the evocation of the metaphor of desire and identity—that incites poetic production, that is, results in the creation of new poetic representations of desire. Werther begins a process of even further reiterations of the trope of male-male desire as he peoples the countryside with his own images and creations of that quintessential male-loving man, Ferdinand/Adonis/Narciß/Werther. Just as Winckelmann merged with a long line of Greek (and male-loving) poets in Goethe's encomium, here Ferdinand and Werther merge with Adonis and Narcissus, and the quotation of male same-sex desire and identity continues on in every new figure Werther infuses into the surrounding countryside. Male desire and identity get perpetually refigured in Werther's imagination and in his poetic production. He enacts for us throughout these passages the *process* whereby the metaphor of desire becomes more and more complex and layered, as more and more male figures converge within it, or, we might say, as they get caught up in its infinite mirroring and figuring of the desiring (here male) self.[47] Here we find a more specific representation of self-fashioning in and through poetic expression, in contrast to the explication of the layers of discourse (predominantly scientific) that function in a circular manner to facilitate the convergence of self and metaphor that we found in *Die Wahlverwandtschaften*. This constitutes a shift from descriptions of how the self attains metaphoricity, to how the self can express its own desire and identity in and through new poetic formulations.

And yet, immediately following this emergence of a male metaphor of desire and/or metaphor of male same-sex desire, Werther's desire shifts and he laments that Venus is missing from this primal experience of love. He decides then that he must, no matter the cost, observe a naked woman as well. His second "Augenschmaus" (feast for the eyes) is also erotically charged.[48] He describes the woman he has hired for this experiment in observation as she removes her clothing before him piece by piece: "Reizend war sie, indem sie sich entkleidete, schön, herrlich schön, als das letzte Gewand fiel. Sie stand, wie Minerva vor Paris mochte gestanden haben . . ." ("She was alluring as she undressed herself, beautiful, splendidly beautiful, as the last article of clothing fell. She stood like Minerva must have before

Paris," MA, 4:1, 643). Here, Werther provides us with fewer descriptions of his responses. His sentences are once again short, repetitive, and not very descriptive. While he mentions various parts and features of Ferdinand's body, he describes the woman's body globally—as beautiful, splendidly beautiful, and alluring. As he observes her, he is laconic and stresses a kind of immobilization whereby he "konnte nur staunen und bewundern" ("could only stare in amazement and wonder," MA, 4:1, 644). Werther discloses that he was left speechless because he could not find himself in her body:

> Soll ich dir's gestehen, ich konnte mich eben so wenig in den herrlichen Körper finden, da die letzte Hülle herab fiel, als vielleicht Freund L. sich in seinen Zustand finden wird, wenn ihn der Himmel zum Anführer der Mohawks machen sollte. Was sehen wir an den Weibern? was für Weiber gefallen uns? und wie konfundieren wir alle Begriffe? (MA, 4:1, 643).

> Should I admit it to you? I could no sooner find myself in that splendid body as the last covering fell off, than perhaps friend L. could find himself in his situation if the heavens should want to make him the chief of the Mohawks. What do we see in women? what kinds of women please us? and how is it that we confuse all of these concepts?

The juxtaposition of Werther's desire for both men and women reveals not only the fluidity of his desire (remember *Die Wahlverwandtschaften*), but (and this is new) that his desire for men is linked specifically to his own sense of self, self-identification, and self-production in the form of poetic creativity. He does not find *him*self in the woman's body, and is, therefore, consequently incapable of metaphoricity as he views a naked woman.[49] The metaphor of desire and identity, the whole string of metaphoric significations, cannot be put into motion because Werther cannot initiate the first step—he cannot find himself in the outside object viewed. Confronted with a female form, he produces few descriptions of his desire and is thoroughly confused. He wonders why men are attracted to women, what kind of women attract men, and he asks how it is that we confuse all of these concepts? Intriguingly, here Goethe clearly foregrounds and privileges the affinity between the two men, as the woman leaves Werther feeling out of place, uncertain of him*self*, and perplexed.

Werther discloses that poetic articulations of desire and identity by men are inextricably linked in Goethean thought to male same-sex desire. A man's desire for other men compels him into layers and layers of metaphoricity. Moreover, these passages demonstrate that visual or specular moments in Goethe's literary production are critical for our understanding of his new expressions of desire and identity. Wellbery has demonstrated convincingly in his recent book, *The Specular Moment,* how the poet's viewing of a woman is linked in Goethe's poetry (specifically in the lyric texts) to the poet's access to an unspeakable, prediscursive language. And while it is true that in a poem such as "Maifest" Goethe alludes to the woman as the source of the poet's "new songs" ("neue Lieder"), the lyric reveals little about the *process* of metaphoric formation that follows that initial pre-linguistic incitement. As Wellbery stresses throughout his study, the specular moment has a distinctly "prearticulate character" (203). What these passages from Werther's letters reveal is how the moment of specularity (and the desire it represents) gets "put into discourse." Moreover, it is clear throughout Goethe's oeuvre that specular reciprocity is not exclusively reserved for the expression of female-male desire. And, finally, and most significantly, these passages foreground the significance of male same-sex desire. Without it Werther cannot find himself in the specular moment (whether shared between himself and a woman or with another man) and cannot begin, therefore, the process of metaphoricity.[50] Indeed, as we shall see, viewing a woman may *incite* the poet to form new expressions of his desire, but the *actual process* of poetic formation is contingent upon verbal exchanges between two men who desire one another. And with this in mind we can turn to the metaphor of the "fisher boy" in *Wilhelm Meisters Wanderjahre.*[51]

Wilhelm recounts the story that interests us in a letter to Natalie.[52] He reminisces about a childhood experience of desire. He and his parents join in some country festivities and Wilhelm is immediately attracted to a fisher boy on their first encounter (MA, 17, 501). They go fishing together and sit side by side, leaning against one another until the fisher boy decides to go swimming: "Er könne, rief er, endlich aufspringend, der Versuchung nicht widerstehen, und ehe ich michs versah war er unten, ausgezogen und im Wasser" ("He yelled as he sprang up that he could no longer stand the seduction and before I knew it, he was down below, undressed and in the water," MA, 17, 501). As Wilhelm views his naked friend, he refers to his own stirring feelings: "mir war wunderlich zu Mute geworden" ("my feelings had become quite strange," MA, 17, 501). And then Wilhelm describes how the fisher boy seduced him:

> Es war umher so warm und so feucht, man sehnte sich aus der Sonne in den Schatten, aus der Schattenkühle hinab ins kühlere Wasser. Da war es denn ihm leicht mich hinunter zu locken, eine nicht oft wiederholte Einladung fand ich unwiderstehlich und war, mit einiger Furcht vor den Eltern, wozu sich die Scheu vor dem unbekannten Elemente gesellte, in ganz wunderlicher Bewegung (MA, 17, 501).

> It was so warm and moist all around that one longed oneself out of the sun and into the shade, out of the cool of the shade and down into the cooler water. Therefore it was easy for him to lure me down there, and I found a not too often repeated invitation irresistible—with some fear of my parents—joined with some shyness in the face of unknown elements. I was in a strange state of excitement.[53]

The seductive warmth, moisture, invitations, and vision of the fisher boy finally join to override Wilhelm's shyness, and he joins his friend in the water. As the boy later leaves the water, Wilhelm, like Werther before him, describes the beauty of the male body that emerges before his eyes:

> . . . und als er sich heraushob, sich aufrichtete im höheren Sonnenschein sich abzutrocknen, glaubt' ich meine Augen von einer dreifachen Sonne geblendet, so schön war die menschliche Gestalt von der ich nie einen Begriff gehabt (MA,17, 501–2).

> . . . and as he raised himself out of the water, and straightened himself up in the high sunshine to dry himself off, I thought my eyes were blinded by a threefold sun, so beautiful was the human figure of which I had never before had a conception.

For the first time, Wilhelm views a beautiful male body and acquires a conception of the male body and his own desire that is entirely new to him.[54] But unlike Werther, who sees himself in Ferdinand, Wilhelm sees the boy seeing him and in the same manner that he sees the boy: "Er schien mich mit gleicher Aufmerksamkeit zu betrachten" ("He seemed to observe me with the same attentiveness," MA, 17, 502).[55] That is, as Lacan might say, Wilhelm is cognizant of being seen and the subject-constructing power of the gaze of the other, and he perceives that gaze of the other as analogous to his own. They are each simultaneously constructing a "Begriff" (a conception) of the other and the other's desire for themselves as they stand viewing one another. And, during this moment of identification, desire takes over: "Schnell angekleidet standen wir uns noch immer unverhüllt gegeneinander, unsere Gemüter zogen sich an und unter den feurigsten Küssen schwuren wir eine ewige Freundschaft" ("Quickly dressed we stood still not yet disclosed before one another, our souls drew together and amidst the hottest kisses we swore an eternal friendship," MA, 17, 502). Their searing kisses attest finally to the mutuality of their desires. And Wilhelm asserts that they were now "unzertrennlich" ("inseparable," MA, 17, 502).

They are inseparable only, however, until the boy leaves to run errands and Wilhelm spends time with the fisher boy's sister. Wilhelm finds her "höchst unterhaltend" ("highly entertaining") and so beautiful that he remarks: "Meine Begleiterin war schön, blond, sanftmütig, wir gingen vertraulich zusammen, faßten uns bald bei der Hand und schienen nichts besseres zu wünschen" ("My companion was beautiful, blond, gentle, we walked along together intimately, took each other's hands and appeared to desire nothing better," MA, 17, 502). While Wilhelm does not express the same intensity of desire for the sister as he did for the fisher boy, he does appear to have forgotten his male object of desire in her presence, and the shift in his desire is reminiscent of the fluidity illustrated in the *Wahlverwandtschaften*.[56]

At this point Wilhelm interrupts the narration of his encounters with the fisher boy and the boy's sister by referring to his present (he is telling this story years later) evaluation of them:

Betracht' ich nach so viel Jahren meinen damaligen Zustand, so scheint er mir beneidenswert. Unerwartet, in demselbigen Augenblick, ergriff mich das Vorgefühl von Freundschaft und Liebe (MA, 17, 503).

> If I observe my situation at that time after so many years, it appears to me enviable. Unexpectedly, in the same instance, I was seized by a nascent perception of friendship and love.

According to Wilhelm, these moments mark his first realizations of desire. They are instances of fluid desire constituting the best and happiest experience of his life. Indeed, he refers to these first experiences of fluid desire as nascent perceptions of an "Originalnatur" ("original nature," MA, 17, 503). As Wilhelm shifts back into the narration of the fisher boy's story, he comments that he intended to tell his male friend all his new discoveries about desire:

> Denn als ich ungern Abschied nahm von dem schönen Kinde, tröstete mich der Gedanke, diese Gefühle meinem jungen Freunde zu eröffnen, zu vertrauen und seiner Teilnahme zugleich mit diesen frischen Empfindungen mich zu freuen (MA, 17, 503).

> Then as I reluctantly said goodbye to the beautiful child, I comforted myself with the thought of revealing these feelings to my young friend, of entrusting them to him, and of enjoying his sympathy and these fresh perceptions at one and the same time.

Wilhelm's desire creates in him a longing to share his feelings and perceptions with his male friend. They incite him to talk about his desires just as Werther's letters induced him to write about his. Wilhelm's incitement to talk about his desire with his male companion becomes more and more urgent. His anxiety about the fisher boy's failure to reappear at the time and destination they had agreed upon earlier is inextricably connected with his desire to tell his friend all about his "sex," or, more precisely here, "desire." Here we might recall Weeks and Foucault and their delineation of a modern compulsion to speak one's desire. Wilhelm manifests Goethe's comprehension that such a compulsion to speak one's self and desire is critical to the poetic formation of senses of a same-sex identified self. As Wilhelm recounts his story further, this compulsion to express his desire and identity verbally gets underscored even more fully.

Wilhelm relates to us that, as he waits for the fisher boy to reappear, he strains to see him: "Ich strengte die Sehkraft möglichst an um seine Gegenwart zu erforschen" ("I strained my power of sight to the utmost in order to determine his whereabouts," MA, 17, 503).

He begins to panic as his friend still does not arrive: "Ich rief, ich ängstigte mich; er war nicht zu sehen und antwortete nicht; ich empfand zum ersten mal einen leidenschaftlichen Schmerz, doppelt und vielfach" ("I yelled, I was anxious; he was not to be seen and did not answer. I felt for the first time a passionate pain, doubled and manifold," MA, 17, 503). Wilhelm experiences for the first time the excruciating pain of the loss of a lover/object of desire. His anxiety over the fisher boy's absence is at least twofold: First, he cannot *see* him. He can no longer see his beautiful body and he cannot see the desiring boy whose gaze met his own and whose gaze constructs him [Wilhelm] as an object of desire.[57] At the same time, without the boy to gaze upon, Wilhelm himself loses an object toward which his desire is directed. Secondly, Wilhelm cannot hear the boy's *answer*, that is, he loses his partner in interlocution and perhaps even worse he loses the object of desire to whom his own expressions of desire are directed:

> Schon entwickelte sich in mir die unmäßige Forderung vertraulicher Zuneigung, schon war es ein unwiderstehlich Bedürfnis meinen Geist von dem Bilde jener Blondine durch Plaudern zu befreien, mein Herz von den Gefühlen zu erlösen, die sie in mir aufgeregt hatte. Es war voll, der Mund lispelte schon um überzufließen; ich tadelte laut den guten Knaben, wegen verletzter Freundschaft, wegen vernachlässigter Zusage (MA, 17, 503–4).

> An immeasurable compulsion to intimate affection, an irresistible need to free my spirit from the image of that blond woman through talking, to rescue my heart from those feelings had already arisen in me and that she invoked in me. It was full, my mouth already whispered to overflowing. I loudly rebuked the good boy for an injured friendship and a neglected promise.

Wilhelm feels an overwhelming compulsion to express his desire (even if it is desire for the sister) to the fisher boy. He needs to give the image ("Bild") of his desire linguistic form. He needs to talk it over or talk it out ("plaudern"). His interlocutor must be a man, in fact, must be his male object of desire. As Mittler recognizes in *Die Wahlverwandtschaften*, "ein liebevoll beschäftiges Gemüt" has "das dringende Bedürfnis . . . sich zu äußern, das was in ihm vorgeht, vor einem Freunde auszuschütten . . ." ("a disposition engaged with loving has the pressing need . . . to express what is going on in him and to pour it out before a [male] friend," MA, 9, 395).[58] Goethe extends his poetic model of desire here in order to illustrate how the putting of desire into discourse requires verbal exchanges between desiring men. Discourse formation is not an auto-discursive process. In each case the desired male interlocutor is essential to the male subject yearning to voice his same-sex desire. Here Wilhelm discloses that, without the fisher boy, his feelings of desire well up inside him, but he has no one to express them to—no one to assist him in the formation of the metaphors of desire that will release him from his immeasurable feelings of longing. Consequently, once the fisher boy disappears, Wilhelm's mouth takes on a whispering life of its own, as the unarticulated emotions he perceives bubble up to his lips and threaten to overflow them. His mouth becomes the site where unformed and directionless desires are threatening to spew forth.

But that does not happen. Wilhelm discovers that the fisher boy's failure to return was not a sign of his infidelity, but has occurred because he has, in the meantime, drowned.[59] Wilhelm's incitement to speech is displaced by his tears. In his frenzy over the boy's death, he attempts to bring his male friend back to life by rubbing his tears into his body. Once he realizes that his efforts are futile, however, he fixes his last attentions on the boy's face, but even more specifically on his mouth:

> In der Verwirrung dacht' ich ihm Atem einzublasen, aber die Perlen-reihen seiner Zähne waren fest verschlossen, die Lippen auf denen der Abschiedskuß noch zu ruhen schien, versagten auch das leiseste Zeichen der Erwiederung (MA, 17, 505).

> In my confusion I thought to resuscitate him, but the pearl rows of his teeth were clamped shut, his lips upon which our departing kiss still seemed to rest, denied even the faintest sign of reciprocation.

Faced with his partner's death, Wilhelm obsesses over his mouth as the site of overwhelming loss. The kiss they exchanged earlier meta-morphoses now into an "Abschiedskuß" (literally a "kiss of separation"). Rather than uniting them in desire, the kiss now rests upon his lover's lips as a sign of their separation; it represents the collapse of their desire as Wilhelm's mouth overflows with emotion and the fisher boy's mouth is closed and incapable of receiving and returning that flow. The clamped teeth, the lips, the departing kiss, and the dead mouth's lack of reciprocation all point back to the critical importance of the desiring male mouth in the poetic formation of desire. The loss lamented here is talk/interlocution and male same-sex desire. The mouth is the metaphor of male desire, that is, male-male desire and the desire to talk about desire. Hot kisses incite the emotions that Wilhelm longs to transform into a language of his desire. The fisher boy is the male counterpart to whom Wilhelm returns his desire, both as kiss and as talk. Indeed, is that not the structure of both of these passages about male same-sex desire and poetic representation? Isn't Werther running his "experiments in desire"—testing out his amorous responses to naked bodies—and then reporting them to his male friend? In fact, couldn't we say that the Werther novel itself has a kiss-and-tell structure? Isn't Werther (both here and in the novel) compelled to relate his sexual adventures to the male friend to whom he addresses his letters?[60] Clearly, kissing and telling, specifically when shared between two men, figures—that is, becomes a metaphor for—the incitement to the poetic formation of male same-sex desire.[61]

The four moments of articulation we have discussed in this chapter demonstrate the processes of expression, the incitements to discourse, and the metaphoric formulations of a Goethean paradigm of identity and desire. In each case metaphorizations are central to the construction and revelation of desire and identity. The three articulations of desire foreground its fluid and protean character. In the cases of Werther and Wilhelm the primal scene of metaphor and desire is also critically connected to expressions of male same-sex desire. The finding of the male-*self* is disclosed as crucial to the proliferation of metaphors of male-male desire. Moreover, both male figures feel a compulsion to kiss and tell, to give their desire (whether for men or women) poetic form, to reveal them*selves* to their male counterparts through the telling of their desire. Accordingly, the Winckelmann essay also revolves around Goethe's desire to "tell" or "spell" all about the "word" (or desire) that is Winckelmann. Indeed, the process of identity-formation is inextricably intertwined with basic compulsions to express desire in metaphoric forms. In fact, these formations are clearly analogous to modern ones in their (self-reflective) concentration on the construction of metaphors of self, identity, and desire and in their incitement to talk about them. In each case the centrality to Goethe's literary production of metaphors of identity and desire is foregrounded. The convergence of processes of articulation, self-fashioning, and identity within the process of the poetic formation of desire—and critically of male same-sex desire— is manifest in each of these crucial moments of articulation. And it is precisely that convergence that makes the Goethean formulations of desire and identity so modern and striking. Finally, and most significantly, these moments of articulation signify a self-reflective process of the linguistic formation of self and desire. That is, in each of these cases, the desiring male subject, and often the man desiring another man, names himself and his desire. Throughout Goethe's literary production, the desiring subject names and speaks himself and his desire. Indeed, in Goethe's conception of the "affinities," male-male desire finds its articulation and is requisite to incitements to express desire and to lend it new poetic forms. Each of the four moments of articulation discussed in this chapter revolves around notions of the need to construct a language, a *Symbolik*, a metaphor of desire and sexual identity. Each accentuates the centrality of male same-sex desire. And each foregrounds the incitement, the need to "spell out," to "encode," and to "speak" desire in all its capacities. In each of these moments Goethe furthers the Winckelmannian project. The Winckelmann essay works to foreground the same-sex desire innate to the Winckelmannian word—manifest in the charade of syllables that is Winckelmann—and announces Goethe's own dedication to further the articulations Winckelmann outlines in his letters to Berg. The *Wahlverwandtschaften* maps out a general metaphor of the fluidity of desire that includes male-male desire and illustrates how metaphors of desire are constructed and proliferated and how they function in different and sometimes competing layers of discourse. The metaphors of desire given contour in both the Winckelmann essay and the *Wahlverwandtschaften* are manifest in both Werther's and Wilhelm's descriptions of their compulsions to give their desires poetic/linguistic forms. Beyond Winckelmann's epistolary struggle to find a language of male-male desire, in these passages Goethe overtly

connects male same-sex desire, poetic production, and poetic articulation. Goethe portrays his characters as they give their desires—
and most often their (male) same-sex desires—new linguistic formulations. It is in moments such as these that Goethe delineates
and extends the Winckelmannian project. He represents incitements
to the poetic signification of male same-sex desire, he creates a language of male-male desire, that Winckelmann only intimated. Finally,
each of these moments of articulation represents a general incitement
to critical expressions of same-sex identity and desire that are even
more overtly formulated throughout Goethe's literary production.
Indeed, with these poetic representations in mind, we can begin a
radical revaluation of the function of male same-sex identity and desire in Goethe's oeuvre as a whole.

chapter 3

MALE INTERLOCUTORS AND
LITERARY ARTICULATIONS
OF MALE SAME-SEX DESIRE

$\mathcal{G}$oethe's notion of the elective affinities—his conception of how desire works—constitutes one of the central structuring mechanisms manifest throughout his literary work. As we have seen, his paradigm of the affinities accentuates the dynamic, transforming, and metamorphosing nature of sexual desire. In Goethe's view, attractions between men and women or men and men are the product of shifting combinations of specific natural inclinations and particular social interactions. The four moments of articulation we discussed in the previous chapter illustrated *in nuce* the basic philosophical presumptions and directions of Goethe's poetic project. They indicated, as well, that Goethe perceived himself as engaged in furthering Winckelmann's linguistic struggles to express same-sex desire and identity and that he understood his poetic production in terms of forming and inciting these new articulations. For these reasons, it is not surprising that many of Goethe's works (and not just *Die Wahlverwandtschaften*) are structured around his notion of the elective affinities and, even more specifically, around his conceptions of the expression of male same-sex desire among male interlocutors. Indeed, as we shall see in this chapter, works as diverse as *Torquato Tasso* (1790), *Götz von Berlichingen* (1773), *Die Wahlver-*

wandtschaften (1809), *Die Leiden des jungen Werthers* (1774), *Egmont* (1788), and *Wilhelm Meisters Lehrjahre* (1796) are structurally contingent upon and evince various permutations of Goethe's model of the elective affinities and male interlocution. Illustrating the structuring effect that Goethe's elective affinities serve in several individual works will allow for a more specific and detailed understanding of the general parameters that we have traced across isolated passages in *Die Wahlverwandtschaften,* the Winckelmann essay, the *Briefe aus der Schweiz,* and *Wilhelm Meisters Wanderjahre.* Moreover, I am principally concerned in this chapter with the specific literary expressions of desire that recur throughout Goethe's oeuvre. With his generalizations about the characteristics of desire and specifically about male same-sex desire in mind, we discover a whole array of new articulations of male-male desire in Goethe's literary production.

For this reason, my analysis of Goethe's notion of the elective affinities consists of tracing several of its permutations in a number of different works. It is, of course, important to keep in mind that the elective affinities (in all of their capacities) do not acquire the same weight in each individual literary production. Nor do I intend to claim that the elective affinities form the structuring principal in all of Goethe's literary works. *Faust I* and *Faust II,* for instance, do not manifest the same tropes of desire and identity. My interest here is also not in new, comprehensive interpretations of Goethe's literary oeuvre, but in tracing new expressions of desire and especially of male same-sex desire in his works to illuminate another way to approach the issue of male-male sentiment in eighteenth- and early nineteenth-century texts. I will be looking at representative expressions of male-female and male-male desire in Goethe's works specifically in order to isolate the types of poetic formulations being made.

While I will refer throughout this analysis to the complex webs of affinities manifest in several of Goethe's literary works, I am principally concerned with the strikingly bold occurrences in his work of elective affinities between men. Goethe's literary illustrations of male same-sex desire are of critical importance, of course, because of the tremendous significance of male-male desire to Goethe's literary project and to his conception of poetic production. Here I am referring to that integral mirroring of male figures, that infinite chain of

significations of male same-sex desire that incite discursive formulations of desire and identity in Goethe's literary aesthetics—the kind
of male-male representations we saw in the Werther and Wilhelm passages in chapter two. It is precisely Goethe's structural allowance for
male-male desire, its poetic expression, and its crucial and inextricable connection to his poetic work that has gone largely unrecog-
nized. Examining Goethe's literary formulations of male-male desire
in detail will accentuate the complex system of metaphoric representations of same-sex desire that informs the structure of many of his
literary productions. And finally, his aesthetic work offers a multi-
layered corpus of formulations of male same-sex desire underscoring
the convergence of senses of self and same-sex desire in various late
eighteenth- and early nineteenth-century texts. In other words, we
will trace here expressions of self and male same-sex desire that many
scholars (following Foucault) have reserved for the later nineteenth
century.

In addition, it is important to keep in mind that Goethe's paradigm of male interlocution provides a counter-example to Sedgwick's
model of homosociality in nineteenth-century English literature (see
Between Men). Sedgwick's notion of a triangle of relationships between two men and a woman (with its basis in Levi-Strauss's an-
thropological work), whereby women are exchanged between men
as they bond with one another, would appear to be universally appli-
cable. But, as we shall see, the German aesthetic tradition revolving
around Goethe accentuates another possibility. In fact, something
like a Sedgwickian notion of cultural homosociality is openly cri-
tiqued in Goethe's *Götz von Berlichingen*. Throughout Goethe's
poetic oeuvre (and we see this in Moritz and in the German dramatic tradition in general), an underlying aesthetic of male same-sex
desire and interlocution operates as the central structuring mechanism. Here we find that male-male desire and male-female desire
are both expressions contingent upon a foundational paradigm of
verbal exchanges between men. This model of desire is not about the
exchange of women, but about expressing an innate, natural desire
between men that gets expressed in spite of women, in addition to
a desire for women, but which precisely does not get reduced to a
"socially acceptable" homosociality. In Goethe's works compulsory

homosociality does not appear to be the most foundational social structuring mechanism. Indeed, as we shall see, Goethe's *Götz von Berlichingen* maps out explicitly the social devastation compulsory homosociality is perceived to cause. One of the critical differences between the model that Sedgwick outlines for nineteenth-century English prose and the one that the German aesthetic tradition foregrounds is that the German/Goethean tradition does not assume that social structure ultimately strives to reaffirm the foundational function of heterosexuality. In other words, Sedgwick outlines the exchange of women as the necessary precursor to bonds between men within a heterosexually oriented social system. The Goethean paradigm, in contrast, accentuates the original and foundational nature of male same-sex desire. Any expression of desire, whether of that between men and/or between men and women, is contingent upon original verbal exchanges between men. So while Sedgwick illustrates how in the nineteenth-century English tradition compulsory heterosexual exchanges allow for bonding between men, Goethe's paradigm highlights how in the German tradition the same-sex desire of men allows for the expression of both same-sex and opposite-sex desire. In essence, while Sedgwick stresses the exchange of women, Goethe foregrounds the exchange of words between men and the fundamental character of male same-sex desire in the formation of discourse and poetry.

Although I concentrated in the last chapter on specific passages in Goethe's literary production that accentuated the metaphoric formation of self, identity, and male same-sex desire, here I will focus on several of Goethe's individual works as literary articulations in and of themselves. They are products of his incitements to the poetic formulation of sexual desires. Each of the literary works addressed here is, in other words, a product of the Goethean project, and I read each one as a representation of his attempts to express the sexual desires alluded to in the *Wahlverwandtschaften*, the Winckelmann encomium, the *Briefe aus der Schweiz*, and *Wilhelm Meisters Wanderjahre*. Because of the complexity of Goethe's paradigm of the elective affinities and its multiple manifestations within the works discussed here, I have chosen to focus in this discussion on its general contours and on specific expressions of male same-sex desire. I am reserving a more lengthy and detailed discussion of identity formation for chapter four. With those things in mind, we can now direct our attention back to *Die Wahlverwandtschaften*.

THE FUNDAMENTAL STRUCTURE OF MALE INTERLOCUTION AND DESIRE IN GOETHE'S NOVELS

While I have already discussed Goethe's general paradigm of the elective affinities/desire in some detail, I want to return now, initially, to an evaluation of the manifold representations of elective affinities and their implications for *Die Wahlverwandtschaften* as a whole. I am particularly interested in the tropes evoked in association with the elective affinities—those that resurface in various permutations throughout Goethe's oeuvre. Moreover, I want to devote particular attention to the emergence of male-male affinities in his literary works, even in those traditionally understood in terms of their profuse expressions of male-female desire and longing. As will become clear in the course of my analysis here, Goethe's works are not premised on the notion that one kind of desire necessarily precludes another, and we find, accordingly, that in each literary text multiple affinities are in operation. I will begin with an investigation of those works by Goethe such as *Die Wahlverwandtschaften, Die Leiden des jungen Werthers,* and *Wilhelm Meisters Lehrjahre* that revolve most overtly around the affinities between men and women, and will then turn to those works such as *Götz, Tasso,* and *Egmont* that accentuate male same-sex desire. What I hope to show in both instances is the critical importance throughout Goethe's work of male-male desire. Indeed, even those texts foregrounding male-female desire have as their *raison d'être* affinities between men, that is, the structure of male-male interlocution manifests itself throughout Goethe's literary production.

We recall that early in the *Wahlverwandtschaften* Eduard and the Captain, as male interlocutors, trace out the chemical nature of the affinities in all of their capacities. Together these two men discuss, explicate, and map out the various affinitive possibilities. They outline the possible trajectories of their desires and they give their desires poetic form, constructing in essence a new language of desire and desire as a metaphor. Moreover, Eduard and the Captain determine *in nuce* the general contours of desire and its possible trajectories throughout the novel. Like the Werther of the Swiss letters, they are in the business of figuring desire, including their own same-sex desire. And like Wilhelm in the *Wanderjahre*, they exhibit a compulsion to share their desires as male interlocutors. It is their compulsion to speak themselves and their desire that constitutes the language, the *Symbolik* that sets the parameters of symbolization for the entire novel. *Die Wahlverwandtschaften* begins with the signification of Eduard's and the Captain's incitement to express their desires and to lend them poetic form. Not only do they discuss the metaphoricity of desire, they themselves enact and symbolize the process of metaphorization and the role of male interlocutors in it. Their conversation about desire sets into motion the poetic process that is *Die Wahlverwandtschaften*. The novel can only begin with the metaphorization of desire, a poetic activity sustained by mutually desiring male interlocutors. The desire that they in turn represent, whether male-male or male-female, acquires new metaphoric forms during the course of their verbal exchanges. And, indeed, the course of the *Wahlverwandtschaften* itself is set into motion by Eduard's and the Captain's incitements to formulate a new metaphor/discourse of desire that includes both same-sex and opposite-sex desire. And even though the novel as a whole appears to stress the attractions between the opposite sexes over same-sex affinities, its foundation, its reason for being, is clearly the male-male desire that functions so fundamentally in Goethe's representations of aesthetic production. And for this reason it is not surprising that *Die Wahlverwandtschaften* is shaped along the lines of the metaphorizations outlined by Eduard and the Captain.

   With this in mind, we can turn initially to several specific expressions of desire in *Die Wahlverwandtschaften*. I will start here with Goethe's descriptions of the desire between the opposite sexes in order to establish how desire operates in general in his work. Later we will see similar linguistic gestures and tropes evoked in order to express a sense of male same-sex desire.

   Of course, the most electric elective bond of *Die Wahlverwandtschaften* is that between Eduard and Ottilie. The novel's plot tags along the course of their developing relationship, and other characters and their affinities for one another appear to be only of secondary significance. The intensity of the attraction between Eduard and Ottilie is immense. Eduard's love for Ottilie is described as infinite and without measure:

> In Eduards Gesinnungen, wie in seinen Handlungen ist kein Maß mehr. Das Bewußtsein zu lieben und geliebt zu werden treibt ihn ins Unendliche. Wie verändert ist ihm die Ansicht von allen Zimmern, von allen Umgebungen! Er findet sich in seinem eignen Hause nicht mehr. Ottiliens Gegenwart verschlingt ihm alles: er ist ganz in ihr versunken; keine andre Betrachtung steigt vor ihm auf, kein Gewissen spricht ihm zu; alles was in seiner Natur gebändigt war bricht los, sein ganzes Wesen strömt gegen Ottilien (MA, 9, 370).

> In Eduard's convictions, as in his actions, there is no more restraint. The realization of loving and being loved drives him into infinity. How changed the view of all the rooms, of the entire surroundings is to him! He does not find himself in his own house any more. Ottilie's presence swallows up everything else: he is completely submerged in her. No contemplation arises before him, no conscience speaks to him. Everything in his nature that had been constrained breaks loose and his whole being streams toward Ottilie.

Eduard perceives nothing outside of Ottilie and is completely lost in her presence.[1] His whole being flows toward her. Indeed, the novel underscores repeatedly the inevitable, natural, and amoralistic character of the mutual attraction between Eduard and Ottilie:

> Eduard hob seine Arme empor: Du liebst mich! rief er aus: Ottilie du liebst mich! Sie hielten einander umfaßt. Wer das andere zuerst ergriffen, wäre nicht zu unterscheiden gewesen . . . Sie standen vor einander, er hielt ihre Hände, sie sahen einander in die Augen, im Begriff sich wieder zu umarmen (MA, 9, 366).

> Eduard raised his arms up into the air: You love me! he cried: Ottilie you love me! They embraced each other. It would not be possible to determine who grasped the other first . . . They stood before one another, he held her hands, they gazed into each other's eyes, on the verge of holding each other again.

Simply being in each other's presence renders their attraction for one another thoroughly irresistible. The specular moment, as Wellbery refers to it, the presence, the visual immediacy of the desired and desiring other determines intractable affinities.[2] Neither Eduard nor Ottilie is concerned with social conventions or with their obligations to Charlotte as Eduard's wife. The elective affinities operate here in their full natural force. Moral or social choice seems impossible, as Eduard insists: "Stünde sie vor mir, in meine Arme würde sie fallen, ich in die ihrigen . . ." ("If she stood before me, she would fall into my arms, and I in hers," MA, 9, 370). And, in fact, for Eduard the attraction continues to grow in its power over him: "Die Notwendigkeit mit Ottilien zu sein, sie zu sehen, ihr etwas zuzuflüstern, ihr zu vertrauen, wuchs mit jedem Tage." ("The necessity to be with Ottilie, to see her, to whisper something to her, to talk to her, grew with each day," MA, 9, 372).

But Eduard and Ottilie are not alone in their experience of puissant passion. Charlotte and the Captain are subject to an equally forceful attraction:

> Denn eigentlich war die Neigung, dieser beiden (Charlotte und der Hauptmann) eben so gut im Wachsen als jene (Ottilie und Eduard), und vielleicht nur noch gefährlicher dadurch, daß beide ernster, sicherer von sich selbst, sich zu halten fähiger waren (MA, 9, 340–41).

> Then actually the passion of these two (Charlotte and the Captain) was growing as much as that (of Ottilie and Eduard) and was perhaps even more dangerous because these two were more serious, more certain of themselves, more capable of composing themselves.

Paradoxically, the affinity coursing between Charlotte and the Captain is even more disturbing and problematic because their moral resistence is stronger, and because they seem to have a more secure sense of who they are and what their social obligations should be. As Eduard is drawn to Ottilie, the Captain feels an overpowering force compelling him toward Charlotte: "Schon fing der Hauptmann an zu fühlen, daß eine unwiderstehliche Gewohnheit ihn an Charlotte zu fesseln drohte" ("Already the Captain began to feel that an unconquerable habit was threatening to bind him to Charlotte," MA, 9, 341). The unraveling of the original affinity between Eduard and Charlotte finds its culmination as they make love to one another while fantasizing about their new objects of desire:

In der Lampendämmerung sogleich behauptete die innre Neigung, behauptete die Einbildungskraft ihre Rechte über das Wirkliche. Eduard hielt nur Ottilien in seinen Armen; Charlotten schwebte der Hauptmann näher oder ferner vor der Seele, und so verwebten, wundersam genug, sich Abwesendes und Gegenwärtiges reizend und wonnevoll durcheinander (MA, 9, 364).

In the shadows of the lamp light inner inclination asserted itself immediately and the power of the imagination asserted its rights over reality. Eduard held only Ottilie in his arms; the Captain floated back and forth before Charlotte's soul, and so the absent and the present, wondrously enough, wove enticingly and blissfully through one another.

The affinities operating in the relationships between Eduard and Ottilie and the Captain and Charlotte highlight certain fantasies about the manner in which desire between the sexes is supposed to work. In both cases desire is represented as a force beyond the control of the parties involved. Here, certainly, desire acts in the manner of chemical affinities. Once the mix starts, it is virtually impossible to halt the chemical reaction. Characters in *Die Wahlverwandtschaften* appear to be propelled solely by their elective (or not so elective) affinities. Eduard is overwhelmed by and driven to desperate lengths by his desires right up until the moment of his death. Ottilie vows (after the accidental drowning of Eduard's and Charlotte's baby) to resist her inclinations—an objective she can only attain by starving herself to death.[3] For Ottilie and Eduard death appears to be the only release from the ravages of their impetuous desires. Charlotte and the Captain, on the other hand, while choosing to uphold social conventions and to honor the bounds of marriage, discover that they cannot relinquish their desire for one another and they cannot restrain it in one another's presence. They can only avoid the inevitable consequences of their desire by refusing to be alone with (in the presence of) one another, which for each of them, is, in a sense, another form of death.[4] Clearly, desire and existence, one's very sense of being, are connected here. Being cut off from desire, unfulfilled desire is death.

Intriguingly enough, while the novel underscores the significance of the visual presence of Ottilie and Eduard and Charlotte and the Captain in the activation and nurturance of their attractions, separations do not have the effect on these lovers of altering their affinities. In sharp contrast to Eduard's insistence during the discussion of the elective affinities that if one of the four of them departed the affinities would rearrange themselves, we find in the novel as a whole that Eduard's severance from Ottilie and the Captain's from Charlotte does not result in a reconstitution of their affections. These affinities are intractable and remain unaffected by the absence of one or more of the four lovers.

The only intimation of a possible threat to the bond established between Eduard and Ottilie is a fleeting reference to her attraction to a Count who visits the estate with his wife. Ottilie is drawn to him because, while the presence of Eduard rendered her oblivious to the world outside, the Count introduces her to its wonders:

> Sie hatte sich ihm genähert, ja sie ward von ihm angezogen, weil sie durch sein gehaltvolles Gespräch dasjenige zu sehen und zu kennen glaubte, was ihr bisher ganz unbekannt geblieben war. Und wie sie in dem Umgange mit Eduard die Welt vergaß, so schien ihr an der Gegenwart des Grafen die Welt erst recht wünschenswert zu sein. Jede Anziehung ist wechselseitig. Der Graf empfand eine Neigung für Ottilien, die er gern als seine Tochter betrachtete (MA, 9, 453–54).

> She had approached him, yes, she had been drawn to him, because she believed that she could see and recognize in his substantial conversation all of those things that had up to that time remained unknown to her. And as she forgot the world in her association with Eduard, the world appeared desirable to her for the first time in the presence of the Count. Every inclination is mutual. The Count perceived an attraction for Ottilie, who he gladly looked upon as his daughter.

Here the same trope of compelling attraction that emerged in the relationships between Eduard and Ottilie and the Captain and Charlotte reasserts itself. Every inclination is mutual, we are told. Or, we might say, for every affinitive action there is an affinitive reaction. But this brief bond does not rise to the intensity of the relationship between Eduard and Ottilie. Nor does it displace Ottilie's feelings for Eduard. Ottilie enjoys the Count's conversation because it has the opposite effect upon her of her rendevous with Eduard. Once in his presence, her desire for him made her forget herself entirely, encounters with the Count make her cognizant of who and where she is in relation to the outside world. The Count, on the other hand, deludes himself with the fantasy that Ottilie is like a daughter to him. His wife certainly is not convinced of the nonerotic nature of his inclinations, and once she perceives what is afoot, we learn that "jetzt war es ihr genug" ("now she had had enough," MA, 9, 454), and she schemes to sever Ottilie from her husband by engineering her marriage with another man. At any rate, Ottilie's fleeting infatuation with the Count signals the fact that while their attraction may be mutual, it is not alike in intensity and direction. And while Eduard's absence and the Count's presence seem to facilitate the new affinity between Ottilie and the Count, this attraction does not threaten the bond between Ottilie and Eduard.

Accordingly, Ottilie appears thoroughly unaffected by the advances of other men in Eduard's absence. Her subsequent relationships with men are marked by the disjuncture between their positive sentiments for her and her disinterest and even disgust for them. The school assistant, for instance, comes to court her and obtains Charlotte's implied consent to Ottilie's return to the school with him—his eventual plan being to marry her so that they can manage the school together. Ottilie is clearly not inclined to participate in this proposal. So while the school assistant "nahm diese Anerbietung freudig auf" ("receives the offer [of Ottilie joining him] with joy"), Ottilie falls silent "ob es ihr gleich vor dem Gedanken schauderte" ("as if she immediately shuddered at the thought," MA, 9, 455). The reaction of the architect who expresses an Eduard-like passion for Ottilie is as unsuccessful as the school assistant:

> . . . es ward ihm so schwer, dieses Haus, diese Familie zu verlassen, ja es schien ihm unmöglich von Ottiliens Augen zu scheiden, von deren ruhig freundlich gewogenen Blicken er die letzte Zeit fast ganz allein gelebt hatte (MA, 9, 443).

> . . . it was so difficult for him to leave this house, this family. Yes, it appeared to him impossible to tear himself from Ottilie's eyes, from their quiet, friendly, favorable glances in which he had lived almost exclusively during the past days.

But like the school assistant he cannot draw Ottilie's attention even

momentarily to himself because her desire remains thoroughly an-
chored to Eduard:

> Das persönliche Verhältnis Ottiliens zum Architekten war ganz rein
> und unbefangen. Seine angenehme und tätige Gegenwart hatte sie,
> wie die Nähe eines ältern Brüders, unterhalten und erfreut. Ihre
> Empfindungen für ihn blieben auf der ruhigen leidenschaftslosen
> Oberfläche der Blutsverwandtschaft: denn in ihrem Herzen war
> kein Raum mehr; es war von der Liebe zu Eduard ganz gedrängt
> ausgefüllt, und nur die Gottheit, die alles durchdringt, konnte dieses
> Herz zugleich mit ihm besitzen (MA, 9, 431).

> Ottilie's personal relationship to the architect was completely pure
> and open. His pleasant and active presence had entertained and
> pleased her like the closeness of an older brother. Her feelings for
> him remained on the quiet passionless surface of blood relations for
> in her heart there was no more room. It was completely filled to the
> limit with her love for Eduard and only God who penetrates every-
> thing, could possess this heart with him at the same time.

In opposition to the discussion at the beginning of the novel of the
elective affinities in which the adding and subtracting of elements
or persons signaled an inevitable reconstitution of affinities, the relationships between Eduard and Ottilie, the Captain and Charlotte,
and those between Ottilie and various other men suggest several
additional critical characteristics of the affinities. While it is true
that the addition of the Captain radically altered the relationship
between Charlotte and Eduard, and that Ottilie's arrival resulted in
the emergence of a new set of female-male affinities, it is also evident
in the novel that once constituted certain affinities (those between
Eduard and Ottilie and the Captain and Charlotte) are impermeable
and intractable. Moreover, while the presence of the desired partner renders the loving subject incapable of resistance, and while the
affinities work in that presence persistently to draw the two lovers
together whether they will it or not, the absence of one of the partners does not inevitably signal the dissolution of their affinity, nor
does it necessarily allow for new additions (new potential lovers)
to displace that desire. What is thoroughly evident throughout the
novel is that the trajectories of desire are unpredictable, that desire
is tremendously powerful and unrelenting in its forging of affinities,

that desires always initiate actions and reactions (but they are not always mutual), and, finally, that one desire does not necessarily preclude another.

Which brings us back to the affinity between Eduard and the Captain. Although both men are depicted in *Die Wahlverwandtschaften* principally in their attraction for women, the novel begins and ends with representations of their immutable and irresistible affinity for one another. This further underscores the fact that female-male desire and male-male desire are not mutually exclusive in Goethe's paradigm of the elective affinities/desires. We recall from the discussion in chapter two that the Captain's arrival triggers the dissolution of the bond between Eduard and Charlotte and an affirmation of the affinity between Eduard and the Captain. The two men then move to a wing opposite from Charlotte and devote their critical emotional energy to one another. And it is in this context that they explicate the metaphoric structures of desire. The arrival of Ottilie exacts a shift in the female-male pairings of the four friends, and the intense relationship between the two men recedes from view. But the affinity between Eduard and the Captain reasserts itself once more at the end of the novel after Eduard returns to the vicinity of his estate in hopes yet of dissolving his marriage and pursuing his desire for Ottilie. Upon his arrival, Eduard immediately calls for the Captain. The novel recounts that:

> Die Freude des Wiedersehens war groß. Jugendfreundschaften, wie Blutsverwandtschaften, haben den bedeutenden Vorteil, daß ihnen Irrungen und Mißverständnisse, von welcher Art sie auch seien, niemals von Grund aus schaden, und die alten Verhältnisse sich nach einiger Zeit wieder herstellen (MA, 9, 486).

> The joy of seeing one another was great. Friendships from youth, like blood relations, have the important advantage, that confusions and misunderstandings of whatever kind they may be, never harm them fundamentally and the old relationships [affinities] reassert themselves in time.

As in the encounters between Eduard and Ottilie and the Captain and Charlotte, the visual encounter, that is, the mere presence of the desired object, initiates an inevitable bonding between the two male subjects. In other words, the same tropes of attraction are deployed here to indicate male same-sex desire that surfaced earlier to designate desire between the sexes. Moreover, the affinity between Eduard and the Captain is one that ebbs and flows—in other words, the original affinity established between them in youth periodically reasserts itself and then recedes from view. During the course of the novel, we find that the affinity between the two men is foregrounded in their discussions of the affinitive qualities of chemical matter and in the structure of metaphoricity. In addition, it asserts itself in the reconstitution of desires right after the Captain's arrival, and then it reemerges finally in the last chapters of the novel when Eduard is in desperate need again of a male interlocutor. Indeed, just like Wilhelm and Werther, Eduard longs to pour his heart out to the man with whom he identifies and who he desires: "Gegen ihn [den Hauptmann] schüttet Eduard sein Herz aus, ihm gesteht er jeden kleinsten Umstand, und so erfährt Charlotte was die Lage so verändert, was die Gemüter aufgeregt" ("Eduard pours his heart out to him [the Captain], confesses every detail, and so Charlotte learns what altered the situation so radically, what excites their hearts," MA, 9, 515). Once again, male same-sex desire facilitates the expression of desire (whether male-male or male-female). Eduard cannot articulate his desire for Ottilie in the presence of Charlotte or to her, but he is able to fashion/create (produce poetically) his desires in the presence of the Captain and within the confines of their verbal exchanges. Indeed, the affinity that Eduard and the Captain share provides the novel with its outer contours. This story of desire, the story of the *Wahlverwandtschaften*, begins and ends with the assertion of the intractable and irresistible affinity between Eduard and the Captain. Male same-sex desire functions as the underlying foundation of the novel; it constitutes the frame of the story that is told. As we know from the discussion of Werther and Wilhelm in chapter two, in Goethe's aesthetics articulations of desire commence, proliferate, and culminate within the confines of male-male desire. In the *Wahlverwandtschaften* this is clearly true. Despite the fact that the novel focuses throughout and predominantly on male-female affinities, it exists as a story that can be told, and that can poeticize desire, only because Eduard and the Captain are drawn to one another as desiring interlocutors. Indeed, as we have seen, without his male counterpart, the potential storyteller (Wilhelm) would be speechless.

Which brings us to Goethe's *Die Leiden des jungen Werthers.* Werther is certainly not speechless. Indeed, while he can claim that the intensity of his emotions prevents him from painting, he has certainly found a way to write. His letters to his friend Wilhelm and the novel they create constitute profuse expressions of his desire for Lotte. Each letter is addressed to Wilhelm, the epistolary interlocutor for whom Werther asserts his affinity in the opening lines of the novel: "Wie froh bin ich, daß ich weg bin! Bester Freund, was ist das Herz des Menschen! Dich zu verlassen, den ich so liebe, und von dem ich unzertrennlich war . . ." ("How happy I am that I am away! Best friend, what is the heart of man! To leave you, you who I so love and from whom I was inseparable . . ." MA, 1:2, 197). And like the Werther of the *Briefe aus der Schweiz,* this Werther also struggles in his letters—within the context of male same-sex desire—to express the new desire that he can hardly articulate:

> "Dir in der Ordnung zu erzählen, wie's zugegangen ist, daß ich eins der liebenswürdigsten Geschöpfe habe kennen lernen, wird schwer halten, ich bin vergnügt und glücklich, und so kein guter Historien-schreiber. Einen Engel! Pfui! das sagt jeder von der seinigen! Nicht wahr? Und doch bin ich nicht im Stande, dir zu sagen, wie sie vollkommen ist, warum sie vollkommen ist, genug, sie hat all meinen Sinn gefangen genommen" (MA, 1:2, 207).

> To explain to you in order what has transpired, how it has happened that I have met the most adorable creation, would be difficult. I am pleased and happy and as such no good narrator of stories. An angel! Ugh! everyone says that about his [beloved]! Right? And still I am not in a position to tell you, how perfect she is, why she is perfect, enough, she has taken all of my senses captive.

Once again the compulsion on the part of the male subject to construct poetic articulations of his desire, to transmit them to his male interlocutor, and the stultifying effect on his speech of the woman's overwhelming presence come to the fore.

As in the *Wahlverwandtschaften,* Werther describes repeatedly in his letters to Wilhelm how compelling his affinity to Lotte is. He recounts how he cannot bear to be apart from her, cannot control his desire to see her, and even interrupts his letter to Wilhelm (his writing of his desire) in order to go to her: "Ich hab's nicht überwinden können, ich mußte zu ihr hinaus" ("I could not overcome it, I had to go to her," MA, 1:2, 208). He feels his "ganze Seele angezogen" "whole soul drawn to her," MA, 1:2, 212) in her presence. A mysterious force pulls him relentlessly to Lotte:

> Ach wie mir das durch alle Adern läuft, wenn mein Finger unversehens den ihrigen berührt, wenn unsere Füße sich unter dem Tisch begegnen. Ich ziehe zurück wie vom Feuer, und eine geheime Kraft zieht mich wieder vorwärts, mir wird's so schwindlich vor allen Sinnen (MA, 1:2, 226).

> Ah how it courses through all of my veins when my finger inadvertently touches hers, when our feet meet underneath the table. I pull back as from fire, and a mysterious force pulls me forward again, all of my senses are giddy.

Just as it did for Eduard and Ottilie, the Captain and Charlotte, and Eduard and the Captain, an irresistible affinity binds Werther to Lotte. Once again, the affinity asserts itself regardless of the will of the desiring subject. Werther cannot keep his hands and feet to himself; they migrate continually back to Lotte. Indeed, as in the *Wahlverwandtschaften*, the extreme intensity of affinitive emotions lead ultimately to the destruction of the desiring subject:

> Wer könnte da wegbleiben? . . . Ich bin zu nah in der Atmosphäre, Zuck! so bin ich dort. Meine Großmutter hatte ein Märgen vom Magnetenberg. Die Schiffe die zu nahe kamen, wurden auf einmal alles Eisenwerks beraubt, die Nägel flogen dem Berge zu, und die armen Elenden scheiterten zwischen den übereinander stürzenden Brettern (MA, 1:2, 229).

> Who could stay away? . . . I am too near in the atmosphere—flash! I am there. My grandmother told a fairytale about the Magnet Mountain. The ships that came too close, were suddenly robbed of their iron material, the nails flew to the mountain, and the poor wretches perished amongst the boards as they crashed down upon one another.

Here Werther enunciates the central metaphor of desire in *Die Leiden des jungen Werthers*. Like the metaphor of the chemical affinities in *Die Wahlverwandtschaften*, Werther relies on another material metaphor—that of a magnetic mountain—to symbolize the force of desire. The mountain destroys the ships that pass by too closely, and the sailors perish in the process. This metaphor captures the essence of Lotte's effect on the men around her and particularly on Werther. His affinity for Lotte is depicted as a thoroughly overwhelming and annihilating force. While in the *Wahlverwandtschaften* the affinities between men and women could only be curbed by subjects striving to escape them through death, in *Die Leiden* these affinities determine the inevitable death or collapse of the male desiring subject. And it is Lotte who serves as the catalyst for such terrific consequences. Werther's all-consuming obsession with her and the impossibility of ever possessing her drive him ultimately to suicide. And Werther is not the only man that Lotte (and the affinity she demands) destroys. As Werther recounts to Wilhelm, he is not the first to succumb to the desire for Lotte:

> Wilhelm! der Mensch, von dem ich dir schrieb, der glückliche Un-glückliche, war Schreiber bei Lottens Vater, und eine unglückliche Leidenschaft zu ihr, die er nährte, verbarg, entdeckte, und aus dem Dienst geschickt wurde, hat ihn rasend gemacht (MA, 1:2, 272).

> Wilhelm! the man about whom I wrote to you, the fortunate unfor-tunate one was a writer for Lotte's father and an unfortunate pas-sion for her, that he nourished, concealed, revealed and was dismissed from service, made him crazy.

While the men who desire her are driven mad or commit suicide, Lotte appears rather impervious to their passions for her. According to Werther's epistolary accounts, his arrival (addition to the chemical mix) has no effect on Lotte's bond with Albert, her fiancé. In fact, her engagement to Albert remains intact and they marry during the course of Werther's continued fascination with Lotte. For her part, Lotte appears drawn to both Werther and Albert and maintains her affinities to them both. A secret force has pulled her to Werther:

> Ein geheimer Zug hatte ihr ihn vom Anfange ihrer Bekanntschaft teuer gemacht, und nun, nach so viel Zeit, nach so manchen durch-lebten Situationen, mußte sein Eindruck unauslöschlich in ihrem Herzen sein (MA,1:2, 282–83).

A secret force had made him special to her from the beginning of their acquaintance, and now, after so much time, after so many shared experiences, his imprint on her heart must be inextinguishable.

At the same time, the presence of Albert incites the renewal of her love for him:

> Die Gegenwart des Mannes, den sie liebte und ehrte, hatte einen neuen Eindruck in ihr Herz gemacht. Sie erinnerte sich all seiner Güte, seines Edelmuts, seiner Liebe, . . . Ein unbekannter Zug reizte sie ihm zu folgen . . . (MA, 1:2, 294).

> The presence of her husband, whom she loved and honored, made a new impression upon her heart. She remembered all of his goodness, his nobility, his love . . . An unknown force enticed her to follow him . . .

Curiously, while Werther's arrival does not effect the dissolution of Lotte's bond with Albert, *Die Leiden* foregrounds how the triangle of desire maintained by these characters does result in the estrangement of Werther and Albert. While the two men initially befriend one another, the dual affinities that Lotte sustains later begin to strain the bonds between the two men. Although both men are still attracted to Lotte, they are repelled by each other: "Albert trat in die Stube. Man bot sich einen frostigen guten Abend, und ging verlegen im Zimmer neben einander auf und nieder" ("Albert entered the room. One offered each other a frosty good evening and each paced in embarrassment up and down the room next to the other," MA, 1:2, 279). While there seems to be no evidence in the novel of an erotic affinity between Werther and Albert, their tolerance of and friendship with one another is subverted during the course of Lotte's attempts to juggle them.

Throughout *Die Leiden des jungen Werthers* (1774) we encounter expressions of the kind of elective affinities that Goethe would first systematize and explicate thirty-five years later in *Die Wahlverwandtschaften* (1809). Both novels stress the fluidity of desire, its ultimate intractableness in certain instances, and the notion that affinities are so strong that they are likely to drive the desiring male subject to despair and/or death. Each novel accentuates a recurrent theme in Goethe's works of the deleterious effects upon the desiring male subject of his fascination with and pursuit of an unattainable woman. And finally, each revolves around the expression of desire to and with a male interlocutor.

Unlike *Die Leiden des jungen Werthers, Wilhelm Meisters Lehr- jahre* is not constructed within a fictional frame of verbal or written exchanges between desiring men. But while the novel is not formally "framed" within that same epistolary structure of male same-sex de- sire, the trope of the male interlocutor resurfaces throughout the novel and, indeed, manifests itself both at the beginning and the end of the work. As we might expect, this later novel provides a more complex model of male-male desire. While it does not oper- ate in the same self-reflective way that was apparent in *Die Wahlver- wandtschaften*, the trope of male same-sex desire repeatedly asserts its significance for the structure of the novel.[5] Moreover, Wilhelm in- teracts with several men who function as male interlocutors (Werner, Jarno, and Lothario) in several different ways. Here, then, the trope of male same-sex desire emerges and reemerges in much greater com- plexity and variety. In order to trace out the implications of the trope in *Wilhelm Meisters Lehrjahre*, I will follow Wilhelm's progression from one male discussant to another, that is, from Werner to Jarno to Lothario.

Wilhelm's early friend, Werner, is the first interlocutor with whom he attempts to articulate his desires and longings. While it is clear from the start that their verbal exchanges revolve around and produce their love for one another, the male same-sex desire they share is also fraught with tensions because of the vast differences between them:

> Werner war einer von den geprüften, in ihrem Dasein bestimmten Leuten, die man gewöhnlich kalte Leute zu nennen pflegt, weil sie bei Anlässen weder schnell noch sichtlich auflodern; auch war sein Um- gang mit Wilhelmen ein anhaltender Zwist, wodurch sich ihre Liebe aber nur desto fester knüpfte: denn ungeachtet ihrer verschiedenen Denkungsart fand jeder seine Rechnung bei dem andern (MA, 5, 60).

> Werner was one of those people tested and secure in their existence, that one tends to call cold people because given causes they neither quickly nor perceptibly flare up. His association with Wilhelm con- stituted a constant dispute, through which their love was only more

tightly bound: then each despite their different ways of thinking, found his confirmation in the other.

Although the affinity between the two men is obvious, it is an affinity based paradoxically on their inability to understand one another:

> So übte sich einer an dem andern, sie wurden gewohnt sich täglich zu sehen, und man hätte sagen sollen, das Verlangen einander zu finden, sich mit einander zu besprechen, sei durch die Unmöglichkeit, einander verständlich zu werden, vermehrt worden. Im Grunde aber gingen sie doch, weil sie beide gute Menschen waren, neben einander nach Einem Ziel, und konnten niemals begreifen, warum denn keiner den andern auf seine Gesinnung reduzieren könne (MA, 5, 60).

> So the one exercised himself on the other. They were accustomed to seeing one another daily, and one could say that the desire to find each other, to speak with one another, was increased by the impossibility of understanding each other. Essentially, because they were good people they pursued together the same goal and could never grasp why then neither could reduce the other to his convictions.

Unlike Eduard and the Captain whose discussions represented a mutual formulation of ideas and desires, Wilhelm and Werner are drawn to one another precisely because they do not understand each other and, consequently, they never really approach one another intellectually and spiritually, that is, neither seems to have any influence upon the other's conceptions or poetic and metaphoric (re)formulations of life and desire.

As we might expect, as Wilhelm falls in love for the first time with Mariane, Werner notes that he comes to visit him less often and is less engaged in their discussions. Although Werner initially blames himself for the waning intensity of their affinity, he soon discovers Wilhelm's secret relationship with Mariane and decides—given her questionable reputation as a "seductive girl"("verführerisches Mädchen," MA, 5, 61)—to confront Wilhelm directly. Despite his efforts to illustrate to Wilhelm all the bitterness of such a foolhardy desire, he accomplishes nothing. Wilhelm is not to be severed from Mariane, insisting that he is as sure of her loyalty and virtue as of his own love. The consequence of their verbal battle over the nature of a relationship with a woman like Mariane results only in the further estrangement of the two men, as Wilhelm departs from Werner feeling "verdrießlich und erschüttert" ("morose and shattered," MA, 5, 61). Here the verbal exchanges with the desired male other do not result in the male subject's metaphorization of himself, in a greater and clearer affinity between the two men, or in any innovative articulation of newly discovered feelings of desire. Wilhelm and Werner, in contrast, talk themselves apart.

Consequently, Wilhelm commences his apprenticeship years without the kind of male interlocutor who could assist him in comprehending and figuring the nature of his own desires. That Wilhelm feels the lack of this sort of male-male incitement to the metaphoric formation of his desires is evident much later in the novel, when he meets Jarno and reveals his yearning to disclose all of his feelings to him. Jarno fascinates him from the very first instance: "Ich wünschte, versetzte Wilhelm, daß ich Ihnen alles, was gegenwärtig in mir vorgeht, entdecken könnte!" ("I wish, Wilhelm replied, that I could reveal to you everything that is presently going on within me!" MA, 5, 190).

But this kind of male-male disclosure does not initially occur, in fact, when Jarno and Wilhelm do discuss Wilhelm's affinities. Jarno castigates him for living with, among others, Mignon, that "albernes zwitterhaftes Geschöpf" ("silly, sexually ambiguous creation," MA, 5, 192). Jarno encourages Wilhelm to relinquish his bonds to such a sexually indeterminate being and offers Wilhelm a bond with himself and a society of men instead. As they are conducting this discussion, one of Jarno's society friends arrives, and Jarno's attention is averted immediately to him:

> Er [Jarno] hatte noch nicht ausgeredet, als ein Offizier zu Pferde eilends herankam . . . Jarno rief ihm einen lebhaften Gruß zu. Der Offizier sprang vom Pferde, beide umarmten sich und unterhielten sich mit einander, indem Wilhelm, bestürzt über die letzten Worte seines kriegerischen Freundes, in sich gekehrt an der Seite stand. Jarno durchblätterte einige Papiere, die ihm der Ankommende überreicht hatte, dieser aber ging auf Wilhelmen zu, reichte ihm die Hand, und rief mit Emphase: ich treffe Sie in einer würdigen Gesellschaft, folgen Sie dem Rate Ihres Freundes, und erfüllen Sie dadurch zugleich die Wünsche eines Unbekannten, der herzlichen Teil an Ihnen nimmt. Er sprachs, umarmte Wilhelm, drückte ihn mit Lebhaftigkeit an seine Brust (MA, 5, 192).

He [Jarno] had not finished speaking, when an officer arrived quickly
on horseback . . . Jarno yelled out a lively greeting to him. The officer
jumped from his horse, the two embraced each other and conversed
with one another, while Wilhelm dismayed over the last words of
his military friend, stood to the side and withdrew into himself.
Jarno flipped through some papers that the newly arrived officer had
handed him. He [the officer] approached Wilhelm, offered him his
hand and called out emphatically: I am meeting you among worthy
company, follow the advice of your friend, and fulfill simultaneously
the wishes of a stranger who cares for you heartily. He spoke it,
embraced Wilhelm, and pressed him enthusiastically to his chest.

Significantly, Jarno's discussion with Wilhelm is interrupted, pre-
cluding him from drawing Wilhelm (as his interlocutor) to a fuller
understanding of the nature of affinities. Jarno and his newly arrived
friend, however, embrace each other and fall, tellingly enough, directly into an intense conversation. Wilhelm, in contrast, falls out of
the conversation, turns in upon himself and stands literally to the
side (as an outsider) of the two other men. Like Jarno, the newly
arrived friend also encourages Wilhelm to join them—to engage essentially in the type of male-male intercourse he and Jarno share.
Jarno's friend expresses his concern for Wilhelm, he speaks to him,
embraces him, and presses him to his chest. Both Jarno and his friend
invite Wilhelm to enter their male society, to join them in conversation, concern, and embrace.[6]

But Wilhelm is incapable of participating in these basic forms of
male same-sex desire and exchange. He is unaffected by the embraces
and words of Jarno's friend. Indeed, he finds the friend's embrace unsettling and fixes his attention on Jarno's incomplete speech instead:

> Die sonderbare Umarmung des Offiziers, den er nicht kannte,
> machte wenig Eindruck auf ihn, sie beschäftigte seine Neugierde und
> Einbildungskraft einen Augenblick; aber Jarnos Reden hatten sein
> Herz getroffen; er war tief verwundet, und nun brach er auf seinem
> Rückwege gegen sich selbst in Vorwürfe aus, daß er nur einen Augen-
> blick die hartherzige Kälte Jarnos, die ihm aus den Augen heraussehe,
> und aus allen seinen Gebärden spreche, habe verkennen und vergessen
> mögen (MA, 5, 192).

The odd embrace from the officer he did not know made little impression on him. It occupied his curiosity and imagination for a
moment; but Jarno's speech had pierced his heart. He felt deeply

wounded and broke into reproaches against himself on his way back—that he had misrecognized and forgotten for an instant the hardhearted coldness that looked out at him from Jarno's eyes and spoke to him through all of his gestures.

Wilhelm dismisses entirely the affinities clearly expressed between Jarno and his friend and those directed toward himself. He concentrates, rather, on Jarno's criticism of Mignon, a judgement that he never has a chance to thoroughly discuss with Jarno but that colors his entire perception of him. Wilhelm does not discern, therefore, the warmth that Jarno expresses, and, indeed, he convinces himself in retrospect that Jarno was cold and callous. He decides, ultimately, that he "verabscheuete die Gesinnungen dieser Männer" ("despised the convictions of these men," MA, 5, 194). Ironically, Wilhelm turns his misrecognition of Jarno inside out and castigates himself for not having seen his frosty demeanor from the start. Wilhelm does misjudge Jarno—not in missing his coldness, but rather in failing to comprehend the significance of his offer.

Subsequently, Wilhelm turns down the opportunity of securing a whole community of male interlocutors and seems incapable throughout the novel of expressing and, even more critically, assessing the character of his desires. Without a male interlocutor like Jarno, Wilhelm's desires remain inarticulable and confused. Indeed, in opposition to Die Wahlverwandtschaften and Die Leiden des jungen Werthers, in which the male protagonists are cognizant of the ramifications of their desires, in Die Lehrjahre Wilhelm is depicted in a series of relationships with women in which he deludes himself— often seemingly willfully—either with the fantasy that an affinity is in operation where none actually exists or with fictionalized notions of the affinities that are present.[7]

Wilhelm stumbles, accordingly, from one disappointing relationship to another. The novel commences with the story of Wilhelm's first love, Mariane, who he finds "unentbehrlich, da er mit allen Banden der Menschheit an sie geknüpft war. Seine reine Seele fühlte, daß sie die Hälfte, mehr als die Hälfte seiner selbst sei" ("indispensable, for he was bound to her with all the bonds of humanity. His pure soul felt that she was half, more than half, of himself," MA, 5, 33). But Mariane has another lover, unbeknownst to Wilhelm. So while she maintains two relationships, Wilhelm allows himself to be misled about the realities of their affinitive bond:

> Wie gern glaubte Wilhelm alles! wie gern ließ er sich überreden, daß sie zu ihm, als er sich ihr genähert, durch einen unwiderstehlichen Zug hingeführt worden, daß sie absichtlich zwischen die Kulissen neben ihn getreten sei, um ihn näher zu sehen, und Bekanntschaft mit ihm zu machen . . . (MA, 5, 62).

> How gladly Wilhelm believed this! how gladly he let himself be convinced that she was drawn irresistibly to him as he came closer to her, that she had intentionally stepped between the backdrops and next to him, in order to see him more closely, and to make his acquaintance. . . .

Wilhelm happily believes in the fantasy of a mutual, inevitable, and exclusive bond between himself and Mariane. He lets Mariane convince him that their love is the result of compelling affinities between them. But, in fact, in contrast to the affinities between Eduard and Ottilie and Werther and Lotte, Mariane and Wilhelm willingly participate in a *fantasy* of attraction. Here we find that the affinities (which, of course, always involve fantasies) can also operate as utter fantasy, as poetic constructs in and of themselves. Wilhelm's bond with Mariane is determined by his desire for and imagination of an ultimate all-consuming affinity, not by any "real" affinity between them. What is particularly significant about Wilhelm's relationship to Mariane is the underlying assumption of the affinities as fictional performances and the participants' inclinations to believe in the fictions they have constructed. Indeed, where no affinities exist, fictions of them can stand in their place. And, as we shall see, in all of his subsequent relationships with women Wilhelm is "gladly" deluded as to the nature of their bonds.

The theatricality of Wilhelm's desire, its innate connection to self-deception and delusion, manifests itself as well in his relationship to the Countess. Their most extensive expressions of mutual attraction occur (like that with Mariane) literally across the stage as Wilhelm performs his various theatrical roles. As the novel recounts it: "Sie [die Gräfin] konnte, wenn er auf dem Theater war, die Augen nicht von ihm abwenden, und er schien bald nur allein gegen sie gerichtet zu spielen und zu rezitieren" ("She [the Countess] could not turn her eyes from him when he was on stage, and he soon appeared to recite and act only in her direction," MA, 5, 175). Neither Wilhelm nor the Countess is interested in a relationship offstage. Moreover, Wilhelm's on stage attraction to the Countess is only one of appearance ("schien"), and her longing for him occurs only when he is on stage—essentially only when he is acting the part of someone else. Goethe alludes here to the performative nature of sexual desire—the desire that is always a socially constructed, staged entity. Here the poetic formation of desire is envisioned in terms of not only the self-fashioning that we found in the *Wahlverwandtschaften*, *Wilhelm Meister*, and *Werther*, but also includes an understanding of self and other as "theatrical" constructions.[8]

Accordingly, we find that Wilhelm is also deluded in terms of his relationship to Mignon.[9] As much as Wilhelm and Mignon would like to insist that they interact with one another as a surrogate father and an adopted daughter, Wilhelm's desire for her and her attraction to him surface relentlessly throughout the course of the novel.[10] From the very first moment that Wilhelm sees her, he is drawn inexplicably and uncontrollably to Mignon:

> Wilhelm konnte sie nicht genug ansehen. Seine Augen und sein Herz wurden unwiderstehlich von dem geheimnisvollen Zustande dieses Wesens angezogen . . . Diese Gestalt prägte sich Wilhelmen sehr tief ein; er sah sie noch immer an, schwieg und vergaß der Gegenwärtigen über seinen Betrachtungen (MA, 5, 97).

> Wilhelm could not look at her enough. His eyes and his heart were drawn irresistibly by the mysterious condition of this being . . . this figure impressed itself deeply upon him, he kept looking at her, grew silent and forgot all of those present during his observations.

Wilhelm perceives the same inevitable attraction for Mignon that characterizes the elective affinities throughout Goethe's poetic oeuvre. Accordingly, he shares with her one of the most erotic moments of the novel. He holds her hands while she crouches before him and rests her head upon his knees. Wilhelm plays with Mignon's hair and notices suddenly that her body is beginning to convulse: "Er hub sie auf, und sie fiel auf seinen Schoß, er druckte sie an sich, und küßte sie . . . die Zuckung dauerte fort . . ." ("He lifted her up and she fell unto his lap, he pressed her against him and kissed her . . . the convulsions continued," MA, 5, 141). But then as Wilhelm clasps her tighter and tighter against his body, her body begins to relax: "Ihre starren Glieder wurden gelinde, es ergoß sich ihr Innerstes, und in der Verwirrung des Augenblickes fürchtete Wilhelm, sie werde in seinen Armen zerschmelzen, und er nichts von ihr übrig behalten. Er hielt sie nur fester und fester . . . ("Her stiff limbs began to relax, her innermost feelings gushed forth and in the confusion of the moment Wilhelm feared that she would melt in his arms and he would retain nothing of her. He held her more and more tightly . . . .," MA, 5, 141). Although their mutual attraction manifests itself here in the most suggestive of physical forms, both Wilhelm and Mignon immediately deny their attraction by repeatedly reasserting their status as father and daughter. While with Mariane and the Countess Wilhelm failed to see the lack of desire, here he refuses to acknowledge the overwhelming affinity that draws him to Mignon. Wilhelm is clearly capable of seeing affinities when they are not there, and missing them entirely when they are.

Wilhelm's succession of confused fantasy relationships with women culminates in his encounter with Natalie. She appears before him briefly, and yet long enough to thoroughly capture his imagination and desire:

> Er [Wilhelm] hatte seine Augen auf die sanften, hohen, stillen, teilnehmenden Gesichtszüge der Ankommenden [Natalie] geheftet; er glaubte nie etwas edleres noch liebenswürdigeres gesehen zu haben (MA, 5, 224).

> He [Wilhelm] fixed his eyes on the soft, high, still, compassionate facial expressions of the one approaching [Natalie]. He believed that he had never before seen anyone more noble or worthy of love.

As he gazes at Natalie, he imagines her as a saint:

> In diesem Augenblicke, da er den Mund öffnen und einige Worte des Dankes stammeln wollte, wirkte der lebhafte Eindruck ihrer Gegenwart so sonderbar auf seine schon angegriffenen Sinne, daß es ihm auf einmal vorkam, als sei ihr Haupt mit Strahlen umgeben . . . (MA, 5, 226).

> In this moment, as he wanted to open his mouth and stammer out a few words of thanks, the lively impression of her presence worked so oddly on his already overwhelmed senses, that it suddenly appeared to him as if her head were surrounded by rays of light . . .

Natalie appears to Wilhelm as a saint-like figure, and when she disappears, it is precisely this divine image that then dominates his imagination, and he fantasizes about finding her again: "Er sah noch . . . die edelste Gestalt, von Strahlen umgeben, vor sich stehen, und seine Seele eilte die Verschwundenen durch Felsen und Wälder auf dem Fuße nach" ("He could still see . . . the most noble figure, surrounded by rays of light, standing before him and his soul hurried after the one who had disappeared," MA, 5, 226–27). Like the Countess, Mariane, and Mignon, Natalie (whose identification Wilhelm does not yet know) functions as a thoroughly fictionalized object of desire. Wilhelm's immediate affinity for her results in both his fantasy of following her and in his actual search for her throughout the remainder of the novel.

Not surprisingly, in Natalie's presence, Wilhelm's current love, Philine, is displaced immediately as the object of his desire:

> Philine war indessen aufgestanden, um der gnädigen Dame die Hand zu küssen. Als sie neben einander standen, glaubte unser Freund [Wilhelm] nie einen solchen Abstand gesehen zu haben. Philine war ihm noch nie in einem so ungünstigen Lichte erschienen. Sie sollte, wie es ihm vorkam, sich jener edlen Natur nicht nahen, noch weniger sie berühren (MA, 5, 225).

> In the meanwhile Philine had stood up in order to kiss the lady's hand. As they stood next to one another, our friend [Wilhelm] believed that he had never before seen such a contrast. Philine had never appeared before him in such an unfavorable light. It occurred to him that she should not come near such a noble nature, much less touch her.

As Natalie gets added to the social mix, the affinities reconstitute themselves, and Wilhelm gravitates decisively to her. She becomes the fantasy woman for whom Wilhelm searches for the rest of the novel. Indeed, as he anticipates meeting her in every new destination, he is continually disappointed to find that she is not there. And yet, despite the fact that Wilhelm knows that Natalie is the partner for whom he has the greatest attraction, his unsuccessful search for her leads him to propose to Therese, a woman who nonetheless cannot drive the images of Natalie and Mignon from Wilhelm's imagination:

> Sie hielten sich fest umschlossen, er fühlte ihr Herz an seinem Busen schlagen, also in seinem Geiste war es öde und leer, nur die Bilder Mignons und Nataliens schwebten wie Schatten vor seiner Einbildungskraft (MA, 5, 546).

> They embraced each other tightly. He felt her heart pounding on his chest. His spirit was desolate and empty, only the images of Mignon and Natalie floated like shadows before his imagination.

Once again, Wilhelm imagines an affinity where none exists and persists in his plans to marry Therese in spite of the images of Mignon and Natalie that animate his imagination/desire. And even though Wilhelm's heart is desolate and empty when he embraces Therese, he does not seem capable of drawing the obvious conclusion and appears oblivious to the exclusivity of his affinities to Mignon and Natalie.[11]

Toward the end of the *Lehrjahre* Wilhelm begins to form a clearer conception of his own desires. The first step in this direction is made when he isolates Lothario as an admirable interlocutor:

> O welch ein Mann ist das! . . . in dieser Gesellschaft hab ich, so darf ich wohlsagen, zum erstenmal ein Gespräch geführt, zum erstenmal kam mir der eigenste Sinn meiner Worte aus dem Munde eines andern reichhaltiger, voller und in einem größern Umfang wieder entgegen, was ich ahndete war mir klar, und was ich meinte lernte ich anschauen (MA, 5, 444–45).

> O what a man he is! . . . in this society, I can well say, I have conversed, for the first time I have encountered the unique sense of my words, as they came to me more richly and fully from the mouth of another. What I have intuited was now clear to me, I learned to see what I meant.

Wilhelm reveals effusively Lothario's role as male interlocutor who will finally draw him to himself and an understanding of his desires. Lothario's mouth (remember the mouth of the boy that Wilhelm will later recount in the *Wanderjahre*) is the source from which Wilhelm's words return to him in more recognizable form. Here (between male mouths and through male same-sex desire) is where the articulation of desire will occur. After talking with Lothario, Wilhelm begins to understand his desires and intuitions for the first time. And while he does not immediately relinquish his delusional attachment to Therese, he does eventually step aside in favor of Lothario. As the novel comes to an end, Wilhelm can finally assert that he truly loves only Natalie (Mignon has died in the meantime) and can suddenly assess his other relationships with women precisely:

> Ja, sagte er zu sich selbst, indem er sich allein fand, gestehe dir nur, du liebst sie [Natalie], und du fühlst wieder, was es heiße, wenn der Mensch mit allen Kräften lieben kann. So liebte ich Marianen, und ward so schrecklich an ihr irre; ich liebte Philinen und mußte sie verachten. Aurelie achtete ich, und ich konnte sie nicht lieben; ich verehrte Theresen, und die väterliche Liebe nahm die Gestalt einer Neigung zu ihr an . . . (MA, 5, 569).

> Yes, he said to himself, as he found himself alone, admit it to yourself, you love her [Natalie] and you feel again what it means when a person can love with all forces. So I loved Mariane and was so crazy about her; I loved Philine and had to despise her. I revered Aurelie and could not love her, I honored Therese, and a fatherly love took the form of an attraction to her . . .

Wilhelm finally isolates Natalie as the true object of his affinitive fancies, and he can also now distinguish the character of his other relationships with Mariane, Philine, Aurelie, and Therese. The critical impetus for Wilhelm's clearer formulation of the nature of his affinities was his verbal exchanges with Lothario. Only after Wilhelm interacts with Lothario, only after their words flow freely from mouth to mouth, can he begin to distinguish the various characteristics of the passionate relationships he has experienced.

Wilhelm's affinities were based throughout the *Lehrjahre* upon his imagination of himself in a particular desiring role. His search for Natalie takes shape during the course of the novel and later under the influence of Lothario's conversation as a search for the kind of inevitable, immutable, intractable love that Werther shares with Lotte and that Eduard fantasizes about with Ottilie. Each of the three novels discussed here is structured around specific notions about the manner in which affinities work. Affinities are perceived to propel the male desiring subject toward his object of love regardless of any moral, social, and geographical obstacles. Affinities are so strong that the desiring male subject may perish in the pursuit of his beloved or may be driven mad by the unattainable woman he cannot expel from his imagination. And, finally, the affinities as fantasy/poetry determine the structure, the progression, and the trajectories of each of these novels. And in each case, underlying the desiring male subject's poetic expression of his sentiments (here largely male-female attraction) is the yearning and the need to share his longings with the male object of his desire. In fact, the trope of the male interlocutor that manifested itself in both the Wilhelm and Werther passages discussed in chapter two reasserts itself as a central structuring metaphor. We discover it in *Die Wahlverwandtschaften* (as its frame), in *Die Leiden des jungen Werthers* (throughout as all letters were addressed to Werther's friend Wilhelm), and in *Wilhelm Meisters Lehrjahre* (as that which was missing as the novel commenced and was discovered by its denouement). Despite the fact that these literary productions focus predominantly on male-female affinities, their fundamental compositions and genesis revolve around the structure of male same-sex desire.[12] Here male-male desire is clearly the prerequisite form of desire allowing for the expression of desire, including male-female desire. In other words, without the structure of male-male interlocution no articulation of desire would occur. Beyond the isolated moments of male interlocution outlined in chapter two, here we find that the fundamental structuring principle, the most innate ordering force of Goethe's literary work is not, as Sedgwick might suppose, heterosexuality underscored by homosocial bonding grounded upon the exchange of women. What we find instead is male same-sex desire and verbal interlocutions shared by men who desire men. In this way Goethe once again turns our presumptions about eighteenth-century representations of a fundamental "heterosexual" foundation for social order and literary structure upside down and inside out.

With that in mind, we can now turn to *Egmont*, *Götz*, and *Tasso* in which the representation of male-male affinities, both as structure and as poetic expression, are even more overtly staged. In fact, in these dramas we will find more specific instances of male interlocutors struggling to express their mutual desires. These are not men in isolation trying to express their own self, but men engaged in conversations as they struggle to understand their relationships to one another.

Struggling to Name an Unnamed Desire: Egmont and Ferdinand

Goethe's drama *Egmont* (1788) is on one level a tragic representation of the historical conflicts leading up to the rebellion of the Netherlands against Spain in the sixteenth century. But it is also, contrary to what Schiller suggested, about passion.[13] Like the other literary works we have considered so far, *Egmont* is also structured around various affinitive tensions. The most obvious of passions in the play are those of Clare for Egmont. Early in the first act she describes at some length how she waits for Egmont to come to her in the evenings and how his presence dispels her reservations about his love:

> Und dann darf ich Egmonten nur wieder ansehn, wird mir alles sehr begreiflich, wäre mir weit mehr begreiflich. Ach was ists ein Mann! Alle Provinzen beten ihn an, und ich in seinem Arm sollte nicht das glücklichste Geschöpf von der Welt sein (MA, 3:1, 261).

> And then I only need to see Egmont again, and everything becomes very comprehensible to me, yes, much more comprehensible. O, what a man he is! All the provinces worship him and should I not be the most fortune creature in the world in his arms?

Egmont's presence, his love, transforms Clare's humble home into a heavenly place: "Diese Stube dieses kleine Haus ist ein Himmel seit Egmonts Liebe drin wohnt" ("This room, this little house is a heaven, since Egmont's love has taken residence there," MA, 3:1, 262). Tellingly enough, Egmont only once briefly alludes to his affection for Clare, describing himself in her presence as " . . . ruhig, offen, glücklich, geliebt und gekannt, von dem besten Herzen das auch er ganz kennt und mit voller Liebe und Zutrauen an das seine drückt. *[Er umarmt sie.]* Das ist dein Egmont!" (" . . . quiet, open, fortunate, loved and known by the best of hearts, that he also knows and with full love and trust presses on his own. *[He embraces her.]* That is your Egmont!" (MA, 3:1, 291). Indeed, neither Egmont nor

Clare express to or about one another the intense affinity that Brackenburg (the man jilted by Clare in favor of Egmont) feels for Clare:

> Jetzt schlepp ich mich an den Augen des Mädchens so hin . . . Könnt ich der Zeiten vergessen, da sie mich liebte, mich zu lieben schien. — Warum hat mir's Mark und Bein durchdrungen das Glück? Warum haben mir diese Hoffnungen allen Genuß des Lebens aufgezehrt, indem sie mir ein Paradies von weitem zeigten. —Und jener erste Kuß! Jener einzige! . . . sie sah mich an—alle Sinne gingen mir um und ich fühlte ihre Lippen auf den meinigen.—Und—und nun—Stirb Armer! (MA, 3:1, 264–65)

> Now I drag along after the girl's eyes . . . Could I forget the times, when she loved me, appeared to love me! —Why did that fortune penetrate to my very marrow? Why have these hopes consumed for me all of the pleasure of life, while showing me a paradise from afar?—And that first kiss! The only one! . . . she looked at me— my senses whirled and I felt her lips on mine—and—and now? Die, wretch!

Brackenburg expresses the desire of a Werther or an Eduard. And, in fact, this passage captures *in nuce* all of the tropes manifest in their affinities: being inevitably drawn to a beloved woman, being rebuffed by her, and being destroyed in the process. Brackenburg, like Werther, is driven by his despair not only to contemplate but also to commit suicide. More importantly, contrasting Brackenburg's effusive descriptions of his passion to the rather bland expressions of sentiments produced by Egmont and Clare casts doubt on the strength and ultimate significance of their affinities. And, although Brackenburg's affinity for Clare is indisputable, it also remains unrequited.

Accordingly, neither Egmont's affinity to Clare nor Brackenburg's obsession with her constitute the dominant expressions of passion in the drama. The most extensive articulation of desire and the most intense incitement to give desire poetic form arises in the final scenes as Egmont awaits execution at the hand of Alba. Alba is a man so vicious and pathetic that he embodies an object of complete revulsion. When he enters the room, everyone draws away from him: *"Herzog von Alba—wie er herein und hervor tritt treten die andern zurück"* (*"Herzog Alba—as he enters and steps forward, all the others step back,"* MA, 3:1, 297). No one establishes an affinity with

Alba in the play, and, in fact, his primary goal is to subvert the bond that is developing between his son and Egmont. In an attempt to deflate his son Ferdinand's crush on Egmont once and for all, he orders Egmont's execution and sends his son to his cell the night before to witness (what he presumes will be) Egmont's psychic collapse. But Alba's scheme fails as Ferdinand and Egmont struggle in these final hours to formulate the nature of their mutual attractions.

Before departing to visit Egmont, Ferdinand recounts his instant affinity for Egmont to his father:

> Egmont kam mit einigen auf den Markt geritten, wir grüßten uns, er hatte ein rohes Pferd das ich ihm loben mußte . . . Unter allen Rittern die ich hier kenne gefällt er mir am besten. Es scheint wir werden Freunde sein (MA, 3:1, 299–300).

> Egmont arrived with some others at the market. We greeted one another. He rode an unbroken horse, which I had to praise. Of all the knights that I know here, he pleases me the most. It appears that we will become friends.

For his part, Egmont assures Ferdinand that he was instantly drawn to him as well: "Mein Freund . . . so nimm die Versichrung, daß im ersten Augenblicke mein Gemüt dir entgegen kam" ("My friend . . . be assured that in the first moments my heart was drawn to you," MA, 3:1, 324). Moreover, the mere sight of Ferdinand and his friendliness affected Egmont so strongly that he was reconciled directly with his arch-enemy Alba: "Du bist so jung und hast ein glückliches Ansehen. Du warst so zutraulich, so freundlich gegen mich, so lang ich dich sah war ich mit deinem Vater versöhnt" ("You are so young and have a fortunate appearance. You were so intimate and friendly to me, that as long as I saw you, I was reconciled with your father," MA, 3:1, 322). As long as Egmont *saw* Ferdinand the affinity to him displaced his hatred for Ferdinand's father. Unlike the relationship between Egmont and Clare, in which there was no expression of a visually motivated, magnetic, assertion of mutual desire, here Egmont and Ferdinand (like Eduard and Ottilie) clearly feel powerfully and willingly drawn to one another.

But the extent and character of their desire remains only partially articulated. While they assert their friendship, it is not initially clear what "friendship" actually means in this context. As the two men struggle to come to terms with their desire for each other, Ferdinand assumes the role of interlocutor or at least accepts the role of the more articulate of the two. At first, however, Ferdinand babbles incoherently and Egmont orders him to pull himself together and to "speak like a man": "rede wie ein Mann" (MA, 3:1, 323). In reply Ferdinand laments that he is not a woman and that he, as a man, is denied the opportunity of expressing his emotions:

> O daß ich ein Weib wäre! Daß man mir sagen könnte: was rührt dich? was ficht dich an? Sage mir ein größeres ein ungeheureres Übel, mache mich zum Zeugen einer schröcklicheren Tat, ich will dir danken ich will sagen es war nichts (MA, 3:1, 323).

> O that I were a woman! That one could say to me: what is stirring you? what is agitating you? Tell me a greater, a more horrific evil, make me a witness to a more terrifying act; and I will thank you, I will say: it was nothing.

As Ferdinand sees it, there is nothing more cruel, nothing more horrible than to deny a man the expression of his sentiments. In the context of Egmont's impending death, Ferdinand isolates the suppression of his emotions as the most horrific of evils. He rejects the notion that only women should have the privilege of articulating their sentiments and challenges Egmont to name a greater evil than forcing a man to repress his feelings. Ferdinand struggles here to redefine the parameters of emotional expression between men. He rejects the conventional assumption of male stoicism, asserting the validity of passionate verbal exchanges. Ironically, of course, Ferdinand assigns women the privilege of speaking their desires in an age that gave women (and particularly women who desired women) virtually no voice. At the same time, Ferdinand constructs a "feminine voice" or a "feminine mode of expression" as one capable of transmitting and formulating his desire for Egmont. His desire subsequently to be a woman—to undo conventional gender boundaries—is intricately connected to his longing to expand the possibilities of the poetic formulation of male same-sex desire. Ferdinand challenges the eighteenth-century suppression of expressions of male same-sex desire. Of course we know that the eighteenth century talked obsessively about perversions, tribades, eunuchs, etc. But what Ferdinand isolates here is the lack of a language of desire between men—the inability of same-sex-identified and desiring men to articulate their emotions. What they did not have was *their own* language of sentiment.

Ferdinand's unexpected injunction to the expression of sentiment confuses Egmont and he can only stammer: "Du verlierst dich. Wo bist du?" ("You are losing yourself. Where are you?" MA, 3:1, 323). Egmont reads Ferdinand's profusions as a loss of control and, subsequently, of self.[14] In a frustrating attempt to clarify the intense sentiments he feels for Egmont and to assert himself, Ferdinand finally blurts out:

> Laß diese Leidenschaft rasen, laß mich losgebunden klagen! Ich will nicht standhaft scheinen wenn alles in mir zusammenbricht. Dich soll ich hier sehn?—dich—es ist entsetzlich! du verstehst mich nicht! Und sollst du mich verstehen? Egmont! Egmont! *[Ihm um den Hals fallend]* (MA, 3:1, 323).

> Let this passion rage, let me lament without restraint! I will not appear composed as everything collapses within me. I should see you here?—you—it is horrifying! You don't understand me? And should you understand me? Egmont! Egmont! *[He falls upon his neck.]*

Ferdinand's extreme emotional frustration manifests itself in his injunction to allow his passions to gush forth—to let himself lament them freely. Egmont is thoroughly confused by Ferdinand's wild and incoherent language and begs him to explicate the secret that is agitating him: "Löse mir das Geheimnis!" ("Solve this mystery for me!" MA, 3:1, 323). Egmont wonders why his fate is so important to Ferdinand, and Ferdinand simply insists: "Kein Geheimnis" ("No secret," MA, 3:1, 324). But Egmont's confusion is also understandable, since, although the force of his desire is manifest in these passages, Ferdinand does not actually name his passion. And so, while he succeeds in unleashing his emotions, he still cannot express them adequately to Egmont. He struggles to lend his outburst coherent form, but stumbles from sentence to sentence, perceiving rather quickly that Egmont does not understand him. He then wonders how Egmont should understand him and resorts finally to repeating Egmont's name emphatically. And as his speech condenses itself into the name of the man he desires, he falls upon Egmont's neck in an embrace. As in Winckelmann's letters, male same-sex passion is practically palpable here, but the specific words to articulate that affinity are lacking. Nonetheless, in the final, desperate moments of the play, Ferdinand makes a last attempt to lend his desire linguistic form:

> Nun hofft ich endlich dich zu sehen und sah dich und mein Herz flog dir entgegen. Dich hatt' ich mir bestimmt und wählte dich aufs neue da ich dich sah. Nun hofft ich erst mit dir zu sein, mit dir zu leben, dich zu fassen, dich—" (MA, 3:1, 324).

> Now I hoped finally to see you and I saw you and my heart flew to you. I had determined you for myself and I chose you anew when I saw you. Now I hoped for the first time to be with you, to live with you, to touch you, you—."

Ferdinand relates here his inevitable affinity for Egmont—an attraction contingent (as we might now anticipate) upon his having *seen* Egmont. Goethe invokes here the same trope of specularity that recurs in his illustrations of male-female desire. Ferdinand *sees* Egmont and his heart flies to him. Moreover, this initial nonelective affinity is bolstered by his subsequent elective determination that Egmont is the man for him. This overdetermination is underscored by the relentless repetition of the word "you" throughout Ferdinand's linguistic/poetic attempt to give the object of his desire specific contours and to hold that "you," that is, Egmont, in place. Ferdinand reinforces the natural affinity that asserts itself in Egmont's presence through his own conscious choice to pursue Egmont as an object of desire. Even more importantly, Ferdinand is finally able to express his desires more cogently. He wants to be with Egmont, he wants to live with him, and he wants to touch him. But nonetheless his ultimate desire remains unexpressed as his sentence never concludes. The last "you—" (in German "dich—") marks only the space in which Ferdinand's articulation of his male same-sex desire fails to acquire linguistic form. The structure of the sentence itself underscores the increasing intensity of Ferdinand's desires as each new desire named expresses his longing to be closer and closer to

Egmont. First he wants to be near him, then more specifically to live with him, then more precisely to touch him, and then? perhaps to embrace him? perhaps to kiss him? or perhaps to make love to him? How far the sentence might go—how much closer Ferdinand may wish to be—remains unarticulated. But the suggestiveness of his final unending sentence in the context of his invocation of stock Goethean tropes of the elective affinities points quite unmistakenly to an even bolder expression of male same-sex desire lurking beyond the grammatical elision ("—").

Egmont foregrounds, above all, not only male same-sex desire—for it really is the most intense desire expressed in the drama—but also the struggle of individual men to articulate their desires to the man for whom they long. Even more significantly, Goethe is clearly accentuating the Winckelmannian project here. *Egmont* stresses the need to find linguistic forms within which to express male-male desire. Ferdinand's final line with its provocative "—" is in and of itself an incitement to poetic formation. It begs the reader and/or audience to fill in the blank, to name the unnamed desire. The fact that Ferdinand does not complete his own sentence implies both that he has not yet reached the point of overtly naming that desire and that the audience/reader ought to join in the process of articulation. Additionally, one can surmise that Ferdinand's unfinished sentence highlights, at the very least, the infinite and coursing nature of such poetic articulations.

However one reads those elliptical dashes, it is clear that *Egmont* moves the issue of male same-sex desire to center stage, indeed, elevates its significance in the final scenes of the drama to the extent that Ferdinand's struggle to express his desire becomes Egmont's assurance that his desire will survive his death. Egmont is reassured as he faces his execution that Ferdinand (and all he represents) will be his legacy. He explains to Ferdinand that they "live" one another and will continue to do so even after Egmont's death:

> . . . sieh mich in diesen Augenblicken an, du verlierst mich nicht. War dir mein Leben ein Spiegel in welchem du dich gerne betrachtetest, so sei es auch mein Tod. Die Menschen sind nicht nur zusammen, wenn sie beisammen sind, auch der Entfernte, der Abgeschiedne lebt uns. Ich lebe dir, und habe mir genug gelebt (MA, 3:1, 326).

. . . look at me in these moments; you are not losing me. If my life was a mirror for you in which you gladly observed yourself, so should my death also be. People are not just together when they are near to one another; even those who are distant and departed from us live [on in] us, I live [in] you and have lived [myself] enough.

Egmont and Ferdinand are not lost to one another. Egmont's life is a mirror for Ferdinand. In Egmont's life (the mirror that is Egmont) Ferdinand identifies himself and his male-male desire. Egmont and Ferdinand have a *life* and a same-sex-identified self. Unlike Eduard and Ottilie or Werther and Lotte, whose desires appear to require death, the passion of Egmont and Ferdinand cannot die, for they, like those men who mirrored themselves in Werther's imagination,[15] live one another—now and even after death.[16] In fact, Ferdinand is only partially correct when he remarks to Egmont: "Ich überlebe dich und mich selbst" (I survive [literally live over or beyond] you and myself," MA, 3:1, 325). Actually, both men live beyond themselves in each other and through the discourse of male same-sex desire; they initiate and offer up to us (as audiences/readers) a linguistic project to continue the expression of male same-sex desire.

EXPRESSING NATURAL DESIRES BETWEEN MEN: GÖTZ AND WEISLINGEN

While Egmont and Ferdinand struggle to give their male-male desire poetic form, Goethe had produced fifteen years earlier a play, *Götz von Berlichingen* (1773), in which male-male desire was even more overtly expressed.[17] Within the context of an almost thoroughly homosocial set of relationships between knights fighting against the dissolution of their lifestyle, Goethe's play foregrounds the erotic affinities sustained by his two main protagonists, Götz and Weislingen.

While other affinities are also manifest in the play, they are represented simply by allusion. We know, for instance, that Götz is married to Elisabeth, but no reference is made to any emotional affinity between the two. Throughout the drama, Götz and Weislingen stress, in contrast, their affinities for one another. Although Götz and Weislingen have been estranged from one another for some time and have been fighting against one another (Götz strove to preserve the institution of knighthood and Weislingen has abandoned knighthood in favor of the new court structure of governance), the early scenes of the play depict their reunion as Götz captures Weislingen and transports him to his castle. Upon arrival, Weislingen immediately remarks how Götz's presence and his return to such well-known halls rekindle his love for Götz:

> O daß ich aufwachte. Und das alles wäre ein Traum! In Berlichingens Gewalt von dem ich mich kaum los gearbeitet hatte, dessen Andenken ich mied wie Feuer, den ich hoffte zu überwältigen . . . Rückgekehrt Adelbert in den Saal, wo wir als Buben unsere Jagd trieben. Da du ihn liebtest, an ihm hingst wie an deiner Seele. Wer kann ihm nahen und ihn hassen? (MA, 1:1, 564)

> O that I would awaken and that all of this would be a dream! In Berlichingen's power from whom I had hardly worked myself free, the thought of whom I avoided like fire, who I hoped to overcome . . . Led back, Adelbert into that hall where we boys romped around. There where you loved him, and hung on him as on your own soul. Who can approach him and hate him?

After his initial admission that he had tried to expunge his feelings for Götz, Weislingen reminisces about how he loved Götz and clung to him as to his own soul. His affinity for Götz is inevitable, for anyone who comes near him cannot possibly despise him. Indeed, for Weislingen, the view of Götz and the castle they once shared evokes all of his old feelings of love.

Weislingen's arrival also triggers Götz's memory of their affinity for one another, and he explains that he finds nothing so pleasurable as remembering

> . . . wie wir Liebs und Leids zusammen trugen, einander alles waren, und wie ich damals wähnte, so sollts unser ganzes Leben sein. War das nicht all mein Trost wie mir diese Hand weggeschossen ward vor Landshut, und du mein pflegtest, und mehr als Bruder für mich sorgtest, ich hoffte Adelbert wird künftig meine rechte Hand sein (MA, 1:1, 565).

> . . . how we bore pleasures and sufferings together, were everything to each other, and how I imagined then that it should be so our

whole life long. Was it not my entire solace when my hand was shot off at Landshut. And you nursed me and cared for me more than a brother would, and I hoped that Adelbert would henceforth be my right hand.

Without overtly saying that he loves Weislingen, Götz outlines here how they shared their pleasures and sufferings, were everything for one another, and how he had hoped that they would retain that intimacy throughout their lives. He further defines Weislingen's affinitive status by describing him as more than a brother: he is Götz's right hand, an integral part of himself. Götz repeatedly hints at both his spiritual and physical affinity for Weislingen, reminding him in one instance how they were accustomed in earlier days to roam around and to sleep with one another: "Zwar vergnügtere Tage werden wir wohl nicht wieder finden, als an des Margrafens Hof, da wir noch beisammen schliefen, und mit einander herum zogen" ("Certainly we will never again discover more pleasurable days than those at the margrave's court, where we still slept and roved around together," MA, 1:1, 564). Here both sentimental and physical desires between men are expressed rather openly. And, indeed, as the earlier affinity between Götz and Weislingen renews itself and as they find themselves in each other's presence, Weislingen insists that Götz has given him back to himself: "Götz, teurer Götz hast mich mir selber wieder gegeben" ("Götz, dear Götz, you have given me back to myself," MA, 1:1, 576). For Götz and Weislingen, their reminiscences about their affinity for one another allow for the expression and reassertion of their desire for one another, for their physical attraction to one another, and to their articulation of each other as integral parts of each other. Moreover, they imply that they are only complete selves within the context of their affinitive bond. And, in fact, in the 1803 revision of *Götz von Berlichingen*, Goethe makes it even clearer that Götz and Weislingen function in the manner of two halves of one self—that they are constantly searching for and are drawn to that other sexual, sentimental half that would render them complete:

Zu ihm Weislingen war mir die Neigung angeboren, wie aus Einfluß der Planeten; mit ihm verlebt ich meine Jugend, und als er sich von mir entfernte, mir schadete, konnt ich ihn nicht hassen. Aber es war mir ein unbequemes Gefühl. Sein Bild, sein Name stand mir überall im Wege. Ich hatte eine Hälfte verloren, die ich wieder suchte. Besser mocht es ihm auch nicht gehen; denn bald als wir uns wiedersahen, stellte sich das alte Verhältnis her, und nun ist's gut . . . (MA, 6:1, 380).

My inclination for Weislingen was born to me, as if out of the influence of the planets. With him I spent my youth, and as he distanced himself from me, as he injured me, I could not hate him. But it was an unpleasant feeling for me. His image, his name stood everywhere in my way. I had lost a half, which I searched for again. It could not have gone much better for him, for as soon as we saw each other again, the old relationship revived, and now it's good . . .

Here Aristophanes's notion of the original splitting of the self into two halves that each then search for their lost half in order to find wholeness and sexual and sentimental fulfillment is invoked in order to assert the primal character of the affinity between Götz and Weislingen.[18] In fact, Götz's articulation of the desire he shares with Weislingen isolates not only the originary character of their affinity, but asserts as well its naturalness. Götz insists that his affinity for Weislingen is innate; he was *born* with an inclination for him. Not only are the expressions of desire between Götz and Weislingen strikingly bold in their references to love, halves of themselves, and intimations of physical closeness, but (at least in the later revision) *Götz von Berlichingen* also states openly that male same-sex desire is an innate, inborn, and natural affinity. While *Egmont* would later reassert the need to continue articulating male same-sex desire, *Götz von Berlichingen* was already producing several rather amazing formulations of male-male desire and was beginning to press on the parameters of a debate on the naturally-versus-socially constructed nature of male same-sex desire that can be traced down (in various permutations) to our present day. Not only do Götz and Weislingen articulate their desire for each other, they also begin to define male same-sex desire in terms of sentimental and physical attractions, in regard to their own senses of self and themselves as desiring beings. This is a phenomenal moment in the history of discourses of male same-sex desire. Beyond the mere expression of self and desire as

linguistic realities, here Goethe refines the definition of the male desiring man to include subtle and specific suggestions concerning the
innateness of male-male desire and its socially constructed nature.

In spite of the intensity and boldness of their desire, Götz and
Weislingen never form a lasting bond with one another. Soon after
their reunion Weislingen returns to court and their bond is severed
anew. But if a sense of their affinitive totality is only possible through
the union of Götz and Weislingen, one might ask: What obstructs
their mutually solicited communion? The answer, it seems, is that
despite their efforts to reaffirm their bonds, the pressures of a society
founded upon what we might call today "compulsory homosociality"
work against them. Regardless of their natural affinity for one another, *Götz von Berlichingen* underscores the reality that there is no
socially sanctioned space in which Götz and Weislingen might enjoy
their desires. The overwhelming counter-presumption of the social
order in which Götz and Weislingen must operate is that each man
must inevitably and finally attach himself to a woman. Accordingly,
Götz is married to Elisabeth and Weislingen pursues several women
at court—and also, indeed, in Götz's very own castle.

The only socially sanctioned bond available to Götz and Weislingen is a substitutive tie mediated through the exchange of Götz's
sister. As he offers Maria to Weislingen in marriage, Götz emphasizes
above all his hopes for continued unity with Weislingen:

> Gebt euch die Hände, und so sprech ich Amen! Mein Freund und
> Bruder! . . . Du siehst nicht ganz frei! Was fehlt dir? Ich- bin ganz
> glücklich; was ich nur träumend hoffte, seh ich, und bin wie träum-
> end. Ach! nun ist mein Traum aus. Mir wars heute Nacht, ich gäb dir
> meine rechte eiserne Hand, und du hieltest mich so fest, daß sie aus
> den Armschienen ging wie abgebrochen. Ich erschrak und wachte
> drüber auf. Ich hätte nur fort träumen sollen, da würd ich gesehen
> haben, wie du mir eine neue lebendige Hand ansetztest (MA, 1:1,
> 574–75).

> Give each other your hands as I say Amen! My friend and brother! . . .
> You don't look very free, Adelbert! What is wrong? I am completely
> happy; that which I only hoped for in dreams I now see, and am as
> if dreaming. Ah! my dream is over! I felt last evening as if I gave you
> my right iron hand, and you held me so tightly that it came out of the

splint as if broken off. I started and woke up. I should have gone on dreaming . . . then I would have seen how you grafted a new living hand on me.

As they exchange hands—Maria and Götz and Weislingen—Maria is understood to bind the two men together. She is the socially acceptable homosocial link (as Sedgwick and Levi-Strauss might insist) who ought to secure their affinity for one another and who allows for at least a possible, sublimated subtext of male same-sex desire. But despite Götz's aim to celebrate their newly arranged and presumably solidified union, his speech reveals relentlessly the tentative and intrinsically unsatisfying character of such an indirect connection. Götz obtains Weislingen's hand (or Weislingen as his lost hand) only through the communal embrace with Maria. In other words, their natural male same-sex desire is muted by and threatened with displacement by a socially mandated homosociality. The insufficiency of the transaction manifests itself in Weislingen's obvious discomfort and Götz's account of a dream that condenses Weislingen into both his lost hand and the man who will once again sever his hand from him. Precisely at the moment of Weislingen's engagement to Maria, Götz relates the underlying import of the moment: that the union between Weislingen and Maria actually signifies a renewed severance of the two men.[19] Upon waking from his dream of separation, Götz may assert that his unity with Weislingen was attained through the betrothal of Maria and Weislingen, but his hestitation discloses the fanciful nature of those visions. As he himself admits, that which he "only hoped for in his dreams"—his fantasy of a reunion with Weislingen—"is over." Accordingly, we later find in the play that Maria fails to cement the bond between Weislingen and Götz and that Weislingen ultimately abandons them both for a life at court.

The social convention of exchanging women reveals itself in *Götz von Berlichingen* as a poor substitute for male same-sex desire. For men like Götz and Weislingen, the somber reality is that they cannot exist within a social order that mandates displacing their desire with forms of homosociality. Indeed, as the tragedy reaches its denouement, all impressions of male-male desire and community dissolve. The final scenes foreground visions not of the affinity between Götz and Weislingen, but of their separation and death. Weislingen and Götz are once again engaged in war with one another. In his last hours Weislingen laments his physical weakness and recounts a poisonous dream in which his hand fails him in a battle against Götz. Berlichingen himself deplores the transition from knightly unity and male-male affinities to a vicious new world of death and division. Unlike Ferdinand and Egmont, Götz and Weislingen will not live beyond themselves. When Götz exclaims of himself: "Du hast dich selbst überlebt" ("You have lived beyond yourself [have outlived yourself]," MA, 1:1, 652), he implies not that he and Weislingen and the passion they represent will live on after them, but that their affinity was of an earlier time, that he (alone) has lasted beyond those days, and that the male same-sex desire he represents will die with him.

The world in *Götz von Berlichingen* sinks to a ghastly state as the community of men turns against itself, inflicting wounds upon its own body (bodies) as hundreds are broken on the wheel, impaled on spears, drawn and quartered, and decapitated. The frustration of male-male desire through compulsory bonds with women and the subsequent repression of natural affinities between men create a gruesome social backlash. The fantasy of male same-sex desire, of securing the lost half and restoring both sentimental and physical wholeness to men desiring men recedes from view as the social nightmare of compulsory homosociality gains a terrifying ascendancy.

Götz von Berlichingen accentuates boldly not only the reality of male same-sex desire, its validity and its naturalness, but also the societal pressures that work against the expression and consummation of that sentiment. While its representations are drastic, the play underscores the point that homosociality cannot operate as a substitute for male-male desire and that, essentially, compulsory homosociality is, for men like Götz and Weislingen, just another name for separation and death. Compulsory homosociality does not ensure social order in *Götz von Berlichingen*, as Sedgwick asserts it does throughout nineteenth-century English literature. In direct opposition to Sedgwick's model, we find that in succumbing to social convention, in allowing Maria to stand between them, Götz and Weislingen war against their once unified and mutually desiring self/selves, until their affinity dies and they with it.

MAKING METAPHORS OF MALE SAME-SEX DESIRE:
TASSO AND ANTONIO

If *Götz von Berlichingen* was about the social subversion of bonds
between desiring men, *Torquato Tasso* is about a different cultural order that actively facilitates the negotiation of affinities between men.
The drama itself is structured around the promotion and actualiza-
tion of an affinity between the two main male protagonists, Tasso and
Antonio. *Tasso* is strikingly self-reflective over the importance of the
erotic bond between Tasso and Antonio, and the negotiation of their
relationship constitutes the crucial trajectory of the play. From start
to finish, it is clear that the entire drama is constructed around the dynamic affinity that slowly develops between the two men. Everyone
in the play is focused on facilitating the bond between Antonio and
Tasso. In fact, in the opening scenes of the drama, the Princess tells
Tasso that her mission is to see him and Antonio allied affinitively
with one another:

> Ihr [Tasso und Antonio] mußt verbunden sein, ich schmeichle mir,
> Dies schöne Werk in kurzem zu vollbringen.
> Nur widerstehe nicht, wie du es pflegst!
> So haben wir Leonoren lang besessen,
> Die fein und zärtlich ist, mit der es leicht
> Sich leben läßt; auch dieser hast du nie,
> Wie sie es wünschte, näher treten wollen
>   (MA, 6:1, 696)

> You [Tasso and Antonio] must be allied. I flatter myself that I will
> be able to complete this beautiful task in short time. Now do not
> resist, as you are wont to do! As we have possessed Leonore for a
> long time, who is fine and delicate, with whom it is easy to let oneself
> live, and this one too you have never wanted to come closer to, as
> she wished.

The Princess, intriguingly enough, not only insists upon a bond between Antonio and Tasso, but informs Tasso that she intends to bring
it off soon and successfully. She orders Tasso not to counteract her
efforts and then slides into a light admonishment of him for not
having taken the opportunity to get closer to Leonore. The juxtaposition she makes between Antonio and Leonore reflects a smooth
slip from one object of desire (male) to another (female). Just as in

the *Wahlverwandtschaften*, such a shift in affinities is recounted as a matter of course, and each potential object of desire, whether male or female, is presented as equally acceptable and plausible.

But Tasso feels no affinity for Leonore. He reminds the Princess that affinities are not something one can fiat into existence. He has done his best, in accord with her desires, but his natural disinterest in Leonore cannot be thoroughly suppressed:

> Ich habe dir gehorcht, sonst hätt ich mich
> Von ihr entfernt, anstatt mich ihr zu nahen.
> So liebenswürdig sie erscheinen kann,
> Ich weiß nicht wie es ist, konnt ich nur selten
> Mit ihr ganz offen sein, . . .
>
>   (MA, 6:1, 696)

> I obeyed you, otherwise I would have distanced myself from her instead of approaching her. As worthy of love as she might appear, I do not know how it is, I could only seldom be completely open with her.

Tasso feels little or no attraction to Leonore, principally because he cannot interact with her openly. In contrast, throughout the drama Tasso freely expresses his affinities for both the Princess and Antonio. And, in fact, his brash articulation of his desires takes both of them by surprise. What the Princess fails to recognize in her attempts to couple Tasso with Leonore and Antonio is that, while Tasso is inclined toward two objects of desire, they are herself and Antonio.[20] And it is precisely these two affinities that he tries to negotiate during the course of the play. As we shall see, Tasso himself slides back and forth between his two objects of desire until he ultimately lands in Antonio's arms.

Tasso relates to the Princess that his first encounter with Antonio leaves his emotions reeling:

> Ich will es dir gern gestehn, es hat der Mann,
> Der unerwartet zu uns traf, nicht sanft
> Aus einem schönen Traum mich aufgeweckt;
> Sein Wesen, seine Worte haben mich
> So wunderbar getroffen, daß ich mehr
> Als je mich doppelt fühle, mit mir selbst
> Aufs neu in streitender Verwirrung bin.
>
>   (MA, 6:1, 692)

I will gladly admit to you that the man who came up to us unexpectedly woke me none too softly out of a beautiful dream. His being, his
words, effected me so wondrously, that I felt myself more than ever
doubled and in a new conflicted confusion with myself.

It is precisely Antonio's being, his presence, and his *words* that shock
Tasso out of his dream-like state of existence and that give him
a sense of being doubled. Antonio's *self* and *word* directly affect
Tasso's sense of his *own self* and unsettle his previously formed notions of himself. He is ultimately confused and fascinated by this initial meeting. Even before his first conversation with Antonio, Tasso
anticipates his role as the desired male interlocutor.

But Tasso's first attempts to establish a bond with Antonio are
thwarted by Antonio's reticence. Tasso's blatant and blunt expressions of his desire for Antonio are more than Antonio can process.
Like Ferdinand, Tasso formulates new and specific expressions of his
desire that his male counterpart does not yet comprehend or trust.
So while Tasso openly admits "Dir biet' ich ohne Zögern Herz und
Hand" ("I offer you my heart and hand without hesitation," MA,
6:1, 701), Antonio acknowledges the value of Tasso's offer but feels
compelled to hesitate:

> Freigebig bietest du mir schöne Gaben,
> Und ihren Wert erkenn ich, wie ich soll,
> Drum lasse mich zögern eh' ich sie ergreife.
> Weiß ich doch nicht, ob ich dir auch dagegen
> Ein gleiches geben kann. Ich möchte gern
> Nicht übereilt und nicht undankbar scheinen,
> Laß mich für beide klug und sorgsam sein.
>
> (MA, 6:1, 701)

You openly offer me beautiful gifts and I recognize their value, as I
should, nonetheless let me hesitate before I seize it. Indeed I do not
know if I can offer you something similar in return. I would not want
to be rushed and do not want to appear thankless. Let me be wise and
careful for us both.

Antonio is more cautious and wants to allow their affinity time to
develop, while Tasso insists upon an instant bond. In fact, Antonio hesitates precisely because he is not sure that he can return the

words and sentiments Tasso has articulated with similar expressions. Nonetheless, Tasso continues to press him:

> Ich weiß, du bist mein Freund, wenn du mich kennst;
> Und eines solchen Freunds bedurft ich lange . . .
> O nimm mich, edler Mann, an deine Brust,
> Und weihe mich, den Raschen, Unerfahrnen,
> Zum mäßigen Gebrauch des Lebens ein.
>
> (MA, 6:1, 702)

I know you would be my friend, when you know me. And I have long needed such a friend. O take me, noble man, on your chest. Initiate me, the rash, inexperienced one in a measured use of life.

Like Wilhelm in the *Lehrjahre,* Tasso recognizes his need for "such a friend"—for a male interlocutor who will guide him through life and desire and toward a sense of himself. Antonio counters that what Tasso demands can only be granted over time: "In einem Augenblicke forderst du, / Was wohlbedächtig nur die Zeit gewährt" ("In one moment you demand that which, well considered, only time grants," MA, 6:1, 702). Tasso rejects Antonio's observations, averring that love grants what time cannot:

> In einem Augenblick gewährt die Liebe,
> Was Mühe kaum in langer Zeit erreicht.
> Noch einmal! Hier ist meine Hand! Schlag' ein!
> Tritt nicht zurück und weigre dich nicht länger . . .
>
> (MA, 6:1, 702)

In an instant love grants what great pains can hardly reach in a long time. Again! Here is my hand! Grasp it! Don't step back and don't refuse any longer . . .

Tasso responds to Antonio's reticence with ever more intense expressions of his passion, asserting that love conquers time and renewing his offer to seal their affinity with the offer of his hand. But Tasso's direct and forceful expression of his desire has the opposite effect. Rather than convincing Antonio of the inevitability of their desire, Tasso's profusions underscore his impression of the distance between them: "Ich gönne jeden Wert und jedes Glück / Dir gern, allein ich sehe nur zu sehr, / Wir stehn zu weit noch von einander ab"

("I gladly grant you every value and every happiness, but I see only too well that we stand yet far too far apart from each other," MA, 6:1, 703). Significantly, Antonio does not reject Tasso's desires, but does underscore their distance from one another. In his thorough frustration Tasso now castigates Antonio for rejecting his offers of trust, adulation, and love:

> Du lästerst, du entweihest diesen Ort,
> Nicht ich, der ich Vertraun, Verehrung, Liebe,
> Das schönste Opfer, dir entgegen trug.
> Dein Gunst verunreint dieses Paradies
> Und deine Worte diesen reinen Saal, . . .
>   (MA, 6:1, 705)

> You make malicious remarks, desecrate this place, Not I, who brought you trust, adulation, love, the most beautiful sacrifice. Your goodwill and your words soil this paradise and this pure hall.

Throughout their discussion of the potential affinity between them, Tasso's expressions of his passion are straightforward, increasingly intense, and more and more precise. By the time that he loses patience with Antonio he is articulating his offer to him in the most exact terms. His original offer of "heart and hand" and "friendship" shifts during the course of his speech to one of "love" and "hand" and finally emerges as one of "trust, adulation, and love." Tasso reads Antonio's reluctance not as caution but as rejection and is deeply wounded. Antonio, on the other hand, perceives Tasso's bold articulations as a sign of his lack of control. He tells Leonore that Tasso "beherrscht / So wenig seinen Mund als seine Brust" ("has as little control over his mouth as his breast [feelings]," MA, 6:1, 724). The conversation between the two men becomes less and less civil and culminates in Tasso challenging Antonio to a duel and being confined in his quarters by the Prince as a consequence. No hope of an affinity between Tasso and Antonio appears to remain as Tasso now rants about his vehement hatred of the man: "Nein, ich muß / Von nun an diesen Mann als Gegenstand / Von meinem tiefsten Haß behalten; nichts / Kann mir die Lust entreißen, schlimm und schlimmer / Von ihm zu denken" ("No, I must from now on consider this man as the object of my deepest hatred. Nothing can snatch from me the pleasure of thinking worse and worse of him," MA, 6:1, 728). And now, even the Princess and Leonore underscore the impossibility of love between these two men.

The Princess suddenly reads their incompatibility across several corporeal signs:

> Es warnte mich mein Geist, als neben ihn [Antonio]
> Sich Tasso stellte. Sieh das Äußre nur
> Von beiden an, das Angesicht, den Ton,
> Den Blick, den Tritt! Es widerstrebt sich alles;
> Sie können ewig keine Liebe wechseln.
>
> (MA, 6:1, 712–13)

> My spirit warned me, as Tasso took a place by his [Antonio's] side. Just look at the external features of the two of them. Look at the face, the tone, the glance, the step! Everything contradicts [works against/resists] everything else. They can never offer each other love.

Leonore concurs with the Princess, pointing out that Antonio and Tasso are innate enemies because nature failed to make one man of them: "Zwei Männer sind's, ich hab es lang gefühlt, / Die darum Feinde sind, weil die Natur / Nicht *Einen* Mann aus ihnen beiden formte" ("They are two men, I have felt this for a long time, who are enemies because nature did not form *One* man out of them," MA, 6:1, 713). With these prophetic words, the question of Antonio's and Tasso's potential affinity to one another appears to have been definitively laid to rest.

As we have seen, Tasso fails in his endeavor to secure Antonio's affection. His words of passion do not incite the intended response. Despite the fact that he names his desire openly and forcefully, Antonio remains reluctant to embrace the idea of an instant affinity. Indeed, one could say that Tasso's profusions of love for Antonio fall on deaf ears, because his expressions of desire are too extreme and too intense. Antonio is not accustomed to the "rash," "warm" words of a poet's "schwellendes Gefühl" ("swelling feeling" MA, 6:1, 705). Tasso's ever more articulate expressions of his desire demarcate the tremendous gulf that exists between the two men. Antonio is not as articulate as Tasso, is not as versed in the expression of desire, and he wonders if he can offer him "ein gleiches" ("something comparable") in return. Tasso is so adept at the verbal expression of his desire that he leaves Antonio behind. Indeed, if Ferdinand marked a shift toward a new kind of emotional exchange between men, a new emphasis on the expression of passion between men, Tasso furthers that project exponentially. And in both cases, the other man confronted with this new language of desire is at least initially hesitant and baffled.

In fact, Tasso's bold articulations of his desire for the Princess are shocking and unsettling to her as well. As in his exchange with Antonio, Tasso directly confronts the Princess with his feelings of affinity:

> Ganz eröffnet sich
> Die Seele, nur dich ewig zu verehren,
> Es füllt sich ganz das Herz mit Zärtlichkeit—
> Sie ist's, sie steht vor mir. Welch ein Gefühl!
> (MA, 6:1, 744).

> My soul opens itself completely, only to honor you eternally. My heart fills completely with tenderness. It is she, she stands before me. What a feeling!

Tasso's expressions of his sentiments for the Princess are even more intense than those he revealed for Antonio. While in both cases he named his desire quite precisely, here the emotions signified by his words surge forth with tremendous force. The Princess is literally frightened by Tasso's outburst and demands that he temper his speech: "Wenn ich dich, Tasso, länger hören soll, / So mäßige die Glut, die mich erschreckt" ("If I am to listen to you any longer Tasso, temper the passion that frightens me," MA, 6:1, 745). But (as we might by now expect) Tasso ignores her injunction entirely, expressing blatantly the love that draws him to her:

> Unsägliche Gewalt, die mich beherrscht,
> Entfließet deinen Lippen; ja du machst
> Mich ganz dir eigen. Nichts gehöret mir
> Von meinem ganzen Ich mir künftig an.
> Es trübt mein Auge sich in Glück und Licht,
> Es schwankt mein Sinn. Mich hält der Fuß nicht mehr.
> Unwiderstehlich ziehst du mich zu dir.
> Und unaufhaltsam dringt mein Herz dir zu.
> Du hast mich ganz auf ewig dir gewonnen,

So nimm denn auch mein ganzes Wesen hin.
[Er fällt ihr in die Arme und drückt sie fast an sich]
    (MA, 6:1, 745).

An inexpressible power that controls me flows from your lips. Yes, you make me completely your own. From now on nothing of myself belongs to me. My eye clouds over in pleasure and light. My senses whirl. My foot no longer holds me steady. You draw me to you irresistibly. My heart pushes ceaselessly toward you. You have won me completely and eternally for yourself. So take now my whole being. *[He falls in her arms and presses her tightly to himself.]*

The Princess is taken so aback by Tasso's boldness—both of speech and of gesture (as he falls in her arms and presses her against himself)—that she shoves him from her and hurries away, ordering him to be gone: "*[ihn von sich stoßend und hinweg eilend]* Hinweg!" ("*[pushing him from her and rushing away]* Away with you!" MA, 6:1, 745). Once again Tasso's brash attempts to secure affinities do not produce the desired result. Unlike Werther and Lotte, Eduard and Ottilie, Charlotte and the Captain, or Ferdinand and Egmont, the Princess and Tasso do not just find themselves falling obliviously into each other's arms. Indeed, this scene culminates in Tasso's remonstrances against himself for actions leading to his total severance and banishment from the Princess:

> Ich bin verstoßen, bin verbannt, ich habe
> Mich selbst verbannt, ich werde diese Stimme
> Nicht mehr vernehmen, diesem Blicke nicht,
> Nicht mehr begegnen.
>
>   (MA, 6:1, 747)

I am disowned, am banished. I have banished myself. I will never hear this voice again, will never again encounter this glance.

As Tasso laments bitterly the Princess's rebuff, Antonio returns in the role of confidant and advisor, that is, as his male interlocutor. And as Tasso pours out his soul and agony to him, Antonio offers him reassurance:

> Laß eines Mannes Stimme dich erinnern,
> Der neben dir nicht ohne Rührung steht!
> Und wenn du ganz dich zu verlieren scheinst,

Vergleiche dich! Erkenne was du bist!
    (MA, 6:1, 747)

> Let a man's voice remind you, a man who stands next to you and
> not without emotion! And when you appear to have completely lost
> yourself, metaphorize [poeticize] yourself! Recognize what you are!

Now, in the moment of his greatest distress, Antonio consoles Tasso
with expressions of his own emotion, and he reminds Tasso that he
is a poet—that he ought to produce a metaphor, recognizing who
he is and expressing himself through poetry. Antonio offers Tasso
his own (man's) voice and guides Tasso back to himself, accentuating
his facility to articulate his feelings of desire. Following Antonio's injunction to poeticize himself, Tasso immediately begins to search his
memory for a man with whom he might compare himself—in whom
he might see himself mirrored. But finding that endeavor fruitless,
he asserts that all that is left to him now is his own poetic ability.
He must fashion his *own self-reflecting* male predecessor. What will
save him from this moment of total despair is his ability, like the
Werther of the *Briefe,* "to people the landscape" with self-mirroring,
self-expressing, male figures of identification and desire. As soon as
Tasso formulates his poetic mission, Antonio offers him freely the
hand he had so longed for in their first encounter: "*[Antonio tritt zu
ihm und nimmt ihn bei der Hand]*" ("*[Antonio walks up to him and
takes him by the hand]*," MA, 6:1, 748). And, in that moment and
with that gesture their affinity is secured. Tasso clasps Antonio in
his arms, and the metaphor that flows from his lips constitutes the
final words of *Torquato Tasso:*

> Zerbrochen ist das Steuer, und es kracht
> Das Schiff an allen Seiten. Berstend reißt
> Der Boden unter meinen Füßen auf!
> Ich fasse dich mit beiden Armen an!
> So klammert sich der Schiffer endlich noch
> Am Felsen fest, an dem er scheitern sollte.
>   (MA, 6:1, 748)

> The helm is broken, and the ship breaks on all sides. Under my feet
> the deck cracks and tears open. I grab on to you with both arms!
> So the sailor clings finally fast to the rock, on which he should have
> perished.

Antonio, as the figure of the desired male interlocutor, coaches Tasso
through his tragedy, through his shipwreck, to a clearer understanding of himself as a poet. He reminds Tasso of his ability to express
his same-sex desire, to lend it poetic contours. Antonio encourages
Tasso to metaphorize, to give his desire metaphoric form. Tasso,
in turn, invokes the metaphor of the shipwreck.[21] Like Werther in
Die Leiden, Tasso likens his catastrophic affinity for an unattainable woman to the collapse and sinking of a ship. But in contrast
to Werther, this desiring male subject does not perish. Here the ravages of the shipwreck are undone as Tasso clings to the rock that is
Antonio. The rock that appeared so inhospitable earlier in the play
now represents the male-male desire and voice that sustains Tasso
and saves him from certain demise.

We can read Tasso's metaphorization of male same-sex desire as
a thoroughly paradigmatic trope. It is precisely this metaphor of literary production, male same-sex desire, and the incitement to poetic
formations of that desire that asserts itself in various permutations
in each of the literary works we have considered here. Except for the
earliest work, *Götz von Berlichingen,* each of the other texts foregrounded the trope of the male interlocutor and his role in guiding and inciting new poetic formulations of male-male desire. And
one could argue that even *Götz von Berlichingen* is implicitly de-
pendent upon a certain structure of male-male interlocution. Each
of the novels discussed was framed in one way or another around
discussions, letters, or even the lack thereof between desiring men.
The most intense exchanges of male same-sex desire, however, are reserved for *Götz, Egmont,* and *Tasso.* While the articulations of male-
male desire in *Götz von Berlichingen* are bold, *Egmont* and *Tasso* are
much more self-reflective about their incitements to expressions of
that desire. *Egmont* introduced new parameters for the expression of
desire between men—pushing the articulations of desire, however,
only so far before resorting to a provocative elision (—). *Egmont*
incites the reader or audience to fill in the blank, to name the unnamed desire. *Tasso* is even bolder. The characters name their desire, they embrace, and Tasso produces the metaphor that is their
desire. Nothing appears to be left unnamed. Tasso's metaphor—not
just the shipwreck but also the verbal exchanges that lead up to it—
and the interactions of Tasso and Antonio in those final moments

capture *in nuce* the implications and contours of male same-sex desire in Goethe's aesthetic production. Just like Eduard and the Captain, Werther (*Briefe*), and Wilhelm (*Wilhelm Meisters Wanderjahre*), Antonio and Tasso figure male-male desire. They outline the structure and genesis of metaphoricity, that is, of poetry. Their desire is not only an incitement to literary production, but their poetry also signifies an incitement to metaphoric formations of male same-sex desire. Even in those works ostensibly only about male-female desire, male-male desire proved fundamental both to the structure of the literary text and to its conceptualization of desire.

Tasso's metaphorization underscores as well how same-sex desire gets put into poetic discourse and how it becomes a metaphor. Within the context of discussions between desiring men, as desiring men fall inevitably and spontaneously into one another's arms, poetry emerges. And it is poetry that sustains Tasso (or the desiring male subject) in the direst of circumstances. It is the imperiled, lost self that male-male desire saves and preserves from the self-annihilating experience of female-male love (think of *Die Wahlverwandtschaften*, *Die Leiden*, *Wilhelm Meister*, *Götz*, and *Tasso*, in which the desiring male subject loses himself in his pursuit of affinities for unattainable women). As Antonio clasps Tasso's hand and Tasso falls into Antonio's arms, the male same-sex desire they signify allows for poetry, for the metaphor that Tasso produces. He, in turn, constructs not only a metaphor of male-male desire, but also a metaphor that reflects what male same-sex desire makes possible: men desiring men can construct a discourse of desire, can speak both their desire and themselves—and that is poetry.

chapter 4

GOETHE AND MORITZ: LITERARY FORMATIONS OF MALE SAME-SEX IDENTITY AND COMMUNITY

*L*iterary formations of male same-sex identity abound in Goethe's aesthetic production, and struggles to formulate new discourses of male-male sentiment are inextricably connected to new articulations of male, same-sex identifications. Although I have for purposes of discussion artificially separated male same-sex desire and identification from one another, in fact, we must keep in mind that the two are, as we would expect, thoroughly inseparable throughout Goethe's oeuvre. Within the context of incitements to the metaphoric representation of male-male desire in Goethe's literary production, the concentration on male same-sex identity and the subtle allusions and significations that repeatedly accompany those identity formations become increasingly more obvious. A constellation of signs and representations of male same-sex identity formation—some of which in isolation might go thoroughly undetected—emerge in the form of systematic groupings or patterns that recur consistently throughout Goethe's oeuvre. For instance, discussions of and allusions to the function of literature and literary signification are evident throughout Goethe's aesthetic production and are intricately conjoined to the expression and proliferation of articulations of male same-sex identity. Significations of literature and the production of literature themselves appear as recurrent poetic paradigms in Goethe's works, which consistently foreground issues of male-male desire and the formation of male same-sex identities. Investigating the codings of same-sex identity that accompany representations of literature and literary processes in Goethe's work reveals a systematic web of significations that operate in conjunction with one another to formulate new articulations of male same-sex identity and desire. More specifically, the paradigm of literature, literature as a model for male-male desire, and literature as an incitement to further expressions of male same-sex identification and attraction are inextricably joined throughout Goethe's oeuvre to notions of childhood experiences. In characterizing the man who desires other men, Goethe focuses on boyhood emulations of men who desire men, the development of boys into male-identified and male-desiring men, visual cathexes, certain kinds of dress, and self-fashioning through poetic formulation. Goethe's representation of same-sex desire and identity demonstrates that men desiring men were perceived to have a specific morphology. As in the case with Winckelmann, Goethe strives to outline throughout his literary work the specific childhood, personal history, personage, and particular type of life that form men who desire men. In his poetic produc-tion, Goethe constructs his own vision of the childhood and boy-hood influences upon the development of persons who will come to desire their own (male) sex. And, at the same time, we discover that the categories of definition are the same ones he deployed in defining Winckelmann's same-sex identity in his encomium. In ex-tending the same-sex desire that is Winckelmann, Goethe produces a complex, systematic pattern or structure of interlinked signifiers and paradigms of same-sex identity. In addition, the convergence of same-sex desire and identity in poetic discourse reveals how the same-sex identified self becomes a metaphor or, more precisely, a set of metaphors. And, finally, the community of men alluded to in the context of Goethe's Winckelmann essay (the boys surround-ing him), in the collaboration of the Weimar Friends of Art, and by Winckelmann's placement within the history of German Classical aesthetics is much more boldly expressed. Here we will trace out how Goethe established the fundamental and critical importance of a *community* of same-sex desiring and identified men and how he and Moritz strove to make that community a reality through new poetic formulations of same-sex identity formations.

But the paradigm of literary creation is not the only one that emerges persistently throughout Goethe's literary production as a sign of male same-sex identity and desire. As we shall see, a carefully defined network of poetic codings of male-male attraction systematically accompanies representations of elective affinities and literary processes in Goethe's work. Once again we must underscore the fact that we are not talking here about representations of sodomy, tribades, mollies, or pederasts, but about the codings of men who identify themselves with and as men who desire other men. Indeed, we are also not talking only about invocations of images of "Greek love." Goethe's codings are specific representations of same-sex identity that are uniquely his own and that are linked to expressions of male-male desire.

And in fact, it is these poetic codings (including the function of literature) that are reiterated in parallel ways in the works of one of Goethe's closest contemporaries, Karl Philipp Moritz. At the end of this chapter we will consider in some detail how Moritz appropriated and transformed exactly those tropes that Goethe relied on to express male same-sex desire and identity formation. In fact, Moritz's novel *Anton Reiser* provides a further literary instantiation and extension of the Winckelmannian-Goethean project of identity and desire. *Anton Reiser* is structured upon poetic codings that are strikingly similar to those that appear throughout Goethe's oeuvre and represent the function of Goethe's literary work as an incitement to further expressions of male same-sex desire and identification. In other words, Moritz must have understood that Goethe's literary work incited and created new poetic articulations of male same-sex desire and identity. Moritz's novel, in conjunction with Goethe's works, points clearly to the critical role that Goethe's literary production played in late eighteenth- and early nineteenth-century attempts to articulate male-male identity and desire. But, even more strikingly, not only do Goethe's literary tropes get rearticulated in Moritz's work, but his literary production, and particularly his *Die Leiden des jungen Werthers*, are the literary topoi evoked in

Anton Reiser as signifiers of male-male desire and identity. Once again, we encounter layers upon layers of tropes signifying male same-sex desire and identity. And in this instance, we see how those tropes begin to take on a life of their own, as other men began to rely on Goethe's figurations of male-male desire. In other words, they continued the "mirroring" of figures of male-male identity in their poetic works in ways that invoke Goethe's literary formations. Just like the Werther of the Swiss letters, these authors began to "people" the literary landscape with male figures, who identify themselves as men desiring men. In order to trace the emergence these specific poetic codings of male same-sex desire and identity in and around Goethe's literary production, it seems appropriate to begin with his general formulations of male same-sex identity in his literary work and then turn to the proliferations of literary topoi of male same-sex identity formation both within his oeuvre and beyond.

The most exciting feature of Goethe's literary production is the proliferation of codings of male same-sex identity formation that are then appropriated by others such as Moritz who understood and extended his poetic articulations of male same-sex identity. As a challenge to Foucault's presumption that same-sex identities emerged for the first time in the later nineteenth century in the form of psychoanalytic, medical, and legal discourses and/or reverse discourses, Goethe's and Moritz's aesthetic project supplies extensive evidence of eighteenth-century male same-sex self-expression and self-identity formation. Above all, Goethe's works strive to trace the childhood desires and identities that operate in forming the same-sex desiring and identified self. In this sense Goethe anticipates in a striking manner later nineteenth-century obsessions with childhood and the fascination with the possible origins of sexual identity in childhood. Think, for instance, of Freud's psychoanalytic theory and its reliance on children's experience to explain "perversions" such as "inversion" in the *Three Essays on Sexuality.* But unlike Freud, Goethe does not provide a judgmental account, does not promote the notion that same-sex desire and identity are abnormal, does not relegate polymorphous perversity to an infantile stage, and finally, does not exclude self-fashioning from his representations. With these things in mind we can now turn to the specific works by Goethe that illustrate same-sex identity formations.

MORPHOLOGIES OF MEN IDENTIFYING WITH AND DESIRING MEN

If male same-sex desire was defined as natural and innate in Goethe's *Götz von Berlichingen* (1773), male same-sex identity formation was already being mapped out in this early play as an integral part of the desiring male subject's youthful development.[1] I will trace the contours of the male identity formation that takes shape in this drama in some detail, because the very same tropes that emerge here are reiterated time and again in Goethe's writings.

In order to explicate the genesis of male same-sex identity formation in *Götz von Berlichingen*, Goethe focuses on the childhood memories and experiences of his male characters. During the course of the play several male characters accentuate the salient erotic identifications of their boyhoods. Each of these accounts concerning the formation of male same-sex identities is different, and yet the crucial moments these men recall share critical similarities. With this in mind, it seems appropriate to examine closely the narratives of male same-sex identification presented in the play.

The first scenes of *Götz von Berlichingen* already focus on the issue of male identity formation. The introduction of the play's hero, Götz von Berlichingen, revolves around two interrelated encounters: one between Götz and a young boy, Georg, who yearns to become a knight, and one between Götz and an adoring monk, Martin. Martin and Georg converse with Götz separately, but both dialogues function to frame, complicate, and mirror the dynamics of male same-sex identification that constitute the central concern of *Götz von Berlichingen*. These preliminary stagings of variant socializations of male love set the scene finally for Götz's and Weislingen's later recollections of their own boyhood dreams, visions, and same-sex yearnings.

Götz's discussions with Georg and Martin detail crucial specular influences upon young men. Both characters sketch out largely analogous descriptions of the visual sensations that ignite their passions and incite their identifications with Götz. They are enamored of ideal knights and they each indicate how eager they are to mimic Götz. Indeed, upon hearing Götz's call, the boy Georg arrives on stage dressed in a man's armor (*"im Panzer eines Erwachsenen,"* MA, 1:1, 552). His masquerade immediately draws Götz's attention, and Georg divulges his compulsion to practice his role as a future knight, admitting how he donned Hans' armor, and, wielding his father's sword, performed fictional battles across the meadows: "Ich nahm ihn leise weg, und legt ihn an, und holt meines Vaters altes Schwert von der Wand, lief auf die Wiese und zogs aus" ("I took it [the armor] quietly away, and put it on, and retrieved my father's sword from the wall, and ran onto the meadow and pulled it out," MA, 1:1, 552). Throughout the play, Georg's identification with Götz as a perfect male and a patriarchal model is suffused with his idealizations of Hans (from whom he gets the armor), of his father (from whom he gets the sword), and of Saint George (from whom he gets his name). The male paragon that Georg envisions is associated predominantly with visual and physical signs of knighthood.[2] The boy's play-acting serves both to make his own fantasies of same-sex identification with Götz visible and to accentuate the performative character of identity formations. Moreover, the signifiers of Georg's same-sex identification are (while at first glance apparently antiquated) quite modern. Goethe points to Georg's dress (armor), his phallic power and desire (sword), and his symbolic existence (name). These three components—dress, phallic power and desire, and symbolic naming—resurface in various accounts of same-sex desire, including psychoanalytic accounts of emerging sexual selfhood, accounts of subcultural activity in the eighteenth century, accounts of cross-dressing in the eighteenth and nineteenth centuries, and drag in our present time. Modern psychoanalytic models, of course, stress phallic identification with or desire for the father (Freud) and the father's name (Lacan). Once again, and in his own fashion, Goethe zeros in on several critical and persistent cultural signifiers of same-sex desire and identity. He understands the importance of "dressing the part," phallic identifications, and the naming of identities. To this extent, we can underscore with Tobin (*Warm Brothers*) that the Age of Goethe—and Goethe in particular—does appear to have set into motion several crucial discursive components of male same-sex identity that can be traced forward to our present day. Interestingly, Goethe's conception of identity formation is also thoroughly modern in its suggestion of the performative nature (Butler) of sexual identity formation. Georg takes armor, sword, and name and wields them all in his own way. He does not passively endure their application to himself by some outside entity (whether witnesses of subcultural activity, psychological observers, etc). Georg actively participates in his own symbolic identity formation.

In a manner similar to Georg, Martin highlights the specular nature of his attraction to Götz. He asserts continuously how imperative it is for him to see his idol: "Wie mir's so eng um's Herz ward, *da ich ihn sah*. Er redete nichts, und mein Geist konnte doch den Seinigen unterscheiden. Es ist eine Wollust, *einen großen Mann zu sehn*" ("How constricted my heart felt *when I saw him*. He didn't say a word and my spirit could still perceive his. It is a pleasure *to see a great man*," emphasis added, MA, I.I, 557). Martin continues by thanking God "daß du mich ihn hast sehen lassen" ("for having let him see," MA, I.I, 556) such a knight. Male same-sex identification is inextricably connected to visual experience (specularity), and Martin foregrounds this when he offers Georg a holy card with a picture of his patron saint on it, instructing him to follow the saint's example. The only "example" that Georg has is the ocular image itself. As the boy views the likeness, he lists the alluring objects that he sees:

> Ach ein schöner Schimmel, wenn ich so einen hätte!—und die goldene Rüstung!—Das ist ein garstiger Drach—Jetzt schieß ich nach Sperlingen-Heiliger Georg! mach mich groß und stark, gib mir so eine Lanze, Rüstung und Pferd, dann laß mir die Drachen kommen! (MA, I.I, 557)

> Such a beautiful white steed, if only I had one like it!—and the golden armor! That is a vile dragon!—I only shoot sparrows now—Saint George! make me big and strong, give me such a lance, such armor and such a horse—then let the dragons come!

Georg's male ideal is a strong knight, bearing armor and carrying a sword. The image of Saint George provides a visual summary of

the desired characteristics or trappings of knighthood. The boy perceives in the visual representation his own potentially ideal body.
Like the child who first conceives of its body as a whole, complete entity in Lacan's mirror-stage, Georg anticipates his own corporeal perfection—physical size and prowess—in the image of the
saint/other man. And in the manner of Lacan's infant, Georg aspires
immediately to become that illusory, perfect body. The simple act
of viewing the male paragon excites Georg's fascination for a kind
of mirror-stage emulation. Peering at the perfect image, the boy discovers who lures him and who he wishes to become. In Goethe's
representation, the ideal image viewed in the "mirror" becomes the
visual template for same-sex desire and identity. That is, it accentuates the reality that Goethe's male subject both desires and identifies
with male paragons who desire other men.

In a separate passage Martin gazes at Götz (as perfect man/
knight) and isolates the same visible signifiers of the male ideal that
Georg did. The monk exclaims:

> Wollte Gott, meine Schultern fühlten sich Kraft, den Harnisch zu er-
> tragen, und mein Arm die Stärke, einen Feind vom Pferd zu stechen!
> —Arme schwache Hand, von je her gewöhnt Kreuze und Friedens-
> fahnen zu führen, und Rauchfässer zu schwingen, wie wolltest du
> Lanze und Schwert regieren? (MA, I.I, 555).

> If only God would fill my shoulders with the strength to bear the
> breast plate, and fill my arms with the strength to knock an enemy
> from his horse! Poor weak hand accustomed till now only to guide
> crosses and flags of peace and to swing censers, how is it that you
> desire to rule lance and sword?

The breastplate functions for the monk as an exteriority, a surface,
a kind of mirror across which and in which he recognizes the ideal
male he loves and would like to be. Martin admits that he is "in euren
[Götzens] Harnisch verliebt" ("in love with your [Götz's] armor"
MA, I.I, 554).

Götz von Berlichingen makes male same-sex identification and
its contingent relationship to specularity and linguistic articulation
visible. As Martin gives Georg the image of the saint he says, "Da
hast du ihn. Folge seinem Beispiel . . ." ("There you have him. Follow

his example . . ." MA, I.I, 557), implying that the boy now has what he needs and wants. The child's identification with and emulation of the men around him require his appropriation of certain crucial visual cathexes to which he endeavors to lend form through narrative expression and physical enactment. As in Lacan's conception of the mirror-stage, the specular image in Goethe's play causes the viewing subject to recognize a desirable (in this case, male) imago. By themselves Georg's and Martin's emulations of the men around them would, of course, not necessarily signify their same-sex desire and identity formation. But we must keep in mind that the man with whom they identify is Götz—a man who desires other men. Indeed, as if to underscore this connection, Weislingen and Götz reminisce about the erotic nature of their youthful relationship (male-male desire) directly after Martin's and Georg's accounts of their identity formations. The drama makes clear that the men that Georg and Martin strive to emulate are men who desire each other, and the development of male same-sex identification manifests itself in the multiple stories the play tells of the cardinal events influencing boyhood relationships.

Indeed, the trope of boyhood same-sex identity formation recurs throughout Goethe's literary production and is a stock component of the youthful experiences of all those men who ultimately come to express their same-sex desire. In *Die Wahlverwandtschaften* Eduard refers to the Captain as his "Jugendfreund" ("friend of youth"), with whom he desired to complete his own sense of self and who was, in fact, his "zweites Ich" ("second self," MA, 9, 293). And the Ferdinand who will eventually come to "live" Egmont asserts that Egmont was the man he emulated in his youth:

> Wie oft hab' ich nach dir gehorcht, gefragt! Des Kindes Hoffnung ist der Jüngling, des Jünglings der Mann. So bist du vor mir her geschritten; immer vor, und ohne Neid sah ich dich vor und schritt dir nach und fort und fort. Nun hofft ich dich zu sehen und sah dich und mein Herz flog dir entgegen (MA, 3:1, 324).

> How often I listened for you, asked about you! The child's hope is the youth and the youth's hope the man. So you rode before me, always before, I observed you without jealousy, and followed after

you, on and on. Now I hoped to see you and I saw you and my heart flew to you.

Similarly, Lerse recounts to Götz that he was following him as a knightly paragon from his youth to the present:

> Von Jugend auf dien ich als Reitersknecht und hab's mit manchem Ritter aufgenommen. Da wir auf euch stießen, freut ich mich. Euren Namen kannt ich, da lernt ich euch kennen. Ihr wißt, ich hielt nicht Stand; ihr saht, es war nicht Furcht, denn ich kam wieder. Kurz ich lernt euch kennen, und von Stund an beschloß ich, euch einmal zu dienen (MA, 6:1, 401).

> From youth on I have served as a knight's servant and have taken up with many knights. That we encountered you pleased me. I knew your name, and I met you then. You know that I did not hold my place; you saw that it was not fear, because I came back again. In short, I became acquainted with you and from that hour I determined that I would serve you some day.

And even Pylades and Orestes in Goethe's *Iphigenia* recount their youth in terms of the beginnings of their male same-sex desire and identity:

> Orest:
> Erinnere mich nicht jener schönen Tage,
> Da mir dein Haus die freie Stätte gab,
> Dein edler Vater klug und liebevoll
> Die halb erstarrte junge Blüthe pflegte;
> Da du ein immer munterer Geselle,
> Gleich einem leichten bunten Schmetterling'
> Um eine dunkle Blume, jeden Tag
> Um mich mit neuem Leben gaukeltest,
> Mir deine Lust in meine Seele spieltest,
> Daß ich, vergessend meiner Not, mit dir
> In rascher Jugend hingerissen schwärmte.
>
> (MA, 3:1, 178)

> Orest: Don't remind me of those splendid days when your house was a sanctuary for me, when your noble father, intelligently and with love, cared for the half-petrified young bloom, when you, always a happy companion, would dart around me, a dark flower, everyday like a light multi-colored butterfly and when you played your joy into my soul, so that I, forgetting my hardship, would revel, swept off with you into youth.

Pylades then replies: "Da fing mein Leben an, als ich dich liebte" ("My life began then, when I began to love you," MA, 3:1, 178). As Pylades makes clear, his *life* begins with his *desire* for Orest. Life and desire are inextricably conjoined discursive/poetic realities. Moreover, both Pylades and Orest acknowledge that their mutual desire and identification was founded upon their desire to replicate the grand deeds of their heroic predecessors:

> Große Taten? Ja,
> Ich weiß die Zeit, da wir sie vor uns sahn!
> Wenn wir zusammen oft dem Wilde nach
> Durch Berg' und Thäler rannten, und dereinst
> An Brust und Faust dem hohen Anherrn gleich
> Mit Keul' und Schwert dem Ungeheuer so,
> Dem Räuber auf der Spur zu jagen hofften;
> Und dann wir Abends an der weiten See
> Uns an einander lehnend ruhig saßen,
> Die Wellen bis zu unsern Füßen spielten,
> Die Welt so weit, so offen vor uns lag;
> Da fuhr wohl einer manchmal nach dem Schwert,
> Und künft'ge Thaten drangen wie die Sterne
> Rings um uns her unzählig aus der Nacht.
>
> (MA, 3:1, 179)

Great deeds? Yes, I know the time when we still saw them before us! When we ran through mountains and valleys after wild game and hoped to track thieves like our forefathers with cudgel and sword. And then evenings leaning against one another we sat on the edge of the broad sea as the waves played up to our feet and the world lay so wide and open before us. And then one of us grabbed his sword and future deeds pressed around us infinitely like the stars out of the night.

Pylades makes it clear that "Ein jeglichter muß seinen Helden wählen, / Dem er die Wege zu Olymp hinauf / Sich nacharbeitet" ("Every one must choose the hero after whom he will work himself up to Olympus," MA, 3:1, 181). In each of these cases the same trope of boyhood emulation signifies male same-sex identity formation. Every boy who develops into a man who desires and identifies with other men recounts his boyhood experiences of male same-sex desire and his longing to emulate male-oriented men.[3] As Egmont suggests to Ferdinand, the lives of men like Götz, Tasso, and Egmont, like those of knights, hunters, and heroes, function as a "Spiegel in welchem du dich gerne betrachtetest" ("mirror in which you gladly observed yourself," MA, 3:1, 326). And, indeed, each of these accounts of male emulation invokes images of the mirroring of male same-sex identities across reflective surfaces such as swords, bodies of water, breastplates, pictures, and mirrors.

Throughout these passages and across several Goethean works, mirrorings of male-male desire and identification revolve around a constellation of signifiers that Wilhelm refers to in the *Lehrjahre* as "Ritterideen" ("ideas of knighthood," MA, 5, 26).[4] Like the other boys discussed here, Wilhelm also performs *himself* in the emulation of heroes: "Ich war wechselsweise bald Jäger, bald Soldat, bald Reuter" ("I was interchangeably a hunter, a soldier, a knight," MA, 5, 26). But we also know from the *Lehrjahre* that Wilhelm's male models are not only hunters, soldiers, and knights; sometimes his male identity formations/performances are predicated on other kinds of cultural heroes such as David and Goliath.[5] Indeed, Wilhelm stresses how his emulations transformed him (at least in his own mind) into his heroes: "Ich ward darüber in meinen Gedanken selbst zum David und Goliath" ("I myself became in my thoughts David and Goliath," MA, 5, 21). Clearly, in each case these accounts of boyhood identity formation foreground the young man's propensity to search for himself mirrored across the surface of a great hero, or great hero's life, and in most cases those heroes desire and identify with men. In this context we should recall Werther's invocation of male paragons of love (Adonis) and self-love (Narciß) as he gazes at the reflection of his friend, Ferdinand, in the lake. And, in each case, Werther identifies himself with those desiring men and expresses his same-sex desire across those ideal images. Indeed, here we must keep Goethe's adulation and imitation of Winckelmann in mind as well, for it is precisely the hero Winckelmann and his struggle to express his male-male desire that Goethe strives to emulate throughout his literary production.

DRESSING THE PART: GÖTZ, EGMONT, WILHELM

But Goethe's boys do not just see themselves as their heroes in/on reflective surfaces, they also practice, perform, and mold themselves into the same-sex desiring men they want to be/become. Georg dresses in a knight's armor, Pylades and Orestes play at being sword-wielding knights, Ferdinand envisions himself riding after Egmont into knightly skirmishes, and so forth. But even more specifically, in several of Goethe's works these performances involve men dressing up (a kind of male-male cross-dressing) and often in another man's clothes. In other words, the performance and emulation of the desired man is further coded in terms of acts of costuming. As Purdy (*The Tyranny of Elegance*) suggests in his analysis of clothing in *Die Leiden des jungen Werthers*, clothing begins to signify a fictional character's interiority (what I would call desires and identifications) in the eighteenth century. This was an interiority that the reading public was completely fascinated by and tried to emulate.[6] In this analysis, I am specifically interested not so much in the broader public response to Goethe's *Werther* novel, but in a more extensive Goethean literary paradigm in which signifiers of clothing, interiority, and emulation converge as an incitement to male same-sex identification, both within his literary work and beyond.[7] With this in mind, we can turn our attention to male dressing in *Götz von Berlichingen*, *Egmont*, and *Wilhelm Meisters Lehrjahre*.

Although Götz seems ready to chide Georg for donning Hans' armor, he actually lapses into praise for his performance: "Was zum Henker treibst du für Mummerei. Komm her du siehst gut aus. Schäm dich nicht Junge. Du bist brav! ja, wenn du ihn ausfülltest. Es ist Hannsens Küraß?" ("What in the devil kind of masquerading are you doing? Come here, you look good. Do not be ashamed, boy. You are good! yes, when you fill it out. It's Hans' breastplate?" MA, 1:1, 552). Not only does Georg mimic Hans, but Götz is clearly impressed by the way that Georg looks after he dresses himself up in Hans' knightly garb. He comments on his appearance, reassures him, and praises him. Georg's masquerade as another man (with all its knightly implications) is both a signification of his identification with Hans and Götz and of the alluring nature of his costuming for other men such as Götz.[8] Georg creates a spectacle of dress that immediately attracts Götz's attention to his body and its desirable appearance. Georg's dressing as another man creates a "sartorial space" for Götz's expression of his pleasure in viewing the young boy's body. Unlike Ferdinand, who stood in the pool before Werther in all his nakedness, here dressing in another man's clothes (armor, actually) highlights the concealed male body as a tantalizing object of desire for other men.[9]

In a similar manner Egmont's dress also draws the attention of a couple of admiring male citizens.[10] As Egmont costumes himself in the Spanish art (that of another culture) as opposed to that of the Netherlands (that of his own countrymen), the men remark not only on his clothes, but also on his masculine beauty. The soldier, Jetter, is immediately attracted by Egmont's clothes and asks his partner: "Hast du das Kleid gesehen? das war nach der neuesten Art, nach spanischem Schnitt." ("Have you seen that costume? it was of the newest fashion, in the Spanish cut," MA, 3:1, 271). The Zimmermeister replies, leaving the clothes aside and focusing on Egmont's body: "Ein schöner Herr!" ("A beautiful man!" MA, 3:1, 271). Egmont's dressing up as another man or in the style of another group of men, like Georg's sartorial performance, is of immediate interest to the men around him—and not for any political reasons, but rather his costuming directs their attention to his beauty and attractiveness as a man. Earlier in the play, Clare and Brackenburg sing a song about following a hero like Egmont into battle—a song in which they both express their desire to dress up like a man and to emulate their ideal: "Wie klopft mir das Herz! / Wie wallt mir das Blut! / O hätt' ich ein Wämslein. Und Hosen und Hut" ("How my heart pounds / How my blood swells! / O if I only had a little vest. And pants and a hat," MA, 3:1, 260). Of course, in Clare's case the song represents a stock trope of the eighteenth century, the cross-dressed woman engaging in military actions. In contrast, Brackenburg's singing reiterates the desire of a man like Martin or Georg to emulate another man—to fashion himself in the image of the man with whom he would like to identify, whose interiority he hopes to emulate and whose body he desires—by dressing the part.[11]

The issue of Egmont's dress is brought to center stage when he appears to Clare, for her private audience, in Spanish dress. He arrives at her apartment dressed so that his Spanish costume is initially concealed: "[Egmont in einem Reutermantel, den Hut ins Gesicht gedrückt]" ("[Egmont in a knight's cloak, his hat pulled down over his face]," MA, 3:1, 287). Intriguingly enough, Egmont hides his Spanish dress, that is, the fact that he is dressed up as another man, beneath a knight's cloak. In other words, two significant codes of male same-sex identification are in operation here. Both costumes, that of the knight and that of the Spanish military, signify male same-sex identification and Egmont's performance of his identification with other men. That Egmont is performing his male-male desire and identification is clear from Clare's reactions. She remarks that today he is noticeably cool and unaffectionate toward her: "Wie seid ihr heute so kalt! Ihr habt mir noch keinen Kuß angeboten" ("How cold you are today! You haven't even offered me a kiss yet," MA, 3:1, 287). At this point Egmont does not reply to her but throws off the first layer of dress: "*[er wirft den Mantel ab und steht in einem prächtigen Kleide da]*" ("*[he throws off the cloak and stands there in a splendid costume]*," MA, 3:1, 288). Clare senses that in this dress Egmont is completely off-limits to her as she exclaims: "Wie prächtig da darf ich euch nicht anrühren" ("So splendid I may not touch you," MA, 3:1, 288). Such a splendid costume underscores Egmont's distance from Clare and their consequent inability to engage in the kind of embraces, kisses, and touching that they might ordinarily enjoy. All that is left to Clare is the spectacle: "Der Sammet ist gar zu herrlich, und die Passement-Arbeit! und das Gestickte . . . Man weiß nicht wo man anfangen soll" ("The velvet is so splendid, and the passementerie and the embroidery. One doesn't know where one should begin," MA, 3:1, 288). Like the two men before her, Clare admires the beauty of Egmont's dress. But they, in contrast, also expressed their admiration for Egmont's body and for Egmont himself. In Clare's case, the usual intimacy with Egmont is subverted by his dressing as another man. Indeed, Egmont's final passionate injunction to Clare—"Sieh dich nur satt" ("Look yourself full," MA, 3:1, 288)—would appear more appropriately addressed to the two men who observed him earlier or to Ferdinand, who clearly lives only to see Egmont. Or perhaps, given the semiotics of these passages, Egmont's visual performance might be better understood as an injunction to the male members of the theater audience. Certainly any man, like Ferdinand, whose greatest desire is to *see* Egmont would welcome the opportunity to see himself (to identify himself in Egmont) to his fullest satisfaction.

With this in mind, I would like to turn to Goethe's *Wilhelm Meisters Lehrjahre*, where we find another overt and complicated literary treatment of male costuming and same-sex identity formation.[12] From the start Wilhelm is obsessed with clothing and dressing up. He glorifies the life of the actor and specifically the "Kleider, Rüstungen und Waffen" ("costumes, armor, and weapons," MA, 5, 58) various characters don. Much attention is devoted to the clothing worn by the women Wilhelm falls in love with, to Mignon's dressing up as a boy (MA, 5, 205), to Wilhelm's Hamlet costume (MA, 5, 321), to his masquerade as the count (MA, 5, 188–89), and to the attire of numerous cross-dressed women. The Baroness, for example, loves to disguise herself "und kam, um die Gesellschaft zu überraschen, bald als Bauernmädchen, bald als Page, bald als Jägerbursche zum Vorschein" ("and always came to surprise everyone as a peasant girl, or a page, or a huntsman," MA, 5, 186). Wilhelm, on the other hand, fetishizes Mariane's male attire (see also MacLeod, 397): "Wie oft ist mirs geschehen, daß ich abwesend von ihr, in Gedanken an sie verloren, ein Buch, ein Kleid oder sonst etwas berührte, und glaubte ihre Hand zu fühlen, so ganz war ich mit ihrer Gegenwart umkleidet" ("How often it occurred that being away from her and lost in thoughts of her, I touched a book or some garment or something else, and thought it was her hand, so absorbed I was in her presence," MA, 5, 72). In fact, clothes are the first sign of sexual identity for Wilhelm. He attempts to read them in his first encounter with Mignon, trying to decide her sex. Initially he is attracted to her (and specifically her clothes) as he thinks she is a boy:

> Ein kurzes seidnes Westchen mit geschlitzten spanischen Ärmeln, knappe, lange Beinkleider mit Puffen standen dem Kinde gar artig. Lange schwarze Haare waren in Locken und Zöpfen um den Kopf gekräuselt und gewunden. Er sah die Gestalt mit Verwunderung an, und konnte nicht mit sich einig werden, ob er sie für einen Knaben oder für ein Mädchen erklären sollte. Doch entschied er sich bald für das letzte . . ." (MA, 5, 90).

> A short silk little vest with cut Spanish sleeves, tight, long pants with puffs looked good on the child. Long black hair in curls and tresses curled and wound around its head. He looked at the figure in wonder,

and could not determine whether he should declare it a boy or a girl. But, in fact, he soon decided on the latter . . .

Wilhelm's first encounter with Mignon accentuates the significance of clothing as a signifier of sexual difference. But, as he experiences it, Mignon's cross-dressing as a boy is confusing. He must determine whether she is a boy or a girl and ultimately declares her a girl despite her boy's clothes. And, finally, it is clear throughout his encounters with Mignon that her attraction for Wilhelm is to a large extent contingent upon the fact that she is wearing boy's clothes.[13]

From the clothing of others, Wilhelm turns his attention to his own clothing: "Er fing nun an über seine Kleidung zu nachzudenken. Er fand, daß ein Westchen, über das man im Notfall einen kurzen Mantel würfe, für einen Wanderer eine sehr angenehme Tracht sei" ("He now began to think about his clothes. He found that a little vest, over which one could if necessary throw a short coat, was a very suitable outfit for a wanderer," MA, 5, 208). In fact, costuming is so important in *Wilhelm Meisters Lehrjahre* that when Felix and Mignon barely escape death by fire, Wilhelm struggles to keep his attention on them and "nicht an die Kleider und was er sonst verloren haben konnte . . ." ("not on the clothes and what else he might have lost," MA, 5, 332).

Dressing up is an obsession that Wilhelm traces back to his youth and his early love of theater. He and his friends were constantly disguising themselves as hunters, soldiers and knights: "Einen Teil meiner jungen Gesellen sah ich nun wohlgerüstet, die übrigen wurden nach und nach, doch geringer, ausstaffiert, und es kam ein stattliches Korps zusammen. Wir marschierten in Höfen und Gärten, schlugen uns brav auf die Schilde und auf die Köpfe . . ." ("I saw some of my young comrades now well armed, the rest were gradually, though less elaborately, equipped, and soon a respectable army came together. We marched in courtyards and gardens, hitting each other on our shields and heads . . . ," MA, 5, 26). As in several of Goethe's literary works, he describes here the early socialization and bonding of boys masquerading as knights. It is this sport, according to Wilhelm, that is inextricably joined to his reading of early novels and his keen interest in *Ritterideen* (ideas of knighthood). Knights, knighthood, and knightly escapades function as ciphers for male-male bonding. Such heroes are the models emulated by boys who grow up to desire and to identify with men who desire men. Historical, literary, and dramatic men provide the heroic templates for the social/sexual development of male-desiring men. In Wilhelm's case, Torquato Tasso's *Jerusalem Delivered* becomes his most favored work and one whose scenes he repeats constantly to himself. In particular, Wilhelm stresses the importance of the literary models Tasso's poem presents to him: "Ich wollte Tancreden und Reinalden spielen, und fand dazu zwei Rüstungen ganz bereit, die ich schon gefertigt hatte" ("I wanted to play Tancred and Rinaldo and found two suits of armor ready that I had already made," MA, 5, 27). Wilhelm desires to be like the greatest of knights. He adopts them as soldierly models and plays them in a theater of his own making. Here the importance of theatrical literary paradigms for male same-sex identification and the development of male-desiring subjectivities are foregrounded.

Indeed, playing hunters, soldiers, and knights is conjoined in Wilhelm's memory with his love of Tasso's poem. More specifically, he reveals that he was enamored above all by the description in *Jerusalem Delivered* of Clorinda:

> Besonders fesselte mich Chlorinde mit ihrem ganzen Tun und Lassen. Die Mannweiblichkeit, die ruhige Fülle ihres Daseins, taten mehr Wirkung auf den Geist, der sich zu entwickeln anfing, als die gemachten Reize Armidens, ob ich gleich ihren Garten nicht verachtete (MA, 5, 26–27).

> Clorinda, in particular, fascinated me in all that she did. Her masculinity-femininity, the quiet fullness of her being had a stronger effect on my developing spirit than the artificial charms of Armida, although I did not despise her garden either.

Wilhelm is most effected by the masculine-femininity of Clorinda and he rejects the other "garden" (with all its sexual innuendoes) offered by the thoroughly feminine Armida. Clorinda is depicted as particularly seductive because of her "Mannweiblichkeit." She evinces a masculinity that Wilhelm finds compelling. And while it is true, as MacLeod has suggested ("Pedagogy," 413), that Goethe evokes for us a sense of oscillation between subjective masculinity and femininity in describing Clorinda in terms of "Mannweiblichkeit," I would suggest that given the context of masquerading, dressing, and cross-identifying that Wilhelm associates with Clorinda, the term actually functions within this text to concomitantly mask and reveal the male same-sex identification and desire Clorinda encodes.[14]

We must keep in mind that Goethe specifically invokes Tasso's Clorinda, a woman who has "altogether disprized the feminine nature and its usages" (Canto Two, #39, p. 35). Clorinda is, indeed, the knightly man Wilhelm aspires to be: "While yet immature with childish hand she tightened and loosened the bit of a warhorse; she managed spear and sword, and in the *palestra* hardened her limbs and trained them to the racecourse. Through mountain path or forest thereafter she followed the tracks of the fierce lion and bear; she followed the wars . . ." (Canto Two, #40, p. 35). Just like Tancred and Rinaldo, Clorinda carves her victories on the bodies of the men who oppose her in war: "Not far off is Clorinda . . . She thrusts her sword into Berlingher's breast to the heart's core where life is lodged; and that stroke made so full a journey to find it that bloodily it issued from his back. Then she wounds Albin where first our nourishment is taken, and cleaves his face for Gallus" (Canto Nine, #68, p. 203). Wilhelm's fascination with Clorinda underscores his desire for knightly valor and for the masculinity such warriors represent. Clorinda is, indeed, characterized by Arsetes as having relinquished all femininity and womanliness: "You grew, and daring and valorous in arms you overcame your sex, and very nature" (Canto Twelve, #38, p.262).

Armida is conversely the totally feminine woman Wilhelm passes over. She deploys "every feminine art" (Canto Four, #25, p. 74). Her enchanting ways capture Rinaldo, who loses himself in the "mirrors of her limpid eyes" (Canto 16, #20, p. 343) and can only be saved from his plight by two fierce knights who force him to gaze upon himself in a shining shield "in which is mirrored for him what manner of man he is become, and how much adorned with delicate elegance: he breathes forth all perfumed, his hair and mantle wanton; and his sword, he sees his sword, (not to speak of other things)

made effeminate at his side by too much luxury, it is so trimmed
that it seems a useless ornament, not the fierce instrument of war"
(Canto Sixteen, #30, p.345). In both instances the women function in Tasso's poem as objects of desire and mirrors of subjectivity
(they determine what kind of men the men become). In each case
objects of desire and identification collapse into one. Wilhelm desires Clorinda and wants to be like her. She represents the desired
male other/self. Armida represents the female object of desire and
threatens Rinaldo with effeminacy, for he sees her/himself in/as his
(female) object of desire. The secret of the cipher "Clorinda" is that
she really functions as a *he*. Within the constellation of signifiers representing male same-sex identification in the *Lehrjahre*, Wilhelm's
fascination with Clorinda, the fact that he chooses her over Armida,
clearly foregrounds his desire for and identification with other men.[15]

Goethe accentuates in these passages the significant influence
that masquerading literary male models have on the developing male
subject and male same-sex identification. Not only does Wilhelm
foreground the connection between masquerading as male literary
heroes and the emergence of male same-sex desire and identification,
the text itself points out how codes of male same-sex identification
can underlie and emerge in a seemingly normative discourse of male-
female affinities.

In this context Wilhelm's fetishization of clothing in *Wilhelm
Meisters Lehrjahre* acquires new significance. While he does not cross-
dress himself, he is attracted almost exclusively to cross-dressing
women. Wilhelm is less fascinated by the women themselves than by
their masculine costuming. Mariane is a case in point. She is described
from the very beginning of the novel as "das weibliche Offizierchen"
("the little female officier," MA, 5, 9). As a cipher of knighthood and
male heroism Mariane stimulates Wilhelm's desire and identity formation. Accordingly, in his first encounter with her he embraces not
her, but her *uniform*: "Wilhelm trat herein. Mit welcher Lebhaftigkeit
flog sie ihm entgegen! mit welchem Entzücken umschlang er die rote
Uniform! drückte das weiße Atlaswestchen an seine Brust!" ("Wilhelm entered. With what enthusiasm she flew to him! With what
delight he embraced the red uniform and pressed the white satin
vest to his breast," MA, 5, 11; see also MacLeod). Wilhelm does

not celebrate Mariane's sexual ambiguity here, but her uniform that makes her a soldier and that codes her as a male object of identification.[16] Like Clorinda, Mariane symbolizes an underlying male object of sexual desire and identification. And while Wilhelm's attraction to Mariane and Clorinda may well indicate his affinity for both men and women, it is clear throughout these passages that his identification with these women is contingent upon their evocation of tropes of male same-sex desire and identification.

The same cross-dressing trope is repeated when Wilhelm first meets Natalie, the woman he refers to throughout the novel as "the beautiful Amazon." She also signifies the male object that Wilhelm desires and admires, and his attention is fixed immediately on her masculine/male dress: "er glaubte nie etwas edleres noch liebenswürdigeres gesehen zu haben. Ein weiter Mannsüberrock verbarg ihm ihre Gestalt; . . ." ("he thought he had never seen anything more beautiful or noble. A man's loose overcoat concealed her figure from him" MA, 5, 224). While Wilhelm ostensibly desires the beautiful amazon (woman), his attention is turned almost exclusively to her coat. Indeed, he notes that her form is concealed from him, leaving only the man's coat as an object for his desire. Moreover, Wilhelm's sense of his own masculinity, his sensual stimulation, and his comfort exert themselves once Natalie drapes her coat over his reclined body: "Dieser lag, in seinen warmen Überrock gehüllt, ruhig auf der Bahre. Eine elektrische Wärme schien aus der feinen Wolle in seinen Körper überzugehen; genug er fühlte sich in die behaglichste Empfindung versetzt" ("He lay quietly on his bier, wrapped in his warm overcoat. An electric warmth appeared to come from the fine wool to his body and he felt transported to a most comfortable emotional state," MA, 5, 226). The man's coat, dress, and costume transport Wilhelm to the highest state of tranquility and self-satisfaction.

As in his childhood, Wilhelm becomes obsessed with the clothing of the male object with whom he identifies. His desire to dress himself in it dominates his concerns:

> Mit der größten Sorgfalt für dieses Gewand war das lebhafteste
> Verlangen verbunden, sich damit zu bekleiden. Sobald er aufstand,
> warf er es über, und sorgte den ganzen Tag, es möchte durch einen
> Flecken, oder auf sonst eine Weise beschädigt werden (MA, 5, 233).

> He combined the liveliest desire to wear the coat with the greatest
> care for it; and as soon as he rose in the morning, he threw it on, and
> took care not to damage it by getting a spot or some such thing on it.

The coat assures Wilhelm that a vision of male same-sex desire and
identity really did appear before him: "Oft kam ihm die Geschichte
wie ein Traum vor, und er würde sie für ein Märchen gehalten haben,
wenn nicht das Kleid zurück geblieben wäre, das ihm die Gewißheit
der Erscheinung versicherte" ("At times the whole story seemed a
dream to him, and he would have considered it a fairy tale if the coat
had not remained to assure him of the certainty of the appearance,"
MA, 5, 233). The man's coat left to Wilhelm attests to the fleeting appearance of a space for male same-sex desire and identity formation.

Finally, Wilhelm connects the vision of the manly dressed Amazon to his childhood memories of male-male bonding and the dressing codes of male same-sex identification. And as in his youth,
Wilhelm is engaged in a constant reiteration of the male-male affinities he perceives in these events and codes:

> Unaufhörlich rief er sich jene Begebenheit zurück, welche einen
> unauslöschlichen Eindruck auf sein Gemüt gemacht hatte. Er sah
> die schöne Amazone reitend aus den Büschen hervorkommen, sie
> näherte ihm . . . Er sah das umhüllende Kleid von ihren Schultern
> fallen; ihr Gesicht, ihr Gestalt glänzend verschwinden. Alle seine
> Jugendträume knüpften sich an dieses Bild. Er glaubte nunmehr die
> edle heldenmütige Chlorinde mit eignen Augen gesehen zu haben . . .
> (MA, 5, 233).

> Over and over again he replayed the event that left such an inextin-
> guishable impression on him. He saw the beautiful Amazon emerge,
> riding out of the bushes, she approached him . . . He saw the coat fall
> from her shoulders, her face and her figure disappeared in a flash of
> light. All his youthful dreams returned and associated themselves
> with this image. He now thought he had seen the noble, heroic
> Clorinda with his own eyes. . . .

As Natalie relinquishes the man's coat to him, Wilhelm remarks that
her form and her face disappear. All that remains for Wilhelm is the
cloak of his desire and the fantasy of the heroic "man," Clorinda. The
fact that the female form/body disappears in Wilhelm's imagined reiteration of the encounter with Natalie/Clorinda underscores "her"

signification of the knightly/soldierly object of desire and identification that fascinates him. Wilhelm rediscovers the male object of his desire in the fantasy of the beautiful Amazon—in his "own" Clorinda!—in the code of dressing as a man. Wilhelm grasps the code of male same-sex identification evinced in the masquerading of his childhood and in his encounter with the beautiful Amazon and repeats the pleasurable scene ad infinitum in his imagination.[17]

Of course, as we saw in chapter three, Wilhelm eventually asserts his affinity to his beautiful Amazon, Natalie. But now that affinity acquires an additional and critical complexity. Despite the fact that Wilhelm's attraction to Natalie suggests on one level his engagement in a male-female relationship, his affinity for several male interlocutors and his desire for male dress, and his longing to dress as another man (in another man's coat) all accentuate his male same-sex desire and identification. In *Die Lehrjahre*, Natalie and the numerous other cross-dressed women of the novel, cannot be read as simply female objects of desire. Even more importantly, their masculine dress, and particularly their knightly attire, invoke the signs of male same-sex identification that recur throughout Goethe's literary production.

Naming and Identifying with Men Who Desire Men

Remarkably (for eighteenth- and early nineteenth-century texts), the men desiring men in Goethe's works are often major cultural icons. These are not the men excoriated by Fanny Hill in Cleland's novel, or condemned in various eighteenth-century pamphlets (see McCormick, *Secret Sexualities*), or castigated by Kant as being "below humanity." These are men revered by society. They are men who have achieved the greatest pinnacles of success. They are Winckelmanns—the men about whom legends, songs, and literature are produced. The tragedy of *Götz von Berlichingen*, for instance, begins with an injunction to repeat once again the great story of Götz: "Erzähl das noch einmal, von Berlichingen" ("Tell again the story of Berlichingen," MA, 1:1, 549). These are stories, legends, myths of which one never grows weary. Egmont also enjoys the adulation of all of his fellow citizens; they recount stories of all the battles he has won and assert that he has proven that he is, above all, a hero: "Dem Helden von Gravelingen" ("To the hero of Gravelingen," MA, 3:1, 249). All of the provinces revel in his deeds and "Die Augen des Volkes sind alle nach ihm gerichtet und die Herzen hängen an ihm" ("The eyes of all the people are directed to him and their hearts hang on him," MA, 3:1, 257). Even Clare wishes she were a boy, so that she could emulate Egmont: "Wär' ich nur ein Bube, und könnte immer mit ihm gehen, zu Hofe und überall hin!" ("If only I were a boy and could always go with him to court and everywhere!" MA, 3:1, 262–63). Indeed, both Clare's and Brackenburg's songs about going into battle emphasize how fortunate they would be to be a hero like Egmont: "Welch Glück sonder gleichen / Ein Mannsbild zu sein!" ("What a fortune without compare, to be a man!" [literally, the image of a man or male paragon] MA, 3:1, 260). There is no greater fortune than to be a "Mannsbild," and this is precisely what the boys in Goethe's literary works are striving to become: paragons of manhood, that is, men who desire and identify with men.

And, in fact, throughout Goethe's poetic production, men like Götz, Tasso, and Egmont are named, that is, the same-sex desire and identity they embody is, contra Kant, articulated and given a name. Within the constellation of tropes of desire and identification that we have discussed so far, the names of these men function as signifiers of male same-sex desire and identification. The individual name becomes a cipher for the male same-sex desire and identification signified by a Götz or an Egmont. As we recall, Ferdinand initially condensed his articulation of same-sex desire into the emphatic calling out of Egmont's name. Moreover, he insists that Egmont is no stranger to him, for he has known his name since childhood: "Nicht fremd! Du bist mir nicht fremd. Dein Name wars der mir in meiner ersten Jugend gleich einem Stern des Himmels entgegen leuchtete. Wie oft hab ich nach dir gehorcht! gefragt!" ("Not foreign! You are not foreign to me. It was your name in my earliest youth that like a star in the heavens shone toward me. How often I listened for you, and asked about you!" MA, 3:1, 324). Egmont's name, like a star in the heavens, guides Ferdinand in the development of his own desires and identifications. And Lerse remarks that he too had followed Götz's name, and, knowing his name, was knowing Götz:

"Ich kannte euren Namen, und da lernte ich euch kennen" ("I knew your name, and I became acquainted with you," MA, 1:1, 605). As Tasso envisions an entire order of heroes and poets joined in desire and identification, he fixes on one youth and wonders "Wer sagt mir seinen Namen?" ("Who will tell me his name?" MA, 6:1, 687). The yearning to name these men who desire and identify with men reveals their function as cultural/literary signifiers of male same-sex desire and identification.

Their names not only signify their male same-sex desire and identification, but also serve as markers, as signs, for the youth who emulate them. Young boys can repeat those names and in each instance rearticulate and reinforce the desire and identification they share. And these names are now everywhere. As Clare suggests, one cannot not name Egmont: "Wer nennt ihn [den Namen Egmonts] nicht bei jeder Gelegenheit? Wo steht er nicht geschrieben? In diesen Sternen hab' ich oft mit allen seinen Lettern ihn gelesen. Nicht nennen? Was soll das?" ("Who does not name it [Egmont's name] at every opportunity? Where is it not written? I have often read it with all its letters in the stars. Not name it? How can that be?" MA, 3:1, 310–11). And, indeed, is male same-sex desire and identification not clearly legible in the spelling out of so many letters throughout Goethe's oeuvre? It does not matter if those letters are A, B, C, and D (*Die Wahlverwandtschaften*), or W-i-n-c-k-e-l-m-a-n-n, or E-g-m-o-n-t, or T-a-s-s-o, or F-e-r-d-i-n-a-n-d, or G-ö-t-z, or W-i-l-h-e-l-m, or W-e-r-t-h-e-r, each still signifies male same-sex desire and identification. Whereas for Kant the naming of same-sex desire was unimaginable, throughout his work Goethe underscores how unthinkable and impossible it would be not to name male same-sex desire and identity. Here we discover that these are names that cannot be suppressed, that are written everywhere, and that must (as Ferdinand insists) be given poetic form. And it is precisely in this context that we should recall Goethe's Winckelmannian project: to spell together the letters of the word that is "Winckelmann." Indeed, that is exactly what Goethe does throughout his poetic production. Sometimes the word/name takes on the form of a Tasso, a Werther, or a Ferdinand, but its meaning is, nonetheless, essentially the same. These are the names that spell male same-sex desire and identification. In Goethe's work names evoke entire stories. Names are codes with legends, myths, and stories condensed within them. These names represent entire lives, ways of living (such as Winckelmann's *Lebensweise*), and they bring these male desiring and identified men to life. These stories are about men who love and identify with other men. They are men who identify themselves as men desiring men. We find here not just a simple "terminological shift" from sodomite to molly or pederast, for instance, but a naming that signifies a vast literary project consisting of multiple stories linked together by common signifiers of male same-sex desire and identity. Goethe's poetic production puts these names, spellings, and stories into poetic discourse and into literary circulation.

A COMMUNITY OF SAME-SEX IDENTIFIED AND DESIRING MEN: TASSO

Throughout Goethe's literary production a constellation of tropes—boyhood memories, reflections of same-sex identifications, performances and emulations of male heroes, dressing as men, and the naming of specific and often knightly heroes—signify male same-sex desire and identity formation. But, in addition to this network of signifiers, Goethe's works also highlight the significant role of literature, of literary heroes, of literary and lyric identifications in the facilitation of male same-sex identity formations and desires. As we know, Wilhelm in the *Lehrjahre* identifies almost exclusively with literary models. In his own mind, he becomes David and Goliath, and the drama he produces about them becomes an integral part of his self-identification:

> Ich ward darüber in meinen Gedanken selbst zum David und Goliath. In allen Winkeln des Bodens, der Ställe, unter allerlei Umständen, studierte ich das Stück ganz in mich hinein, ergriff alle Rollen, und lernte sie auswendig, nur daß ich mich meist an den Platz der Haupthelden zu setzen pflegte . . . (MA, 5, 21).

> In my thoughts I myself became David and Goliath. In all corners of the ground, the stalls, under all kinds of conditions I studied the drama completely into my self, grasped all the roles, and learned them

by heart—only that I usually tended to put myself in the role of the
major heroes . . .

In the same manner, he identifies with Tancred and Rinaldo in Tasso's
Jerusalem Delivered: "Ganz konnte ich das Gedicht nicht lesen, es
waren aber Stellen die ich auswendig wußte, deren Bilder mich um-
schwebten . . ." ("I could not read the whole poem, but there were
passages I knew by heart, whose images floated around me," MA,
5, 26). In Goethe's poetic work, literary and lyric representations of
heroes have a particularly strong effect on the developing male subject's identity formations and desires. Indeed, one of the Harfner's
songs so affects Wilhelm that he can barely keep himself from rushing to embrace him:

> Er trug das Lied mit so viel Leben und Wahrheit vor, daß es schien, als
> hätte er es in diesem Augenblicke und bei diesem Anlasse gedichtet.
> Wilhelm enthielt sich kaum, ihm um den Hals zu fallen, nur die
> Furcht, ein lautes Gelächter zu erregen, zog ihn auf seinen Stuhl
> zurück . . . (MA, 5, 126).

> He performed the song with so much life and truth, that it appeared
> as if he had created in it this moment and on this occasion. Wilhelm
> could scarcely restrain himself from falling upon his neck, only the
> fear of evoking loud laughter pulled him back onto his chair . . .

The power of the literary/lyric representation almost pulls Wilhelm
out of his chair and into the Harfner's arms. Indeed, the Harfner's
representation of *life* and *truth* trigger Wilhelm's same-sex desire.
Once again, Goethe connects life, self, and desire metaphorically.
And, in this context, we can also think of Tasso and Antonio and
their embrace under the force of Tasso's final metaphor of male-male
desire. As Elpenor suggests in an eponymous drama, such narratives,
such metaphors, incite the male subject's desire to desire and to
emulate the male model immortalized:

> Wenn ich vor dir am Feuer saß und du erzähltest von Thaten alter
> Zeit, du einen Guten rühmtest, des Edlen Wert erhobst; da glüht es
> mir durch Mark und Adern, ich rief in meinem Innersten: O wär' ich
> der, von dem sie spricht! (MA, 2:1, 363)

> When I sat before you at the fire and you recounted the deeds of
> old times, and praised a good man, and highlighted the worth of a

noble man, then it glowed in my marrow and veins. I called out in my
innermost self—if only I were he, about whom she speaks!

For Elpenor, the poetic representation effects his *innermost self* and
compels him to *identify* with the male hero depicted. He ultimately
wishes he were the hero.

And it is precisely the poet, and, indeed the poet's mouth, that
is the source of the metaphors of male same-sex identification that
compel young boys to emulate male models. Pylades summarizes
this succinctly in *Iphigenia:*

> Wir möchten jede Tat
> So groß gleich tun als wie sie wächst und wird,
> Wenn Jahre lang durch Länder und Geschlechter
> Der Mund der Dichter sie vermehrend wälzt.
> Er klingt so schön was unsre Väter taten,
> Wenn es in stillen Abendschatten ruhend
> Der Jüngling mit dem Ton der Harfe schlüft;
> Und was wir tun, ist, wie es ihnen war . . .
> Wir eilen immer ihren Schatten nach,
> Der göttergleich in einer weiten Ferne
> Der Berge Haupt auf goldenen Wolken krönt.
>
> (MA, 3:1, 179)

> We would like to replicate each deed as greatly as it grows and be-
> comes after it has rolled and turned and multiplied through lands and
> races in the mouths of poets. It sounds so beautiful what our fathers
> did. When reposing in the evening shadows, the youth laps [slurps]
> them in with the tones of the harp. And what we do, is, what it was
> for them . . . We always scurry after their shadows . . . that crown the
> mountain top on golden clouds like gods in the distance.

From the mouths of the poet great deeds and heroes issue, roll, turn,
and multiply. At the same time, the poet becomes the quintessential male interlocutor and object of male-male desire. His mouth
is the erotically charged site from which male figures of emulation
pour forth. The male listener responds by emulating and playing the
part of those heroes: "Und was wir tun, ist, wie es ihnen war . . . wir
eilen immer ihren Schatten nach . . ." ("And what we do, is, what it
was for them . . . we always scurry after their shadows . . ."). In the
male poet's mouth the deeds of a multitude of forefathers sound so

beautiful that the young male listener's mouth laps and slurps them in eagerly to the sound of the harp. Recall the Harfner whose music practically propelled Wilhelm out of his chair and into his arms. And remember Wilhelm's obsession with the fisher boy's mouth as the site of erotic exchange between the two boys who desired one another and needed to lend that desire metaphoric form. And then there was Lothario's mouth—that source from which Wilhelm's own words flowed back to him, but in a more precise linguistic and conceptual form. And finally there is Antonio's manly voice and its guiding effect on the poet Tasso, and Tasso's voice, the male poet's voice, as the site in which metaphors of male-male desire acquired poetic form. All of these mouths (poetic and heroic) join in Goethe's literary production to signify male same-sex desire and identity formation.

And it is precisely poetic and heroic male mouths that search each other out throughout Goethe's literary production. In *Torquato Tasso* we find the most comprehensive summation of the poetic interlocution between poets and heroes. The Princess underscores how heroes and poets live for one another (remember Ferdinand living Egmont) and search one another out: "Wie Held und Dichter für einander leben,/Wie Held und Dichter sich einander suchen..." ("How hero and poet live for one another, how hero and poet search for one another..." MA, 6:1, 693). In fact, the poet perceives the lyric signifiers of male-male desire and same-sex identification as ones poured into him by/through the heroes/knights who inspire him:

> O könnt ich sagen, wie ich lebhaft fühle,
> Daß ich von euch nur habe, was ich bringe!
> Der tatenlose Jüngling-nahm er wohl
> Die Dichtung aus sich selbst? Die kluge Leitung
> Des raschen Krieges—hat er die ersonnen?
> Die Kunst der Waffen, die ein jeder Held
> An dem bescheidenen Tage kräftig zeigt,
> Des Feldherrn Klugheit und der Ritter Mut,
> Und wie sich List und Wachsamkeit bekämpft,
> Hast du mir nicht, o kluger, tapfrer Fürst,
> Das alles eingeflößt, als wärst du
> Mein Genius, der eine Freude fände

Sein hohes, unerreichbar hohes Wesen
Durch einen Sterblichen zu offenbaren?
  (*Tasso*, 6:1, 684)

> If only I could say, how vividly I feel that what I bring I have solely
> from you. The youth without achievements—could he have drawn
> poetry out of himself? The bold direction of swift, chaotic war—
> did he envision that? The art of weaponry so mightily displayed by
> every hero on every modest day, the cunning of the captain, and the
> knight's courage, and how cunning and vigilance are subdued, did
> you not, O wise and brave Prince, inspire all of these things in me
> [literally, pour them into me]? —as if you were my Genius who finds
> his pleasure in revealing his high, his unattainably high being through
> a mere mortal man.

All of the poet's "Ritterideen" flow from the heroes who infuse him
with their essence/life, and it is the hero's very being that the poet
returns to him in the form of poetry. Not only heroic deeds but
heroic words "die sichern Worte des erfahrnen Mannes" ("the certain
words of the experienced man," MA, 6:1, 693) flow from the hero
into Tasso and back out again as metaphor. And at this moment Tasso
can assert that what fills his soul, what moves him most deeply, are
the stories and lives of past heroes. Antonio, of course, is Tasso's
central focus, and it is their mouths that ultimately sustain the male
same-sex desire and identification that Wilhelm lost upon the lips of
the dead fisher boy. It is, in essence, their mutually desiring selves, as
they live each other, that flows back and forth between the mouths
of the poet and his heroic model.

And yet Tasso does not envision the lyric flow of *word* and *self*
between poets and heroes as an isolated or purely individual event.
Same-sex identity formations do not simply form between two men
who desire and identify with one another. Throughout Goethe's
work community is foregrounded as an essential foundation for
same-sex identity formation. Such formations occur within a society
of men who share the same desires. According to Tasso, male-male
discourses of desire and identification reiterate themselves throughout history and poetry (and certainly also in Goethe's own aesthetic
production). Tasso fantasizes about a community of men—poets
and heroes—who join together in their male same-sex desire and
identifications. He imagines himself in that community:

Dort will ich einsam wandeln, dort erinnert
Kein Auge mich ans unverdiente Glück.
Und zeigt mir ungefähr ein klarer Brunnen
In seinem reinen Spiegel einen Mann.
Der wunderbar bekränzt im Widerschein
Des Himmels zwischen Bäumen, zwischen Felsen
Nachdenken ruht: so scheint es mir, ich sehe
Elisium auf dieser Zauberfläche
Gebildet. Still bedenk' ich mich und frage,
Wer mag der Abgeschiedne sein? Der Jüngling
Aus der vergangnen Zeit? So schön bekränzt?
Wer sagt mir seinen Namen? Sein Verdienst?
Ich warte lang und denke: Käme doch
Ein andrer und noch einer, sich zu ihm
In freundlichem Gespräche zu gesellen!
O säh ich die Heroen, die Poeten
Der alten Zeit um diesen Quell versammelt!
O säh' ich hier sie immer unzertrennlich,
Wie sie im Leben fest verbunden waren!
So bindet der Magnet durch seine Kraft
Das Eisen mit dem Eisen fest zusammen
Wie gleiches Streben Helden und Dichter bindet.
Homer vergaß sich selbst, sein ganzes Leben
War der Betrachtung zweier Männer heilig,
Und Alexander in Elisium
Eilt den Achill und Homer zu suchen.
O, daß ich gegenwärtig wäre, sie,
Die größten Seelen nun vereint zu sehen!

    (MA, 6:1, 687)

There I will wander alone, no eye will remind me of my undeserved
fortune. And if by chance a clear fountain shows me there a man
in its pure mirror, resting in thought and crowned wondrously in
the reflection of sky between the trees, between the rocks, then it
appears to me as if I see Elysium formed upon that magic surface.
I will ponder quietly and ask: who may this departed one be? The
youth of ancient times? So beautifully crowned? Who will tell me
his name? His accomplishments? I will wait long and think: if only
another one and yet another one would come and join him in friendly
conversation! O to see the heroes and the poets of ancient times
gathered around this fountain [literally, source or mouth]. O to see
them here forever inseparable from one another as they were united
in life! In just the same way the magnet joins iron things with iron
things fast together—as like striving binds heroes and poets. Homer

forgot himself, and his whole life was dedicated to the thought of two men, and Alexander in Elysium hurries to search out Achilles and Homer. O if only I could be there to see those greatest of souls united together.

Not surprisingly, Tasso's vision of a unified male community begins with his observation of a young male figure mirrored in a fountain. The beautiful young poet/hero bedecked with a wreath is, of course, both Tasso (who is presented with a wreath in the opening scenes of the play) and the male object of his desire. It is upon this mirroring surface that Tasso sees Elysium formed and reflected before his very eyes. Tasso's rhetorical question about the identity of this youth—his longing to hear him named—points to the crux of the Goethean-Winckelmannian literary project: to name the male-male desire and the same-sex identification that these mirrored and mirroring boys represent. Simultaneously, we must not forget that Tasso, as a poet, is also invoking the image of a beautiful, young, male body reflected upon a watery surface. He reproduces for his audience, for his listeners, or for his readers the poetic and alluring simulacrum of male same-sex desire and identification. And he begs us to reflect upon the question: Who is mirrored in the fountain? Tasso? Another young hero? Or the reader/listener as they themselves perceive the image reflected back upon them from/through/across the surface of Tasso's poetic vision?

But Tasso does not just invoke the trope of male same-sex desire and identification by now so familiar to us. In his imagination Tasso calls forth an entire community of men. One by one he envisions poets and heroes of old gathering around this *Quelle* (source, mouth), gathering around this watery reflection, and gathering around Tasso—and more specifically Tasso's mouth—as he recites his lyric vision. It is precisely, around this metaphor of male-male desire, at the site of the desiring male mouth that the affinities between all of these men are confirmed. Tasso sees these heroes and poets "fast bound to one another," "eternally inseparable," and tied to one another with the force of a magnet. And, indeed, Tasso's words work like a magnet (a metaphor of affinities), fusing these men together in a common pursuit ("ein gleiches Streben"). Like Homer, Alexander, and Tasso (and Goethe in relation to Winckelmann), these men devote their lives to the observation and love of great men. And, as Tasso voices his own desire to join these men in their community, he reiterates the desire he hopes to pass on to the listener or reader: "If only I were there to see all of these great souls bound together." Tasso seems to want to say "If only I were one of them . . ." and in a sense, he does say it, to the extent that he is, as a poet, engaged in the process of creating images of himself, of giving himself metaphoric expression in the form of all of the poets and heroes he calls forth.

Tasso's utopic fantasy is one of a community of poets, heroes, and, one might add, art historians (like Winckelmann) bound to one another by their affinities and identity formations—living, observing, talking to, and desiring one another. Indeed, the first thing these men do upon appearing around the fountain is to begin a conversation, to reiterate the flow of words that invoked their presence in the first place. And it is only after this male-male discourse is set into motion that Tasso observes how strong their affinitive bonds have become. And it is precisely this conversation that engenders Tasso's string of observations and metaphors describing the magnetic affinities that fuse these men together. Tasso's mouth is, in other words, set into motion by the preceding male-male verbal exchanges. And as the source of the poetic formation of their desires and identifications, his poetry calls and recalls these men back to one another. Tasso's poetry serves as the linguistic mirror in which past and future communities of men can merge and in which they can discover their affinities and same-sex identifications flowing back to them in newer and clearer poetic forms. The literary mirror serves as the focal point around which men who desire men can form larger social bonds and identifications.

Curiously, Tasso initially fears losing himself in this community of male same-sex identification, but he reasserts ultimately the literary process of self-formation at the end of the play in which he quite literally finds himself in Antonio's arms and as an author of metaphors of male-male desire. But, even more significantly, Tasso adds himself to a long line of poets and heroes who people the Elysium he fashions in and through his poetry. Like Winckelmann, he joins a vast community of men who desire and identify with other men. Moreover, Tasso joins a community of self-fashioning, male-desiring men within Goethe's poetic oeuvre. Tasso not only embraces Antonio, he embraces all of those heroes and poets who people Goethe's aesthetic production: Ferdinand, Egmont, Götz, Wilhelm, Weislingen, Lothario, the fisher boy, Eduard, the Captain, and Jarno. Indeed, the implication seems to be that Elysium would emerge once the poetic heroes of Goethe's works affirmed their affinity to all the poets and heroes of the past and future. And Goethe's poetic legacy incites the reader/audience to fashion itself in the image of a Tasso—to form its identity within this community of men, within a complex network of men desiring men, forming same-sex identifications, and speaking its desire and community.

Throughout Goethe's literary and aesthetic oeuvre we have discovered a specific community of men in which men desire men and through which they come to form male same-sex identifications. The recurrent trope of representation or paradigms of male same-sex identification surfaces consistently and systematically in work after work. Boyhood stories of visual cathexes and emulations determine the development of men who desire and identify with men. The poetic process facilitates the creation of both poetry (male-male desire) and a male community of literary heroes and poets (male same-sex identification). These discursive realities join together with a number of codings, especially of knights, knightly ideas, emulations, mirroring, names and naming, and manly dress. All of these codings work together with clearer and clearer expressions of male same-sex desire (as we saw in chapter three) throughout Goethe's writings to encode and articulate the literary convergence of senses of self, same-sex identification, and male-male desire. Literature and/or literary and lyric representations acquire a special function in Goethe's work. As an infinite mirroring process, literature and its poetic codings, its figuring of men who desire men, and its establishment of male same-sex identities establish a network, a *Symbolik* that characterizes Goethe's literary production. The implications of Goethe's *Tasso* is that Goethe's work should be placed within a tradition of literary mirrorings and codings of male same-sex desire and identification that extends from the ancients to the present and beyond. Moreover, Goethe's representations of male same-sex identity and identity formation are strikingly modern in their understanding of the significance of the symbolic construction of desire, identity, and community. Goethe intuits how all of these formulations are intertwined, interdependent, and necessary for the self-fashioning of the same-sex identified and desiring man. And, finally, Goethe approaches a type of identity politics through the radical assertion of the innateness and naturalness of same-sex desire, identity, and community.

MORITZ AND GOETHEAN METAPHORS OF SAME-SEX IDENTITY FORMATION

One of the most interesting questions is, of course, whether or not Goethe's poetic codings of male same-sex desire and identity acquired a life outside of his own work. While it would be beyond the purview of this study to try to outline all of the possible reiterations of Goethe's literary figuring of male-male desire and same-sex identity, it does make sense, perhaps, to look at one specific example: Karl Philipp Moritz and his novel *Anton Reiser*. I have chosen Moritz's *Anton Reiser* for several reasons. Goethe and Moritz were involved in rather lively and extensive interactions during their stay in Italy between 1786 and 1788. During this period Moritz was busy completing *Anton Reiser*, and Goethe was busy working on *Wilhelm Meister, Tasso, Iphigenia,* and *Egmont*. In fact, Moritz's *Anton Reiser* appeared in four parts. The first in 1785, the second and third in 1786, and the fourth in 1790. Goethe, for his part, was working principally on *Tasso, Iphigenia,* and *Egmont,* but he was also gathering materials and conceptualizing *Wilhelm Meister*. It is clear from Goethe's letters to Frau von Stein during this period that he was reading *Anton Reiser* and that it was of great benefit to him in his conceptualization of *Wilhelm Meister*. Indeed, scholarship generally insists that Goethe rethought and reconceptualized his *Wilhelm Meister* against the negative model of the theater-obsessed young hero of *Anton Reiser*. And yet at the same time we must keep in mind that Moritz had not yet completed the fourth part of his novel before meeting with Goethe in Italy between 1786 and 1788. The question of who influenced whom in their respective conceptualizations of their literary works becomes more complex when we take into consideration the fact that Moritz and Goethe were also deeply involved in major aesthetic discussions. In fact, Goethe would later claim that Moritz's essay *Über die bildende Nachahmung des Schönen* (1788) was actually generated by their conversations and was largely his contribution to a theory of Classical aesthetics. The convergence of thought and formulation manifest in Moritz's and Goethe's works of this period makes it virtually impossible to decide whether the influence flowed in one direction or the other or if it was not simply mutual. Nonetheless, though we cannot decide in larger terms whether *Anton Reiser* influenced *Wilhelm Meister* more than *Wilhelm Meister* influenced *Anton Reiser*, we can say that there are certain poetic codings and tropes in *Anton Reiser* that Moritz could only have derived from Goethe's literary production. Indeed, many of the poetic representations that we have traced back to Goethe's early works such as *Werther* and *Götz von Berlichingen* reappear throughout *Anton Reiser*. In fact, we must keep in mind that Goethe was not just working on *Wilhelm Meister* and Moritz was not just working on *Anton Reiser* and they were not just reading each other's work, but that Goethe was also working on *Tasso* and *Egmont*, two plays, as we have seen, that put male same-sex identification and desire at center stage. In this context I would be so bold as to suggest that Goethe and Moritz were operating as two male interlocutors developing an aesthetic system and in particular an aesthetic system that foregrounds male-male desire and same-sex identification.[18] And for this reason, it is not at all surprising that Moritz's *Anton Reiser* invokes an understanding of Goethe's larger literary project, that is, it is also involved in the poetic coding of male-male desire and same-sex identification and specifically foregrounds and emphasizes the role of the literary process in the facilitation of that aim. With these things in mind, we can turn our attention directly to the textual evidence of Moritz's *Anton Reiser*.

Just like Goethe's literary heroes and much in the manner of *Wilhelm Meister*, Moritz's *Anton Reiser* recounts its title character's fascination with and emulation of various literary heroes. As we might expect, this reading induces Anton Reiser to act out the scenes he has read:

Mit einer Art von wehmütiger Freude las er nun, wenn Helden fielen, es schmerzte ihn zwar, aber doch deuchte ihm, sie mußten fallen. Dies mochte auch wohl einen großen Einfluß auf seine kindischen Spiele haben. Ein Fleck voll hochgewachsener Nesseln oder Disteln waren ihm so viele feindliche Köpfe, unter denen er manchmal grausam wütete, und sie mit seinem Stabe einen nach dem andern herunter hieb (Moritz, AR, 51).

With a manner of melancholy pleasure he now read how heroes fell and it certainly caused him pain, but it also occurred to him that they had to fall. This must have also had a great influence on his childish games. A patch of land full of highly grown nestles and thorns were so many enemy heads to him—amongst which he sometimes raged cruelly—and with his sword he mowed them down one after another.

In addition to reiterating the kinds of performances that were characteristic of the young men in Goethe's literary works, *Anton Reiser* also invokes the trope of names and naming that so systematically accompanied those performances in Goethe's oeuvre:

Wenn er auf der Wiese ging, so machte er eine Scheidung, und ließ in seinen Gedanken zwei Heere gelber oder weiser Blumen gegeneinander anrücken. Den größten unter ihnen gab er Namen von seinen Helden, und eine benannte er auch wohl von sich selber. Dann stellte er eine Art von blinden Fatum vor, und mit zugemachten Augen hieb er mit seinem Stabe, wohin er traf (Moritz, AR, 52).

When he went to the meadow, he made a division, and in his thoughts he allowed two armies of yellow or white flowers to advance upon each other. He gave the names of his heroes to the largest of them, and one of them he actually named after himself. And then he imagined to himself a kind of blind fate and with his eyes shut he thrashed with his sword whatever he hit.

Significantly, Anton Reiser does not just name his heroes. He also names one of those heroes after himself, underscoring the kinds of identifications and emulations he is beginning to form. And it is precisely this desire to identify himself in and as his literary heroes that compels Anton to begin theatrical productions:

Als er von P[yrmont] wieder nach Hause gereist war, schnitzte er sich alle Helden aus dem Telemach von Papier, bemalte sie nach den

Kupferstichen mit Helm und Panzer, und ließ sie einige Tage lang in Schlachtordnung stehen, bis er endlich ihr Schicksal entschied, und mit grausamen Messerhieben unter ihnen wütete, diesem den Helm, jenen den Schädel zerspaltete, und rund um sich her nichts als Tod und Verderben sahe (Moritz, AR, 52).

When he had traveled from Pyrmont back to his home, he cut all of the heroes of Telemach out of paper, painted them with helmets and armor, and let them stand for days in battle readiness until he finally decided their fate, and with cruel slashes of a knife he raged amongst them, splitting the helmet of one and the skull of another, and saw all around himself nothing but death and destruction.

Just like the young boys in Goethe's literary works, Anton is fascinated by and drawn to military heroes and knights. These are the figures he feels compelled to emulate and to enact. Later in the novel we will discover that precisely these kinds of identifications explain Anton's fascination with theater and his own role in it as an actor:

Und dann konnte er [Anton] auf dem Theater alles sein, wozu er in der wirklichen Welt nie Gelegenheit hatte—und was er doch so oft zu sein wünschte—großmütig, wohltätig, edel, standhaft, über alles Demütigende und Erniedrigende erhaben—wie schmachtete er, diese Empfindungen, die ihm so natürlich zu sein schienen, und die er doch stets entbehren mußte, nun einmal durch ein kurzes täuschendes Spiel der Phantasie in sich wirklich zu machen. Das war es ohngefähr, was ihm die Idee vom Theater schon damals so reizend machte (Moritz, AR, 173–74).

And then he [Anton] could be everything in the theater that he did not have an opportunity to be in the real world—and those things that he so often wished to be—generous, kind, noble, steadfast, raised above everything that is humiliating and demoralizing. How he longed now once through a short deceptive play of fantasy to evoke those sentiments in himself that appeared to him to be so natural and with which he always had to go without. That was what made the idea of theater so enticing to him even at that early stage.

As he sees it, on stage he can be all of those things that he cannot be in the real world. The play allows for at least the illusion that his fantasies might be real. Indeed, throughout the novel it becomes clear that Anton understands acting not in terms of representing characters, but in terms of identifying with and being the characters portrayed. We recall here that Wilhelm identified himself with several literary characters, including David and Goliath and Hamlet. In a similar manner, Anton identifies himself with an entire string of male literary heroes, including Philotas, Ugolino, Hamlet, Macbeth, Lear, and Guelfo, and in each case Anton completely identifies himself with the literary figures he would like to portray.

Goethe emphasized the significance of the literary process and the creation of metaphor in the establishment of male same-sex identification and the solidification of male-male desire. But Moritz shifts attention in *Anton Reiser* to the function of literature as a vehicle of exchange between men who desire and identify with one another. Each and every one of Anton's relationships with men is described in terms of the literary works they read together. So, for example, with his friend Philipp Reiser, Anton reads Shakespeare, Kleist, and Goethe. With his friend Neries he reads Klopstock and Zachariäs. With his friend Winter, Anton enjoys many evenings of Fielding's *Tom Jones*. Finally, in the case of his friend Iffland, we are told that it is the love of theater that binds the two men together: "Jetzt waren sie beide fast unzertrennlich, und Tag und Nacht beisammen" ("Now the two of them were almost completely inseparable—and were together day and night," Moritz, AR, 296). Each of Anton's relationships with men revolves around shared literary readings and performances, and it is precisely their literary exchanges that incite their affinities for one another. Anton expresses this critical link between male-male desire and literary readings or exchanges quite distinctly in the description of his relationship with Neries:

> Nach und nach aber bildete sich bei ihm eine ordentliche Liebe und Anhänglichkeit an den jungen N[eries], welche durch dessen wahre Freundschaft für Reisern immer vermehrt wurde, so daß sie sich immer mehr, auch in ihren Torheiten, einander näherten, und von ihrer Melancholie und Empfindsamkeit sich wechselweise einander mitteilten. Dies geschahe nun vorzüglich auf ihren einsamen Spaziergängen, wo sie nur gar zu oft zwischen sich und der Natur eine Szene veranstalteten, indem sie etwa bei Sonnenuntergang die Jünger von Emmaus aus dem Klopstock lasen, oder an einem trüben Tage, Zachariäs Schöpfung der Hölle, u.s.w. (Moritz, AR, 377).

> Slowly but surely a strong love and attachment to the young Neries
> grew in him. These sentiments grew even more and more because of
> Neries's true friendship for Reiser, such that they became ever closer
> to each other (and even in their crazy acts) and told each other more
> and more about their melancholy and sensitivity. This occurred pre-
> dominantly on their walks alone, during which they often acted out
> a scene between themselves and nature in which they (approximately
> at sundown) read out of Klopstock's *The Disciple of Emmaus* or on a
> dismal day from Zachariäs's *Creation of Hell*, etc.

Anton connects his growing love and inclination for Neries specifically to their solitary wanderings and performances of scenes from
literary works that they are reading such as Klopstock and Zachariäs.
For Anton it is the flow of literature between men that cements their
bonds.

In describing his relationship to Philipp Reiser, Anton provides
us with a virtual anatomy of male-male desire and specifically its
formation during literary exchanges between men. Initially Anton
and Philipp are drawn to one another through their mutual readings of Shakespeare, particularly of *Hamlet*: "der Shakespear knüpfte
zwischen Philipp Reisern und Anton Reisern das lose Band der
Freundschaft fester" ("Shakespeare connected fast the loose bond of
friendship between Philipp Reiser and Anton Reiser," Moritz, AR,
226). Immediately following the revelation about Shakespeare's facilitation of their affinities, Moritz clues us in to Anton's pressing desire to share all of his feelings and thoughts with a male interlocutor:

> Anton Reiser bedurfte jemanden, an den er alle seine Gedanken und
> Empfindungen richten konnte, und auf wen sollte wohl eher seine
> Wahl gefallen sein, als auf denjenigen, der einmal seinen angebeteten
> Shakespear mit durchempfunden hatte! (Moritz, AR, 226)

> Anton Reiser needed someone to whom he could direct all of his
> thoughts and feelings and upon who else then should his choice fall
> than upon that person with whom he had experienced the Shake-
> speare he so adulated!

Anton longs to express his innermost feelings to the man with
whom he has shared the most intimate Shakespearian moments.
Like Werther and Winckelmann before him, he is compelled to write
down his thoughts, giving his male same-sex desire poetic form. The

literary mode that Anton chooses is that of a diary, specifically a diary that is structured in the form of letters to his friend Philipp. Indeed, Anton's principal intention in writing his diary letters to Philipp is to lend his feelings and thoughts linguistic form, or, as he phrases it: to clothe his feelings and thoughts in words (" . . . er suchte . . . was er empfunden hatte, und noch empfand in Worte einzukleiden," AR, 229). Indeed, his compulsion to "clothe" his thoughts in words is connected directly to his desire to express his sentiments to his male friend: " . . . er fing an, ein unbeschreibliches Vergnügen daran zu empfinden, Gedanken, die er für sich gedacht hatte, nun in anpassende Worte einzukleiden, um sie seinem Freunde mitteilen zu können" (" . . . he began to feel an indescribable pleasure in clothing ideas he thought on his own in fitting words in order to relate them to his friend," AR, 226). Just like Ferdinand in Goethe's *Egmont*, Anton expresses here his yearning to express his male-male desire in linguistic form. And, indeed, this meticulous anatomy of Anton's desire culminates in a letter to Philipp in which he expresses explicitly and precisely his love for his friend:

> Als plötzlich ein Jüngling vor mir stand—den Freund verkündigte sein Blick—Empfindung sprach sein sanftes Auge—schleunig wollt' ich entfliehen—aber er faßte so vertraulich meine Hand—und ich blieb stehn—er umarmte mich, ich ihn—unsre Seelen flossen zusammen—Und um uns ward's Elysium (Moritz, AR, 230).

> As suddenly a young man stood before me—his glance announced a friend—his soft eye spoke of sentimentality—and I wanted to immediately flee—but he took my hand so trustingly into his own— and I remained there—he embraced me, I him—our souls flowed together—and all around us was Elysium.

Here, for the first time, Anton expresses openly his feelings for Philipp. He describes the paradise he experiences when they embrace one another and their souls flow together. Significantly, his final words, "um uns wards Elysium" are quoted from Klopstock's ode *Rosenband* (1753). Anton's invocation of his literary predecessor, Klopstock, is important for several reasons. First and foremost we must keep in mind that Klopstock was famous in his era for his new poetic expressions of emotions. By quoting Klopstock, Anton alludes implicitly to his own project, that is, creating new poetic codings of male same-sex desire. Anton not only quotes Klopstock, he also calls up the figure of Klopstock. Like Tasso before him, Anton also attempts to lend form to his desire through the invocation of a literary poet/hero worthy of emulating. Finally, Anton's quotation of Klopstock is significant to the extent that it underscores the function of literature to incite new articulations of desire and to facilitate erotic bonds between men. And, in this context, the literary quotation is of tremendous importance. It is, of course, literary reiterations that flow back and forth between Anton Reiser and his various male objects of desire. His own expression of desire for Philipp, his account of how Philipp took his hand, how they embraced, and how their souls flowed together, culminates in and finds its fullest expression through Klopstock's poetry. Or, perhaps more precisely, Anton finds a way to express his desire for Philipp through his quotation of Klopstock's poetry. And indeed, it is such reiterations and quotations of literary predecessors that manifest themselves throughout Moritz's novel. In fact, the layers of quotation are often so dense it is virtually impossible to determine where one quotation leaves off and another begins. Of course, we must keep in mind here that Moritz is also quoting Goethe's *Werther* novel, in which a famous evocation of Klopstock occurs. While in Goethe's novel Charlotte refers to Werther as Klopstock—indicating that he is a man of emotion and sentimental self-expression—Moritz clearly cites Klopstock within the context of desire expressed between men. Goethe and Klopstock were venerated during their age for introducing new sentimental languages to German letters. These passages in Moritz's novel link Goethe and Werther and Klopstock to a discourse of sentimentality at exactly that point in which it expresses male same-sex desire.

Moreover, the quotation does not stop there. Anton's description of his feelings for Philipp Reiser, for instance, in which he recounts how Philipp takes his hands, how they fall into each other's arms, how their souls flow together, and his final invocation of Klopstock's poetry, could easily be read as a condensed quotation of the final scenes of Goethe's *Torquato Tasso*. We recall that in Goethe's play, Antonio takes Tasso's hand, Tasso falls into Antonio's arms, and, at that precise moment, Tasso creates the metaphor, the poetry that is their male same-sex desire. And, of course, Moritz's quotation of Goethe does not stop there. Throughout these passages Moritz has invoked paradigms of male-male desire, and the poetic coding of that desire, which as we have seen are thoroughly characteristic of Goethe's literary production. With these quotations in mind, we can now turn our attention to Anton's obsession throughout the novel with Goethe's literary work, *Die Leiden des jungen Werthers*.

Of all the literary exchanges and reiterations in Moritz's novel, the most significant one occurs when Philipp Reiser gives Anton a copy of Goethe's *Die Leiden des jungen Werthers*. Anton is immediately fascinated by the Goethean text. He carries it with him wherever he goes and he is constantly reading it. And although Goethe's text recounts the story of a love between a man and a woman, Anton Reiser is able to translate the language of the *Werther* text to his own relationship with Philipp Reiser and, in fact, it is precisely Goethe's novel that evokes Anton's poetic feelings for Philipp:

> Er bekam sie [*Die Leiden*] im Anfange des Sommers durch Philipp Reisern in die Hände, und von der Zeit an, blieben sie seine beständige Lektüre, und kamen nicht aus seiner Tasche.—Alle die Empfindungen, die er an dem trüben Nachmittage auf seinem einsamen Spaziergange gehabt hatte, und welche das Gedicht an Philipp Reisern veranlaßten, wurden wieder lebhaft in seiner Seele (Moritz, AR, 244).

> He received it [*Die Leiden*] at the beginning of the summer from Philipp Reiser and from that time forward it remained his constant reading and never came out of his pocket. —All of the sentiments that he had felt on those dismal afternoons during his solitary wanderings and that occasioned the poem to Philipp Reiser were revived in his soul.

Tellingly, the only thing that Anton Reiser does not seem to understand about Werther is his suffering, that is, his love for Lotte:

> Was aber nun der eigentlichen Leiden Werthers anbetraf, so hatte er dafür keinen rechten Sinn . . . weil es ihm unmöglich fiel, sich selbst jemals, als ein Gegenstand der Liebe von einem Frauenzimmer zu denken (Moritz, AR, 245).

> But in regard to the actual sufferings of Werther, for that he had no real understanding, because it seemed to him impossible even at that time to think of himself as an object of a woman's love.

Except for his love for a woman, Reiser identifies completely with Werther: "Kurz, Reiser glaubte sich mit allen seinen Gedanken und Empfindungen, bis auf den Punkt der Liebe, im Werther wieder-zufinden." ("In short, Reiser believed that he could find all of his thoughts and sentiments except for that point about love in Werther," Moritz, AR, 246).[19] Although many readers would assert that the focus of Goethe's *Werther* is precisely Werther's obsessive love for Lotte, Anton's fascination with the text lies elsewhere. Anton clearly identifies with Werther and sees Werther's expressive personality as a reflection of his own: "Was Wunder also, daß seine ganze Seele nach einer Lektüre hing, die ihm, sooft er sie kostete, sich selber wieder-gab!" ("It was no wonder that his whole soul hung on the reading that gave him as often as he enjoyed it back to himself!" Moritz, AR, 247). Even more significantly, Werther's language, that is, his expression of his desires, becomes Anton's mode of articulation to the extent that Werther's speech is so thoroughly integrated into his own that he can no longer distinguish one from the other:

> . . . indem ihm die Wendungen und selbst die Gedanken in diesem Schriftsteller durch die öftere Wiederholung so geläufig wurden, daß er sie oft für seine eigenen hielt, und noch verschiedene Jahre nachher bei den Aufsätzen, die er entwarf, mit Reminiszenzien aus dem Werther zu kämpfen hatte, welches der Fall bei mehrern jungen Schriftstellern gewesen ist, die sich seit der Zeit gebildet haben (Moritz, AR, 246–47).

> . . . to the extent that the expressions and the thoughts in this writer [Goethe] became so common with him through repetition that he often held them for his own. And even many years later while writing essays he had to fight with reminiscences out of Werther—that was the case for many young authors who trained themselves after that time.

Anton's quotation of Goethe's *Werther* becomes so complete that even years later he has to fight against the rearticulation of Werther's language when trying to create his own modes of expression. Even more importantly, it is precisely Werther's speech that Anton returns to Philipp Reiser. In other words, the literary quotation that flows between these two men, allowing them to articulate and formulate their desire, is a Goethean one. The process of literary exchange

comes full circle as Anton writes to Philipp Reiser in what he refers
to as the tone of Werther's letters: "Dies Schreiben war denn ganz
im Tone der Wertherschen Briefe" ("This writing was completely
in the tone of Werther's letters," AR, 392). In Anton's hand, the
Werther tone gets transformed or translated into an expression of
male-male desire. We recall that in Goethe's novel, Werther addressed
his letters to a male interlocutor, but that they articulated his desire
for a woman, Lotte. In Anton's case his letter captures the tone of
Werther's letters, but now these expressions of love are addressed
directly to another man:

> Jetzt, mein Lieber! bin ich in einer Lage, welche ich mir nicht reizen-
> der wünschen könnte. Ich blicke aus meinem kleinen Fenster über die
> weite Flur hinaus, sehe ganz in der Ferne eine Reihe Bäumchen auf
> einem kleinen Hügel hervorragen, und denke an Dich, mein Lieber
> usw (Moritz, AR, 392).

> Now my beloved! I am now in a situation that I could not wish to be
> more alluring. I look out of my little window over the wide meadow
> outside and see in the far distance a row of trees shooting up from a
> small hill and I think about you, my Love.

As we might expect, the expression of male same-sex desire in and
through Werther's language inspired Anton to create poetry: "Und
nun war auf einmal, der beinahe zur Ruhe gebrachte Dichtungstrieb
bei Reisern wieder angefacht" ("And now suddenly, Reiser's almost
completely sleeping poetic desire was rekindled," Moritz, AR, 392).

Not only does Moritz's text invoke the tropes of male-male desire and literary figuration that are so familiar to us from Goethe's
texts, he also employs Goethe's text as his central literary trope.
In other words, Moritz does not just use the same patterns of poetic codings to articulate male-male desire and same-sex identification, but allows Goethe's work itself to signify those processes.
Moritz clearly understood the Goethean project, that is, he understood Goethe's incitements to the poetic coding of male same-sex
desire and identification, and he deployed Goethe's own works in
order to replicate and further that process.

At least literarily, it is thoroughly evident that Moritz and Goethe
shared a language of male same-sex desire and same-sex identification, which Moritz clearly connects to Goethe's literary production

and in particular to *Werther.* In his poetry of male same-sex desire and identification Goethe's new formulations function as the quintessential language of the expression and connection of sentiments and same-sex identifications between men. In essence, Moritz reads Goethe as Goethe reads Winckelmann. In each case the next male desiring and identified poet spells together the poetic/aesthetic discourse of his predecessor lending it even greater and clearer contours and foregrounding its function to express male-male desires and same-sex identifications. If Goethe translated Winckelmann into new poetic forms, that is, put him and his desires and identifications into a literary discourse, then Moritz spelled together Goethe and foregrounded the function of Goethe's poetry in cementing relationships between men. In other words, we begin to see a line of connection forming between cultural poets and heroes not unlike the one that Tasso envisions in Goethe's play. The literary fantasy of a community of men who desire and identify with men begins to acquire a real, actual existence.

In this context Moritz's suggestion in *Anton Reiser* that many young authors of his day emulated and struggled with their own production of a language reminiscent of Werther's acquires additional significance (AR, 246–47). It begs the question: To what extent do these new poetic formulations that Moritz and Goethe clearly associate with male-male desire and same-sex identification represent a much larger cultural phenomenon? We can begin by wondering whether similar injunctions to new metaphoric formations of male-male desire and same-sex identification are in operation and serve to shape what has traditionally been referred to as the late eighteenth-century Werther craze. In other words, in the context of the Goethe-Moritz project outlined here, we must reevaluate the implications of the eighteenth-century European fascination with Goethe's Werther. What is the possible significance lying behind the eighteenth-century obsession with Werther and dressing up in his clothes? Why was just about everyone doing it? And beyond the general significance of dressing up as Werther and the identification with him as a new sentimental subject, could it be that some participants in the Werther craze were dressing as this other man because they desired and identified with men desiring men? And, perhaps more precisely, to what extent might a community of men have adopted the language of Goethe's *Werther* in order to inaugurate new representations of male same-sex desire and identity—an action in accord with Goethe's literary project? Indeed, it is clear from Goethe's own correspondence that he himself employed what he referred to as Werther's "babbling" in his letters to other men:

> O Bruder! Nennbaare aber unendliche Gefuehle durchwuehlen mich—und wie ich dich liebe fuehlst du da ich unter alten Linden in dem Augenblick dein Gedencke. Das Erbaermliche Liegen im Staube, Friz! Und das Winden der Wuerme. Ich schwoere dir bei meinem Herzen! Wenn das nicht Kindergelall und Gerassel ist der Werther und all das Gezeug! (an Friedrich Leopold Graf zu Stolberg, October 26, 1775)

> O brother! Expressible but infinite feelings burrow through me and how much I love you, Fritz, you feel as I think of you under the old lindens at this moment. Pitiful lying in the dust, Fritz! And the squirming of worms. I swear to you by my heart! If that isn't the childlike babbling and rattling of Werther and all that stuff!

While traditional scholarship may have assumed that Goethe is referring here to and deploying a general language of sentimentality, we can now read it with the underlying implications of Werther's language of desire in mind. We can see the same-sex desire evoked in the Werther passages in the *Briefe aus der Schweiz* and Anton Reiser's appropriation of this Goethean-Winckelmannian language in terms of its explicit illustration of the poetic fashioning of male same-sex desire and identification. Goethe's letter provides further evidence of the emergence of this "Werther language" outside of the realm of purely literary representation.

It certainly lies outside of the purview of this study to track down further manifestations and/or quotations of Goethe's poetic discourse of male same-sex identification and desire in German Classicism. The links, however, that we have drawn between Winckelmann, Goethe, and Moritz illustrate an aesthetic project of incredible depth and compass. Winckelmann first foregrounded the struggle to articulate same-sex affinities that Goethe then recognized as his own literary project. We find throughout Goethe's work not only representations of a pervasive desire to create new poetic formulations of male same-sex desire and identification, but also integral structural manifestations and explications throughout his dramatic and prose works of the function of the male interlocutor. These were combined with subtle poetic codings (including costuming, naming, knightly ideas, etc.). Moritz, finally, deploys Goethe's new poetic formulations of same-sex desire and identity, underscoring Goethe's own literary production as a coding of male same-sex identity and desire. These poetic ventures constitute a vast aesthetic project through which and in which the desiring male subject recognizes himself, formulates himself, and binds himself to other men of like sentiment in a community of men. Even if this genealogy of same-sex desire and identity formation could only be traced thus far from Winckelmann to Goethe to Moritz, given the preeminence and influence of these figures on new poetic formulations in the realms of literary scholarship, art history, aesthetics, and in the history of same-sex activities and expressions, the implications are quite significant. And here we have discovered for the first time in the eighteenth and early nineteenth centuries a highly self-conscious and sophisticated project of male same-sex identification, desire, and self-fashioning. For after all, we cannot forget that what is manifest here in literary representation is an attempt to spell together the male same-sex desire and identification that was the real man, Winckelmann. And it is critically significant that Goethe and Moritz are compelled to give the male same-sex desiring self a literary space for self-expression. It is there in the late eighteenth and early nineteenth century in those new literary formations and not in legal discourse, not in medical discourse, and not in psychoanalytic discourse that a particular male subject—one who desires other men—begins to speak and identify himself. And that is, as we know from Goethe's *Torquato Tasso*, poetry.

Epilogue: From Tasso to Tadzio

Men Desiring Men has traced a new language of male same-sex desire and identity from its inception (Winckelmann), through its development (Goethe), to its reiteration and extension (Moritz) in German Classical aesthetics. In shifting our attention away from descriptions of same-sex activity (and specifically of sodomy) and towards literary representations of same-sex desire and the self-fashioning of men who desire men, we have been able to map out a vast and detailed "Symbolik"—a new poetic language of male same-sex identity and desire. Moreover, what we have discovered is a consciously constructed aesthetic project that traces the manner in which same-sex desire and identity acquired poetic and linguistic form. Goethe, Winckelmann, and Moritz demonstrate clearly that the eighteenth and early nineteenth centuries did concern themselves with the processes of the self-fashioning of same-sex desire and identity formation. The poetry that they created was the result of a highly self-conscious longing to develop their own language of same-sex desire, identity, and community. These discoveries suggest a need to reevaluate the writings of eighteenth- and early nineteenth-century writers within the context of their own discourses of same-sex desire and identity and in consideration of the broader fascination of the era with literary representations of self, desire, self-fashioning, and community.

Winckelmann's struggle to express and name his own same-sex desire and identity in his letters to Berg became the template for Goethe's attempts to spell Winckelmann in his encomium. But even more significantly, Winckelmann's struggles to fashion himself in and through his letters provided the basic outline for a new poetic language of male same-sex desire, identity, and community in the discourse we call German Classical aesthetics. Goethe's literary production manifests his conscious attempts to expand, further, and translate the word that he perceived was Winckelmann. His poetry provides a genealogy of this new language, demonstrating how various literary figures attempt to express their own same-sex identity and desire through poetry and how specific metaphoric representations of a new self became bolder and more precise throughout his literary production. Indeed, in Goethe's novels and dramas we find confirmations and reiterations of Tasso's vision of the poet as the source (mouth) of new namings, of self-expressions, and of the poetic bonding of men who identify with and desire men. Moritz furthered and translated Goethe's language of same-sex desire and identity into his own language of male-male desire and same-sex identification in *Anton Reiser*. In particular, he appropriated the language of desire expressed by Werther in Goethe's famous novel, applying it specifically to relationships between men. Moreover, Moritz evokes Goethe's "Symbolik"—of which his new Werther language is a crucial part—as the quintessential trope of male same-sex desire and identity. Like Goethe's literary figures, Moritz's are in search of male interlocutors to whom and through whom they can express their male same-sex desire. In each case a predecessor's language is modified, developed, and translated into a new and often more precise language of same-sex desire, identity, and community. Goethe reads and translates "Winckelmann" and Moritz in turn reads and translates "Goethe." Indeed, in accord with Tasso's vision of the bonding of heroes and poets (men desiring men) across time, Winckelmann, Goethe, and Moritz suggest a line of translations that might continue on indefinitely as other authors appropriate and create discourses of male same-sex desire and identity.

Indeed, one wonders where such a line of poets, of men desiring men, might lead to or end. In Tasso's conception the string of poets would extend back to the ancients and infinitely forward into the future. But beyond Moritz, did German and European or non-European poets influenced by Winckelmann and Goethe recognize, appropriate, and extend this language of male same-sex desire and identity? Did any other poets gather, so to speak, around the watery, self-reflecting, mirroring source we call German Classical discourse and in so doing join in the process of naming the desire that Oscar Wilde would later claim dare not speak its name?

While it lies outside the purview of this study to trace all of the possible reiterations of the Winckelmann-Goethe-Moritz language of same-sex identity and desire, one seems almost compelled to wonder if the young boy, Tadzio, in Thomas Mann's *Tod in Venedig* (1912) is not a metaphoric reiteration of Tasso. Tadzio, we recall, is the beautiful boy desired by the poet Aschenbach. One wonders if Tadzio is a "respelling," a new metaphorization, of Tasso and those other fictional men desiring men who get articulated in German Classical aesthetics? Is "Tadzio" one of the names reflected back to Tasso as he gazes into the watery Quelle ("mouth," "source")—that place where men desiring men from all ages join in conversation and identification with one another? In other words, is Tadzio the symbolic progeny of that line of men who desire men and who get spelled out in German Classicism, including Winckelmann and then Götz, Egmont, Ferdinand, Werther, Wilhelm, Anton, and finally Tasso?

We recall, of course, that Mann originally conceived of *Tod in Venedig* as a literary representation of the aged Goethe and his obsession with the little girl in Marienbad who he was absolutely determined to marry (July 4, 1920, *Briefe*, vol. 1, 177). Moreover, during the writing of *Tod in Venedig* Mann recounted reading *Die Wahlverwandtschaften* five times (July 4, 1920, *Briefe*, vol. 1, 176). At some point during this process, Mann shifted the principle desire depicted in his novella from that of an aged man for a little girl to that of an old man for a young boy. He explained that he wanted to intensify the effect of the novella by shifting to a "forbidden love" (July 4, 1920, *Briefe*, vol. 1, 177). He further clarified that his fascination with the *Wahlverwandtschaften* had to do with its style and the balance it achieved between "Sinnlichkeit und Sittlichkeit" ("sensuality and morality"). But given the fundamental and structural accentuation of same-sex desire in *Die Wahlverwandtschaften,* we could surmise that Mann recognized at some level the implications of Goethe's famous text for the expression of same-sex desire. Moreover, in an interview with Pesti Napló, Mann recounted that during the time he was preparing to write *Tod in Venedig,* he refamiliarized himself with Goethe's works in general (see Angermeier, 13). Given Mann's concentration on Goethe during this period, one might also speculate that he ultimately discovered a German Classical language of male same-sex desire and identity that in turn inspired his own writing. At any rate, we can say definitively that Mann was a well-versed student of Goethe and within that context we can certainly wonder about the possible connections between "Tadzio" and "Tasso."

Tadzio is, of course, not a poet, but he certainly seems reminiscent of the beautiful boys Tasso, Werther, and Wilhelm envision reflected upon watery surfaces. In fact, we recall that in Werther's and Tasso's visions of beautiful boys, the poet's own self-image merges with that of the boys they view (in metaphors of self, love, and self-love) and in that instant they feel compelled to name both the boys they see and their own same-sex desire. Tasso, for instance, immediately queries: "Who will tell me his name?" With this in mind, it seems hardly accidental that Thomas Mann's novella of male same-sex desire depicts Aschenbach's first encounter with Tadzio in Venice. Not only do they first come together in a watery location,[1] but Aschenbach is immediately consumed by the task of trying to decipher Tadzio's name. Because he only hears it uttered from a distance, he spends considerable time trying to decide if the name is "Adgio," "Adgiu," "Tadzio," or "Tadziu":

> Zu erraten, zu erforschen, welcher Name es sei, der ungefähr »Adgio« lautete, schien dem ernsten Mann eine angemessene vollkommen ausfüllende Aufgabe und Beschäftigung. Und mit Hilfe einiger polnischer Erinnerungen stellte er fest, daß »Tadzio« gemeint sein müsse, die Abkürzung von »Tadeusz« und im Anrufe »Tadziu« lautend (*Tod in Venedig,* 39).

To guess, to discover which name it was that sounded approximately like "Adgio," appeared to the serious man to be a reasonable and fully fulfilling task and occupation. And with the assistance of a few

Polish memories he determined that "Tadzio" must have been meant, the shortened form of "Tadeusz," which sounded when called like "Tadziu."

Just like Goethe's poets, Aschenbach is engaged immediately in the process of spelling and naming his young male object of desire. And, indeed, in precisely those moments in which Aschenbach struggles to name Tadzio, Tadzio goes bathing:

> Tadzio badete. Aschenbach, der ihn aus den Augen verloren hatte, entdeckte seinen Kopf, seinen Arm, mit dem er rudernd ausholte, weit draußen im Meer; denn das Meer mochte flach sein bis weit hinaus. Aber schon schien man besorgt um ihn, schon riefen Frauenstimmen nach ihm von den Hütten, stießen wiederum diesen Namen aus, der den Strand beinahe wie eine Losung beherrschte und, mit seinen weichen Mitlauten, seinem vollgezogenen u-Ruf am Ende, etwas zugleich Süßes und Wildes hatte: »Tadziu! Tadziu!« Er kehrte zurück, er lief, das widerstrebende Wasser mit den Beinen zu Schaum schlagend, zurückgeworfenen Kopfes durch die Flut; und zu sehen, wie die lebendige Gestalt, vormännlich hold und herb, mit triefenden Locken und schön wie ein Gott, herkommend aus den Tiefen von Himmel und Meer, dem Elemente entstieg und entrann: dieser Anblick gab mythische Vorstellungen ein, er war wie Dicterkunde von anfänglichen Zeiten, vom Ursprung der Form und von der Geburt der Götter (*Tod in Venedig*, 39).

> Tadzio bathed. Aschenbach, who had lost him from view, discovered his head and his arm which he stretched out like an oar, far out in the sea; for the sea was shallow for quite a ways. But one was already concerned about him, the voices of women called to him from the huts, and repeated this name that practically possessed the beach like a rallying-cry and which had with its softened consonants and it's drawn-out "u" sound something simultaneously sweet and wild: "Tadzio!" "Tadzio!" He turned back, he ran, churning the waves into foam with his legs, his head flung high. And to see the living form emerge out of the depths of heaven and sea, emerging from and outrunning the element, virginally pure and austere, with dripping locks and beautiful as a god. This vision evoked mythical presentations, it was like poetic tidings from primal times, from the origin of form, and from the birth of the gods.

Like Werther and Wilhelm before him, Aschenbach observes the beautiful body of his male object of desire as he bathes. And in accord with the German Classical paradigm, Aschenbach's adulation of this young male body acquires its most direct expression as he emerges from the water. Tadzio appears to him to be as beautiful as a god. Indeed, like Werther and Tasso, Aschenbach isolates this "Anblick," this visual moment, as one of mythical and metaphoric significance. Tadzio, the sight of him, and the desire he represents and evokes are all *Dichterkunde* ("poetic tidings and proclamations") come down from ancient times, from the very source of form, and the birth of gods. Like Tasso, Aschenbach envisions a poetic genealogy that reaches from the beginning of time to himself and beyond.

Given the many metaphorical connections and reiterations of the poetic language of Winckelmann, Moritz, and Goethe that resurface in Mann's *Tod in Venedig*, it is not at all surprising that Aschenbach ultimately expresses a conception of elective affinities reminiscent of that invoked throughout Goethe's literary production:

> Irgendeine Beziehung und Bekanntschaft mußte sich notwendig aus-bilden zwischen Aschenbach und dem jungen Tadzio, und mit durch-dringender Freude konnte der Ältere feststellen, daß Teilnahme und Aufmerksamkeit nicht völlig unerwidert blieben (*Tod in Venedig*, 56).

> Some sort of relationship and acquaintance necessarily had to form between Aschenbach and the young Tadzio, and with intense joy the old man could determine that his sympathy and attentiveness did not remain fully unanswered.

An attention, an interest, an attraction, and a fascination inevitably arise between Tadzio and Aschenbach as they observe each other on the seashore. As we have seen throughout Goethe's work, this unavoidable rise of same-sex affinities between men is ultimately determined through their reciprocal exchanges of looks of desire:

> Aschenbach erwartete täglich Tadzios Auftreten, und zuweilen tat er, als sei er beschäftigt, wenn es sich vollzog, und ließ den Schönen scheinbar unbeachtet vorübergehen. Zuweilen aber auch blickte er auf, und ihre Blicke trafen sich. Sie waren beide tiefernst, wenn das geschah. In der gebildeten und würdevollen Miene des Älteren verriet nichts eine innere Bewegung; aber in Tadzios Augen war ein Forschen, ein nachdenkliches Fragen, in seinen Gang kam ein Zögern, er blickte zu Boden, er blickte lieblich wieder auf, und wenn er vorüber war, so schien ein Etwas in seiner Haltung auszudrücken,

daß nur Erziehung ihn hinderte, sich umzuwenden (*Tod in Venedig,* 56–57).

> Aschenbach waited daily for Tadzio to appear and at times he acted when it occurred as if he were preoccupied and let the beautiful boy pass apparently unnoticed. But at times he also looked up and their glances met. They were both deeply serious when that happened. The cultured and dignified mien of the elder man disclosed nothing about his inner emotions, but in Tadzio's eyes there was a query, a reflective question, he hesitated in his gait, he looked to the ground, he glanced up again charmingly, and when he was past, it appeared that something in his bearing suggested that only good upbringing hindered him from turning around.

As Thomas Mann describes it, the "innere Bewegung"—the desire—both Aschenbach and Tadzio feel for each other as their glances meet finds outer expression only in Tadzio's physical reactions.

Throughout *Tod in Venedig* the expression and impact of visual reciprocities increase in intensity. In fact, the desire figured by the visual exchanges in the novella acquires its boldest expression in a thoroughly Goethean moment. As Tadzio smiles at Aschenbach for the first time, Aschenbach sees him as Narcissus gazing at his own reflection:

> Freude, Überraschung, Bewunderung mochten sich offen darin malen, als sein Blick dem des Vermißten (Tadzio) begegnete—und in dieser Sekunde geschah es, daß Tadzio lächelte: ihn anlächelte, sprechend, vertraut, liebreizend und unverholen, mit Lippen, die sich im Lächeln erst langsam öffneten. Es war das Lächeln des Narziß, der sich über das spiegelnde Wasser neigt, jenes tiefe, bezauberte, hingezogene Lächeln, mit dem er nach dem Widerscheine der eigenen Schönheit die Arme streckt,—ein ganz wenig verzerrtes Lächeln, verzerrt von der Aussichtslosigkeit seines Trachtens, die holden Lippen seines Schattens zu küssen . . . (*Tod in Venedig,* 57–58).

> Joy, surprise, admiration might have painted themselves on his face as his glance met the missed Tadzio—and in this second Tadzio smiled: he smiled at him, openly, trustingly, a speaking, winning smile with slowly parting lips. It was the smile of Narcissus bent over the mirroring water—a smile profound, infatuating, lingering as he stretched out his arms to embrace his own beauty in the reflection—a slightly

pursed smile—a smile pursed by the futility of his intention to kiss the cold lips of his shadow . . .

Tadzio's speaking smile, his slowly parting lips are reminiscent of the proliferation of male mouths (those sources of the expression of male same-sex desire) throughout Goethe's poetic production. And, as in Goethe's poetry, here the alluring male mouth is inextricably connected to the mirroring and verbalizing of male same-sex desire. As Tadzio offers his smile to Aschenbach, Aschenbach sees it as that of Narcissus bent over the mirroring pool. Like Tasso, Werther, and Wilhelm before him, Aschenbach envisions his object of desire in a reflection upon a pool that mirrors both the man desired and the man desiring him. Tadzio and Aschenbach merge in a mutual reflection/identification. Recall that Tadzio is looking at Aschenbach and Aschenbach sees him looking at him in a kind of narcissistic mirroring. In other words, while Tadzio looks at Aschenbach, Aschenbach superimposes on them the image of Narcissus looking into a pool. This has the effect of positioning Tadzio as Narcissus and Aschenbach as the pool into which he gazes. And so, Aschenbach is the shadow/reflection (of himself) that Tadzio strives to kiss. Self, love, and self-love converge in this metaphor of Narcissus/Tadzio kissing himself/Aschenbach/the shadow. As Aschenbach sees Tadzio's smile and mouth, as it appears to speak to him, he invokes metaphoric representations of men desiring men in order to formulate the desire that Tadzio's smile and glance signify for him. In this most intense moment of recognition Aschenbach is able to articulate precisely and clearly his own same-sex sentiments. He finally blurts out "Ich liebe dich" ("I love you," *Tod in Venedig*, 58). Here Aschenbach proves himself capable of expressing what Ferdinand could not in *Egmont*. While Ferdinand's increasingly direct expression of his desire for Egmont ultimately ended in a provocative elision, Aschenbach openly states his desire. As in the German Classical metaphorization of male same-sex desire, here visual reciprocity and figures of male mouths join and incite a new (at least for Aschenbach) formulation and/or expression of men desiring men.

Indeed, strikingly enough, as Aschenbach observes the beautiful body of Tadzio, he feels compelled (like Werther and Tasso) not just to speak his desire, but to create literature—to produce, in addition, a poetic language of male same-sex desire. And as he strives to capture Tadzio in a few pages of prose, Aschenbach becomes aware for the first time that "Eros is in the word." He remarks that desire and language are intricately connected, that the source of his poetry is his desire for Tadzio, and, in fact, that this desire is an inherently discursive and poetic phenomenon:

> Nie hatte er die Lust des Wortes süßer empfunden, nie so gewußt, daß Eros im Worte sei, wie während der gefährlich köstlichen Stunden, in denen er, an seinem rohen Tische unter dem Schattentuch, im Angesicht des Idols und die Musik seiner Stimme im Ohr, nach Tadzios Schönheit seine kleine Abhandlung,—jene anderthalb Seiten erlesener Prosa formte, deren Lauterkeit, Adel und schwingende Gefühlsspannung binnen kurzem die Bewunderung vieler erregen sollte. Es ist sicher gut, daß die Welt nur das schöne Werk, nicht auch seine Ursprünge, nicht seine Entstehungsbedingungen kennt; denn die Kenntnis der Quellen, aus denen dem Künstler Eingebung floß, würde sie oftmals verwirren, abschrecken und so die Wirkungen des Vortrefflichen aufheben (*Tod in Venedig*, 52–53).

> Never had he felt the pleasure of the word so sweetly, never had he known so well that Eros is in the word, than during the dangerously precious hours in which he sat at his crude table under an awning with his idol in view and the music of his voice in his ear. There forming his little essay in accord with Tadzio's beauty—that page and a half of premier prose that was so honest, so noble, and so emotionally moving that it would soon excite the wonder of many. It is certainly good that the world knows only the beautiful work and not also its origins and not the conditions of its inception; for the knowledge of the sources from which the artist's inspiration flowed would often confuse and repulse them and thereby undo the effects of excellence.

Interestingly enough, Mann's suggestion in this passage about the unknown sources of beautiful literature and the fact that readers do not recognize the same-sex desire that underlies it might easily be read as a comment about Goethe's, Winckelmann's, and Moritz's aesthetic production and traditional receptions of German Classical discourse. Simultaneously, it could be read as a commentary *avant la lettre* on the reception of *Tod in Venedig*. German scholarship has often "overlooked" or "downplayed" the same-sex desire that constitutes the foundation of these poetic productions. And indeed, as Mann conceives it, if the world does not recognize the same-sex desire that incites poetic production, it can enjoy beautiful poetry without becoming confused and scandalized. Nonetheless, as in German Classical poetry, in Aschenbach's prose it is evident that same-sex desire and word, self and metaphor, are inextricably intertwined. Mann certainly reiterates and furthers the German Classical notion that expressing male same-sex desire and identity is a poetic act. The same-sex desiring self, while in and of language, also fashions itself in language and particularly in poetry. Like Goethe, Winckelmann, and Moritz before him, Mann recognized that Eros is in the word.

Following Winckelmann and Goethe (and Tasso, Werther, and Ferdinand), Mann and Aschenbach strive to capture male same-sex desire in poetry. They illustrate how male same-sex desire, that is, Eros, is both the genesis of and the principal foundation of the word. Moreover, we know desire and ourselves as desiring beings in and through words. In this context, Mann's fascination with the *Wahlverwandtschaften* is thoroughly understandable. *Die Wahlverwandtschaften*, as we recall, is centrally concerned with the depiction of desire as metaphor and as determined by the circular process of metaphoricity. The desiring self is in and of language and metaphor. Moreover, Eduard and the Captain strove to "put themselves," that is, their same-sex desires, into poetic formulation. Mann clearly recognized this process. In his essay "Zu Goethes Wahlverwandtschaften" ("On Goethe's *Elective Affinities*") he highlights in particular the tremendous "Kenntnis des Menschenherzens" ("knowledge of the human heart," "Zu Goethes," p. 638) displayed in the novel. Indeed, he claims that throughout German literature one finds no clearer "Mischung von Eros und Logos" ("mixture of Eros and Logos," "Zu Goethes," p. 639). And it is specifically this knowledge of the human heart and its convergence with Eros and Logos that Mann emphasizes in conjunction with *Tod in Venedig*. In a letter to Carl Maria Weber (July 4, 1920, *Briefe*, 176–80), Mann alludes persistently to the significance of the convergence of Eros and Logos, desire and word, life and spirit in *Tod in Venedig*. In a manner strikingly similar to the *Wahlverwandtschaften*, *Tod in Venedig* depicts the articulation of male same-sex desire and identity and underscores the sense that poetry is a product of desire, and, even more specifically, that metaphors are generated by a fundamental desire between men. Indeed, Mann describes the polarity he perceives between Eros and Logos, desire and word, life and spirit as being not only quintessential for poetic production, but also as an often essentially masculine or male venture. Throughout his letter to Weber, Mann accentuates that desire and word, and the polarity between them, are fundamental. In fact, this polarity is not essentially connected, as one might expect, to divisions between genders. That is, "das Männliche braucht nicht notwendig vom Weiblichen angezogen zu werden" ("the masculine is not necessarily attracted by the feminine," *Briefe,* 178). As Goethe perceived of desire as desire in *Die Wahlverwandtschaften,* here Mann insists that the tension between Eros and Logos is a fundamental structure of desire and articulation that does not require a primal attraction and/or distinction between masculine/male and feminine/female. In fact, among men desiring men in the German aesthetic tradition, no assumption of a necessary attraction to feminized men is manifest. According to Mann, men who desired other men, such as Michelangelo, Frederick the Great, Winckelmann, August von Platen, and Stefan George are not feminine men and are not attracted to feminine men (*Briefe,* 178). In these cases Mann perceives a polarity between Eros and Logos that has interest and meaning principally for men (*Briefe,* 178). The problem of erotics and beauty is, for Mann, one of a polarity between life and spirit, Eros and Logos. Attractions between men and women, men and effeminate men, and men and masculine men are all possibilities within the basic polarity of desire and word. Like Goethe in *Die Wahlverwandtschaften,* Mann delineates in his letter to Weber a conception of male same-sex desire in which it functions as neither "above" nor "below" heterosexual desire, but as an equally natural, probable, and fundamental desire. At the same time, in *Tod in Venedig* Mann foregrounds, as did Goethe, the crucial role of male same-sex desire and its articulation in the production of poetry. And like Goethe, he seems particularly interested in expressions of male same-sex desire that are not contingent upon gender polarities. Mann assures Weber, as well, that he had no intention in writing *Tod in Venedig* to deprecate male same-sex desire. In fact, he argues one could only accomplish that if one were to insist that it was "unnatural" (*Briefe*, 178). But he adds that that is an assumption "den schon Goethe triftig zurueckgewiesen hat" ("that Goethe has already rejected convincingly," 178). Mann does not indicate where Goethe so persuasively demonstrates that male same-sex desire is natural, but as we know, he does so throughout his poetic production and certainly unequivocally in *Die Wahlverwandtschaften*.

Mann clearly evokes throughout *Tod in Venedig* and in his discussions of it, the German Classical discourse on male same-sex desire formulated by Winckelmann, Goethe, and Moritz. *Tod in Venedig* does appear to directly reiterate and extend their languages of male same-sex desire and community. Mann, one could surmise, is another poet in the genealogy of poets envisioned by Tasso. Moreover, Mann articulates even more clearly in *Tod in Venedig* the love that the poet feels for his male object of desire. In contrast to Ferdinand, whose expressions of love culminate in an elliptical omission, or to Tasso, whose metaphor might be perceived as ambiguous, Aschenbach clearly states his love for Tadzio ("I love you"). In his letter to Weber, Mann extends and clarifies even further the fundamental relationship between Eros and Logos. He explicates a complex understanding of the basic nature of desire, separating it from gender and insisting that Goethe has already demonstrated convincingly that male same-sex desire is thoroughly natural. Finally, Mann insinuates that this understanding of desire is based on his own notion/spirit (Logos) and experience/life (Eros): "Sagen Sie mir, ob man sich besser 'verraten' kann. Meine Idee des Erotischen, mein *Erlebnis* davon ist hier vollkommen ausgedrueckt" ("Tell me, if one can 'betray' oneself any better. My idea of the erotic, my experience of it, is completely expressed here," *Briefe*, 179). In the context of Mann's letter to Weber, his *Tod in Venedig*, and Goethe's *Wahlverwandtschaften*, it becomes clear that Mann was also struggling to formulate a language of Eros and Logos that would allow him to express his own same-sex desires.[2] Intriguingly enough, although Mann wrote after the proliferation of sexological discourses of the later nineteenth century, like Winckelmann, Goethe, and Moritz, he, too, seems more interested in finding and developing a language of himself, in fashioning and articulating his own desire. Mann, it appears, discovered a model of the poetic self-fashioning of the same-sex identified man in German Classical discourse. This does not mean that Mann did not also resort at times to contemporary medical and psychoanalytical descriptions of male same-sex desire. In 1918, for instance, he invoked the sociomedical terminology of his day in suggesting that his own poetic production expressed his "inversion."[3] In fact, we find that Mann appropriated both German Classical descriptions and contemporary ones of pathology to represent male same-sex desire in *Tod in Venedig* and in his letter explaining the novella to Carl Weber. But he is also careful in his letter to Weber to qualify the limitations of the "medical sphere" (what Foucault would call medical discourse) in defining male same-sex desire. He juxtaposes those medical conceptions to the profound spiritual and cultural self-expressions of men such as Michelangelo, Winckelmann, von Platen, and George. In *Tod in Venedig*, as we have seen, Mann returns rather persistently to a Goethean notion of male same-sex desire as fundamental to poetry and as an incitement to the self-fashioning of men who desire other men. Mann's *Tod in Venedig* constitutes a salient reminder that even in ages when discourses of Freudian psychoanalysis or sodomy are in ascendancy, there is more than one language of male same-sex identity and desire, and German Classical poetry has something essential to say to us about the self-fashioning articulations of men desiring men.

NOTES

CHAPTER 1

1. Ironically, it seems that despite their extensive efforts to express their same-sex desires and identities, the German Classicists never seem to have settled on a specific name for themselves. Perhaps they did not perceive a need for such designation. And because they did not give themselves a particular name, like others current in their time, such as "warm brothers," "holy pederasts," or "sodomites," I have chosen to refer to their expressions of desires for and identities with other men as *same-sex* desires and identities. In addition, I often use the term "male-male desire" as interchangeable with "male same-sex desire." I have tried with this choice to avoid more politically charged and historically specific terms such as queer and homosexual. Regardless of the fact that the German Classicists did not give themselves and their same-sex desires and identities a single name, they did strive to express their desires and to identify and define themselves as men desiring men. Indeed, although they did not call themselves by a single name, naming their desire and naming (spelling out) men who desired men formed one of the crucial foundations of their linguistic and poetic productions.

2. See, for instance, Weeks and Dollimore.

3. We should keep in mind here the anachronistic character of the term "homosexuality" when applied to eighteenth- and early nineteenth-century notions of desire. As Foucault suggested in *The Use of Pleasure* (187), "homosexuality" is a plainly inadequate notion to describe the experience, forms of valuation, and categorizations of other historical eras.

4. I am using the term "heterosexuality" here anachronistically as a short-hand way of indicating the importance of the sexual relations between husbands

and wives within the eighteenth-century conceptualization of marriage and its boundaries.

5. As cited in Diderot's "On Women" (1772), 312.

6. Compare Gillis ("Married but not Churched," 31): "In this sexual telos the eighteenth century has come to occupy a special place, for it is seen as a turning point, the moment when, to use Lawrence Stone's term, a new 'affective individualism' finally pushed aside the ancient obligations to kin and community, permitting men and women for the first time to construct relationships on the basis of personal likes and dislikes. The eighteenth century is perceived as the moment when traditional arranged marriage gave way to the modern love match, when sexuality was finally domesticated, and when the nuclear family based on companionate marriage became the central focus of social and emotional life."

7. Scholars often stress how few cases of "sodomy" are on record. See, for instance, Hull (36) and Derks (10), who stress the veritable absence of court records of trials against sodomites in the German states of the eighteenth century. In fact, Derks stresses how he searched in vain for trial records: "Der einzige Strafprozeß von symptomatischen Wert, der um den bedeutenden deutschen Komponisten Johannes Rosenmüller, fällt bereit ins 17. Jahrhundert; ein zweiter Prozeß um den Rechtsanwalt Franz Desgouttes von 1817 ist in der Hauptsache ein Mordprozeß. Ein dritter Fall, der des Berliner Schauspielers Albert Wurm, endete mit einem Freispruch. Weiteres Material war nicht zu finden" ("The only trial of symptomatic worth—that of the important German composer Johannes Rosenmüller—occurred in the seventeenth century; a second trial—that of the lawyer Franz Desgouttes in 1817—was essentially a murder trial. A third case, that of the Berlin actor Albert Wurm, ended with an acquittal. Further material was not to be found"). Rey (129) recounts that seven sodomites were burned to death in France between 1715 and 1781. Moreover, police records provide evidence of 20,000–40,000 "sodomites" the police had under surveillance at one time or another between 1725 and 1780. Penalties, however, were being relaxed, and many of the culprits brought in were simply released (144). Coward (235) describes a "pattern of minimum intervention" in France and notes in conclusion a relative "lack of interest in homosexuality" in the eighteenth century (250). One exception to this appears to have been Holland, where waves of prosecutions occurred in 1730 and 1764 (van der Meer, 189) resulting in 600–800 prosecutions (van der Meer, 190). Trumbach ("Sodomitical Subcultures," 113), in fact, notes that it "appears as though England and Holland, the two most modernizing societies of the early eighteenth century, were also the two to experience the most intense waves of sodomy prosecutions." See also Greenberg, 313.

8. Kant shifts here to an allusion to the waste of sperm that crimes of *sexus homogenii* involve. His allusion to issues of spermatic economy is important here because, while he refers originally to these activities as crimes committed by both sexes, his focus on matters of spermatic economy reveals that he is concerned principally with men. As in many instances in the eighteenth century, same-sex desire between women gets ultimately glossed over. Indeed, we will find this tendency throughout Goethe's work as well and will discuss it in more detail in chapter two.

9. Foucault reminds us in the *Order of Things* (120) about the importance of "naming" for the eighteenth century. He points out that "the fundamental task of Classical 'discourse' is *to ascribe a name to things, and in that name to name their being.*" Indeed, he summarizes (311) that for the Classical age "the possibility of knowing things and their order passes, . . . through the sovereignty of words . . . ,'" which "form rather a colourless network on the basis of which beings manifest themselves and representations are ordered." In this context we can understand more clearly Kant's concern about what kinds of sexual activities get "named."

10. Coward (237–38) recounts that in Paris punishments for sodomy were not revealed to the public because of the officials' fear that such announcements would teach the ignorant public that such activities existed and would result in the perpetration of such acts. The *Treatise of Hermaphrodites* (1718), attributed to Giles Jacobs (cited in McCormick, *Secret Sexualities,* 18), begins with the assurance that the text will not incite "masculine-females to amorous trials with their own sex; and I am persuaded there will not be one single HERMAPHRODITE the more in the world, on account of the publishing of this TREATISE." So Kant was certainly not alone in his fear of the naming of certain sexual realities.

11. For a collection of seventeenth- and eighteenth-century texts addressing "other sexualities" see McCormick, *Secret Sexualities.*

12. In their introduction to *Sexual Underworlds of the Enlightenment* Rousseau and Porter (1) remind us of the swell of libertine thought that was developing in eighteenth-century Europe: "Not least through Linneaus's highly influential taxonomy, eighteenth-century biology came to recognize the fundamental sexuality of all living beings, and in Erasmus Darwin's evolutionary theories a vision of cosmic organic progress found expression which enshrined sexuality as the fundamental agent of progress, order and happiness in the universe . . . New currents of philosophical hedonism, led by Lamettrie, d'Holbach and Diderot, and of utilitarianism, systematized by Jeremy Bentham, gained ground, advancing the view—popularized in novels such as John Cleland's *Memoirs of a Woman of Pleasure*—that sex was a basic mode of human enjoyment, and that whatever forms of sexual expression created more pleasure than pain—be they modes traditionally labeled as visions, sinful or unnatural—were ipso facto desirable and good." Haggerty (*Men in Love,* 6–11) outlines the limits of libertinism for studies of eighteenth-century love between men because of the inherent paradigms of power manifest in the discourse of, for example, Rochester (and one could add de Sade). He also emphasizes that discourses of libertinism were not about love and identity. I would add that discourses of libertinism accentuate precisely modes of sexual conduct and political discourses that are fundamentally *not* about forming *specific* sexual identities. Edmiston (155) tentatively suggests that one might find some evidence of something like a "homosexual" identity formation in de Sade's character Bressac in *La Nouvelle Justine.* I have chosen not to foreground libertinism, as opposed to other literary and philosophical descriptions of eighteenth sexual desire, in this study because the evidences of identity formations in libertine discourse appear to be minimal and because libertinism is less important to the German than to the English and French traditions.

13. Haggerty (*Men in Love*) addresses issues of the containment of same-sex sexuality in the writings of Gray, Beckford, and Walpole.

14. Of course, Foucault implies that there is something like *a single* homosexual identity or interior, which is a problematic notion from both historical and synchronic perspectives.

15. All translations from the German are my own unless otherwise indicated.

16. As G. S. Rousseau's mention of *bougre* might imply, writers in the eighteenth century often located the origin of sodomitical acts at some other national site and quite often in France, Italy, Bulgaria, or Turkey. See for example Derks (96) and G. S. Rousseau ("The Pursuit of Homosexuality," 136 and 143) where Rousseau suggests that in England the original home of same-sex attachments was thought to be Italy or Turkey. Sodomy was often considered the "Italian menace." Consider finally McFarlane (55), who writes: " . . . sodomy is repeatedly represented as coming from elsewhere, a kind of foreign infection erupting within the social body, but the source of which is definitely outside of that body. Just as the representation of sodomy and the sodomite is refracted through the social structures of the gender and class hierarchies, it also intersects with a discourse of xenophobia, a xenophobia directed particularly toward the Catholic countries of France and Italy."

17. G. S. Rousseau is using modern conceptions to describe eighteenth-century phenomena. I try throughout this study not to apply terms such as "heterosexuality," "homosexuality," "bisexuality," "gay," or "lesbianism" anachronistically. Since these terminological distinctions did not exist in the eighteenth and early nineteenth centuries, I have opted in most instances to use historically accurate terms or to refer to same-sex desire. Occasionally, I will use "heterosexual" or "homosexual" in quotation marks or in accord with their use by other scholars.

18. Rousseau (*Pursuit of Homosexuality*, 140) also points out here that "the 'philosophic,' if seemingly secular, idea that excessive masturbation was the chief cause of homosexuality flourished throughout the eighteenth century." See also Greenberg, 367.

19. See Derks, 25–27, 61–62, 88, 96, and 141.

20. What is striking throughout this study of Goethe, Winckelmann, and Moritz is that they rarely seem to address the issues of gender and feminization in their delineation of a male same-sex desiring self. In stark contrast to the accounts of subcultural activity in the eighteenth century, these German Classicists do not seem to concern themselves with notions that men who desire men might be more "feminine." Nor do these men necessarily appropriate female characteristics or practices. The men desiring men described by the German Classicists are, if anything, typically hyper-masculine. Indeed, in Goethe's work, any concentration on gender issues seems to be relegated to the depiction of masculinized women. And any anxiety about gender confusion is also generated predominately by women passing as men.

21. Trumbach ("Sodomitical Subcultures," 110–111) explains the rise of homosexual subcultures in terms of population base: "First, although large Italian cities of at least 60,000 people had well-developed homosexual subcultures from the High Middle Ages, it was not possible for a northern European city to support a homosexual subculture with a population of less than 100,000, and it was not really until the seventeenth century, when the great capital cities of the north began to surpass 200,000 people, that in them appeared continuous, well-developed homosexual subcultures."

22. Keep in mind that accounts of eighteenth-century subcultures are often provided by witnesses called in criminal proceedings to testify against those involved in subculture activities. A contemporary epistolary/literary account by Johann Friedel, *Briefe über die Galantieren von Berlin auf einer Reise gesammelt von einem österreichischen Offizier 1782*, is exemplary in this respect. Friedel attests to the existence of a subculture of "warme Brüder" or "warm brothers" (men attracted to men) in Berlin as early as the 1780s. His account is essentially a moral diatribe against the behavior of "warm brothers." Friedel insists that his main purpose was to warn others, to spare them, and to protect them from such abominable activity: "Den Neuling zu warnen, ihm die verborgne Schlange aufzudecken, ihn von seinem oft zu schnellen Unglücke zu retten, das war meine Absicht" (To warn the uninitiated, to uncover the hidden snake, to save him from an often too quick misfortune, that was my intention," 5). He enjoins boys and girls to recognize the "Häßlichkeiten" ("horrors," 5) of such desires that he himself can only "verachten, verabscheuen" ("abhor and loathe," 142). For after all, the actions of such men are "so weit außer dem Gleise der Natur" ("so far outside of the boundaries [literally, tracks] of nature," 143) and "fast kein junger wohlgebildeter Knabe ist vor dieser Herren sicher" ("almost no young well-bodied boy is safe from these men," 141–42). While Friedel's account suggests that a subculture of men attracted to men existed in Berlin in the 1780s, it provides us with no objective or first-hand account of its characteristics or any evidence about the nature of any possible group identifications the "warm brothers" might have established. In fact, outside of a few references to the "warm brothers" kissing one another, Friedel is content to moralize. See also Patterson ("The Rage of Caliban"), who outlines in some detail the unreliability of extant accounts of eighteenth-century sexual subcultures.

23. See Haggerty's introduction for a summary of scholarly debates about the nature of eighteenth-century quotations of "Greek love." Many scholars consider these quotations of male friendship to be stylistic (see the collection of essays by Mauser and Becker-Cantarino, for example). I agree with Haggerty that in cases such as those of Gray, Walpole, Beckford—and I would add Winckelmann, Goethe, and Moritz—invocations of Greek love and male friendship are appropriated precisely in order to facilitate the expression of desire between men.

24. Recent German scholarship, including Alice Kuzniar's *Outing Goethe and His Age*, Detering's *Offenes Geheimnis*, Robert Tobin's *Warm Brothers*, and essays by Simon Richter, has begun to outline the contours of an eighteenth-century German culture of homosociality and homoeroticism as it revolves around certain key figures such as Winckelmann and Frederick the Great.

25. Although Haggerty refers throughout his study to the moments in which the emergence of same-sex identities in passages of eighteenth-century English literature are manifest, he seems to play it down some in the introduction, emphasizing that "a certain sexual sensibility emerges in the eighteenth century that begins to have recognizable contours" (2).

26. Because Goethe, Winckelmann, and Moritz do not distinguish between "friendship" and "love" in their delineation of men desiring men, I will respect that lack of distinction throughout this book. Indeed, I feel that attempts in scholarship to dismiss the passion they express as "mere" friendship has distorted our sense of

the same-sex desire they struggled to articulate. The kinds of systematic expressions of male same-sex desire produced by these Classicists are in no way simply formulaic phrases of *Empfindsamkeit* (sensibility). As we shall see, these men developed their own individual languages of same-sex desire and openly struggled to articulate themselves and to describe that struggle. The poetic languages these men developed to express themselves emerged and evolved throughout their literary and aesthetic production. And, as we shall see, for instance, in the discussion of Goethe's *Elective Affinities*, scholars have described the relationships depicted there between men and men as friendships and between men and women as love relationships—even though Goethe describes all of the relationships in the novel in the same manner. He does not distinguish the relationships between men as friendships. Scholarship has felt compelled to do that.

27. See Todd, *Sensibility*; Wegmann, *Diskurse der Empfindsamkeit*; Sauder, *Empfindsamkeit*; Ellis, *Politics of Sensibility*; and Baasner, *Der Begriff 'sensibilité.'*

28. Several recent studies have outlined the connection in the eighteenth century between new generic innovations and new senses of how subjectivity can be fashioned through aesthetic experience. See, for instance, von Muecke, *Virtue and Veil*; Wellbery, *The Specular Moment*; Gustafson, *Absent Mothers*; and Purdy, *The Tyranny of Elegance.* Luhmann (*Love as Passion*, 135) points out as well the link between literature and codings of intimacy in eighteenth-century German literature: "More than ever before, personal elements began to enter into literature, and literature was in turn interpreted with reference to the personal element . . . The semantics of intimacy seems for the time being to consist of a structured chaos, a fermenting and self-stimulating mass that inspired everyone to reach their own conclusions and thus opened the way for individualization beyond its mere self-presence in feeling."

29. Consider, for instance, Bruce Smith (*Homosexual Desire*, 17), who maintains that "we miss the imaginative dimension to sexual experience if all we attend to is moral discourse, legal discourse, and medical discourse, with their narrow interest in sex as a physical act . . . only poetic discourse can address homosexual desire." G. S. Rousseau ("Pursuit of Homosexuality," 161) maintains that "literature broadly conceived nevertheless remains one of the most sensitive barometers—however inaccurate its measurements and distorted its antennae—of the climate of opinion and feeling in an age." One could, of course, make the same argument of inaccuracy about any text—literary or not. That is, is not every text a fiction? See also Goldberg (*Sodometeries*, 20).

30. I would like to quibble with Tobin (*Warm Brothers*) on terminology here. I would not call the eighteenth-century male desiring and identified man a "homosexual," although I think that Tobin and I are talking about the same person when he says "homosexual identity" when referring to the eighteenth century and I say "male same-sex identity." Technically, if Tobin really means here "an homosexual identity"—I would agree that you cannot find a late nineteenth- and twentieth-century notion of homosexual identity in the eighteenth century—because the concept has an historical specificity. But just because that particular same-sex identity is specific to the later nineteenth century and beyond, that does not mean that same-sex desiring and identified men were not articulating themselves in the later eighteenth and early nineteenth centuries.

CHAPTER 2

1. Kristeva makes comments to this effect in an interview in 1984. See Oliver, 140.

2. Foucault outlines this compulsion to order and classify in the *Order of Things*, pp. 125–65.

3. In this way Goethe's model of sexual desire is reminiscent of Greek models of unbifurcated desire as illustrated by Foucault in the *Use of Pleasure* (188), in which he writes of the Greeks: " . . . they did not recognize two kinds of 'desire,' two different or competing 'drives,' each claiming a share of men's hearts or appetites . . . To their way of thinking, what made it possible to desire a man or a woman was simply the appetite that nature had implanted in man's heart for 'beautiful' human beings, whatever their sex might be."

4. Weeks summarizes this succinctly: "Social processes construct subjectivities not just as 'categories' but at the level of individual desires. This perception . . . should be the starting point for future social and historical studies of 'homosexuality' and indeed of 'sexuality' in general" (Weeks, "Discourse," 111).

5. Anyone familiar with Goethe's literary and scientific work can recognize how these two discourses meld throughout his intellectual production. One need only think of *Faust, Wilhelm Meister's Apprenticeship, The Elective Affinities, The Theory of Colors, On Granite*, and countless poems.

6. Armstrong and Tennenhouse point out both the potential for further study implied by Foucault's analysis and the fact that he often ignored the significant effects of literature. Foucault fails to consider "the historical impact of literature" ("A Novel Nation," 341–42).

7. See notes in the Münchner Ausgabe edition of Goethe's works, p. 1061. Throughout this study I refer to the Münchner Ausgabe [hereafter abbreviated MA] whenever possible. When I quote texts by Goethe unavailable in the MA edition, I rely on the Weimarer Ausgabe [hereafter abbreviated WA].

8. Herder does mention Winckelmann's death in his eulogy of 1777, *Denkmal Johann Winckelmanns*, but does not mention the possible same-sex encounter surmised to be associated with it. See the Suphan Edition of Herder's works, vol. 8, pp. 437–83. The specific passage on Winckelmann's death is on p. 480.

9. All of the letters I cite in the following passages are contained in collections of letters that Goethe insisted that his readers should review (see MA, 6:2, 400–1) unless otherwise indicated.

10. While one might assert that these are expressions of formulaic sentimentality, Winckelmann's letters offer impressive and recurrent structural evidence of his struggle to identify and to express his same-sex desire, which in their extensiveness, intensity, persistence, and individuality demonstrate that they are not to be dismissed as merely formulaic in nature. See also Detering, 39–77.

11. This letter is not contained in the collections of letters Goethe referred his contemporaries to, but would have been available to them in the *Monatschrift von und für Mecklenburg*, 1791 (See *Briefe*, vol. 1, 519).

12. Goethe would not have known about this letter, which was published in 1866 (see *Briefe*, vol. 1, p. 518). I quote it here, nonetheless, because it reiterates impulses of the other letters to which Goethe did refer his readers.

13. By this I mean that Goethe does not quote the letters to Berg, but he does encourage his readers to familiarize themselves with them (See MA, 6:2, 400–1).

14. Sweet's insistence that Winckelmann's homosexuality "was never admitted by his contemporaries" is refuted by more recent studies of the art historian by Richter, Kuzniar, et al.

15. One famous exception to this is Mephisto's sodomitical desire for the angels in the final scene of *Faust II* See Falkner.

16. For a comprehensive investigation of Goethe's use of the term "Wahlverwandtschaften," see Adler's book, *Eine fast . . . .* Adler focuses on the meaning of the term itself in *Die Wahlverwandtschaften,* its scientific sources, and its use in autobiographical works such as the *Italienische Reise* and *Dichtung und Wahrheit.* In this study I am interested in assessing the model of the "Wahlverwandtschaften" both in its function in the novel of the same name and as a model manifest in other literary works by Goethe. In other words, I focus on the "elective affinities" as a metaphor and a structural paradigm in Goethe's aesthetics of male same-sex desire.

17. The tremendous complexity of Goethe's *Elective Affinities* and the vast amount of secondary literature on this novel make it impossible to provide a comprehensive review of the novel's significance in this study. I am specifically interested in the issue of discourse formation and sexual desire as it is outlined in the discussions of the metaphor of the "Wahlverwandtschaften." This metaphor is critical, as we shall see, as a structuring mechanism throughout Goethe's oeuvre.

18. Miller, *Adriadne* (207). See also Wellbery ("Die Wahlverwandtschaften," 307, 312–13), who argues that Goethe's novel outlines a "neue Form des Begehrens" ("new form of desire"). I would add that Goethe introduces both a new form of desire and that he outlines a paradigm of desire that allows for desire in all its capacities, permutations, and divergences.

19. For a comprehensive overview of the reception of Goethe's novel through 1832, see Härtl.

20. In this context we recall, of course, Kant's anxieties about naming what he considered to be acts of sexual deviance.

21. Adler (*Eine fast . . .*) provides an extensive summary of the scientific notions of sympathies, affinities, and "Wahlverwandtschaften" in Goethe's age as they relate to chapter four of his novel.

22. See Adler, *Eine fast . . .* , 170.

23. Compare Lore Metzger (474), who writes: "Thus the narrative borrows its central metaphor from the behavior of chemical elements that is itself an analogical discourse (Gleichnisrede) based on human, or, rather, male anthropomorphism, man's imposing his will and willfulness on inanimate as well as animate nature, a doubling of metaphorical relations that emphasizes the primacy of the symbolic order of language in this fictional mirror of a social microcosm." Many scholars refer to the narcissistic underpinnings of these passages, including J. Hillis Miller (167), von Thadden (154), Noyes (133).

24. Wellbery ("Die Wahlverwandtschaften," 302) also mentions in passing how this passage evinces a sense of the subject's "Verstricktsein im Bilde" ("entanglement in the image," here, I would say, metaphor).

25. In this sense, think of the disjuncture that is developing here—i.e., between

something like the accepted Cartesian understanding of the self and Goethe's modern conception of metaphoric metamorphoses of the self.

26. Compare for example von Thadden, who also notes this injunction to "Selbstbezug" as narcissistic, but who applies it more exclusively to Eduard. Zons, Schlaffer ("Namen und Buchstaben"), and Winnett foreground the mirroring character of the affinities and of the letters OTTO, which (or variations of which) occur in the names of all four characters and that of Eduard's and Charlotte's son.

27. In this context we might consider the Harfenspieler [Harp Player] in Goethe's *Wilhelm Meister's Apprenticeship Years,* who without bonds with others is trapped within his own "empty self": "Seit vielen Jahren hat er [der Harfenspieler] an nichts, was außer ihm war, den mindesten Anteil genommen, ja fast auf nichts gemerkt, bloß in sich gekehrt, betrachtete er sein hohles, leeres Ich, das ihm als ein unermeßlicher Abgrund erschien . . . ich sehe nichts vor mir, nichts hinter mir, rief er aus, als eine unendliche Nacht, in der ich mich in der schrecklichsten Einsamkeit befinde." ("For many years the harp player had not concerned himself with anything outside of himself, yes, took practically notice of nothing, simply turned in upon himself, he observed his hollow, empty self, which appeared to him as a immeasurable abyss—I see nothing in front of me, nothing behind me, he yelled out, other than an infinite night in which I find myself in the most horrible loneliness," MA, 5, 438).

28. Adler (*Eine fast,* 145–46) summarizes this succinctly: "Der Text greift nicht ein isoliertes Beispiel aus der Chemie heraus, sondern wendet eine ganze Typologie auf die Gesellschaft an. Er verwandelt eine naturwissenschaftliche Typologie in ein soziologisches Modell" ("The text does not just pull an isolated example out of chemistry, but applies an entire typology to society. He transforms a typology of the natural sciences into a sociological model"). While Adler is certainly correct here, he doesn't draw any conclusions about what this means in terms of Goethe's conceptions of identity and desire in a social context.

29. By way of contrast we could compare the shifts between male-female and male-male desire as they are related in Friedrich Schlegel's *Lucinde.* In Schlegel's novel the main protagonist, Julius, slides back and forth between affinities for men and women. His desire for men, however, is qualified as not quite right for him: "Junge Männer aber, die ihm einigermaßen glichen, umfaßte er mit heißer Liebe und mit einer wahren Wut von Freundschaft. Doch war das allein für ihn noch nicht das Rechte" ("He embraced with hot love and a fury of friendship young men who were to some degree like him. But that was for him not quite right," *Lucinde,* 126). After sliding back and forth between intense relationships with men and women, Julius finally finds the woman "die einzig war und die seinen Geist zum erstenmal ganz in der Mitte traf. Seine bisherigen Leidenschaften spielten nur auf der Oberfläche, oder es waren vorübergehende Zustände ohne Zusammenhang. Jetzt ergriff ihn ein neues Gefühl, daß dieser Gegenstand allein der rechte und dieser Eindruck ewig sei" ("who was unique and who affected the core of his heart for the first time. His previous passions had only played on the surface or they were transient conditions without connection. A new feeling seized him, that this object alone was the right one and this impression would be eternal," *Lucinde,* 150–52). In Goethe's notion of the elective affinities the shifts from one type of desire or another are not isolated as "not quite right" (male-male desire) or "just

right" (female-male desire); they are simply presented without moral or judgmental qualifications.

30. Earlier in their discussion Charlotte argued conversely that desires are uncontainable, while Eduard asserted that the intellect could control them (MA, 9, 292). This shifting of positions is less important than the palpable anxiety the main characters evince about the unalterable nature and directions of desire.

31. See for instance von Thadden (158), who provides one of the most explicit acknowledgments of the same-sex coupling overtly mapped out here: "denn zunächst entstehen neue gleichgeschlechtliche Frauen- und Männerpaare und die neue Verbindung zu Liebespaare vollzieht sich erst von dieser Ausgangsbasis . . ." ("at first new same-sex pairs of women and men emerge and the new connection between pairs of lovers completes itself first from/out of this point of departure"). What von Thadden does not do is follow through with an explication of the implications of these illustrations of same-sex desire.

32. This may well provide yet another explanation for Thomas Mann's fascination with Goethe's *Wahlverwandtschaften* during his writing of *Der Tod in Venedig*. Intriguingly enough, studies tracing the influence of Goethe's novel on Thomas Mann's novella have entirely missed the fact that both works (to different degrees, of course) illustrate the possibility of male same-sex desire. For instance, Thomas (106) insists that the two works diverge radically from one another in that Mann introduces homosexual desire while Goethe's novel is thoroughly focused on heterosexual normativity. Following suit, Zmegac (156, 162) maintains that what connects the two works is that both could be held to be "unsittlich" ("immoral"). See also Wertheim's comparison of Goethe's *Wahlverwandtschaften* and Mann's *Der Tod in Venedig*. I will return to this issue in greater detail in the epilogue.

33. Throughout the novel the letter "O" resurfaces in various contexts as a sign of Eduard (whose given name is Otto), the Captain, whose first name is Otto, and Ottilie. So not only can desire be refigured, but the signifiers representing subjects can be reassigned or have multiple signifieds. Many scholars have discussed the significance of the letters OTTO; see for instance W. Kittler, Zons, Schlaffer ("Namen und Buchstaben"), and Winnett.

34. J. Hillis Miller (171) writes similarly: "The basic paradigm of *The Elective Affinities* is the following: human relations are like the substitutions in metaphorical expressions. Or, to put it the other way, since metaphorical analogies are reversible: the laws of language may be dramatized in human relations." We might also consider here Diana Fuss's comment in the introduction to *Inside/Out* (2), where she points out that one of the critical insights of Lacanian psychoanalysis is "that any identity is founded relationally." Here Goethe expresses that relationality in his insistence upon the analogous character of desire and language—a notion that approaches Lacan's conception of the inextricable conjunction of language and desire. Indeed, Goethe is downright Lacanian in his representation of a metaphor of desire in which "people" and "letters" course along an infinite chain of linguistic expressions.

35. In this context we can recall the Lacanian conception of the subject's entrance into language/the Symbolic order. Once the subject leaves the Real and enters the Symbolic order, he or she is caught in a symbolic chain of signification in which

and through which she or he views both her- or himself and the outside world. There is no way to perceive reality outside of the structure of signification.

36. By this I do not mean to suggest that the novel does not underscore that one can make moral or ethical choices about one's behavior—only that desire is a slippery thing that cannot be willed in one direction or another. For an excellent discussion of necessity and freedom in *Die Wahlverwandtschaften*, see Michelsen.

37. Scholars have noted this before. See, for example, Wolf Kittler (252), Lindner (32–33), and the notes to the MA, 9, 1203.

38. There are two additional remarkable instances of female same-sex desire in Goethe's works. The most positive description occurs in his *Unterhaltungen deutscher Ausgewanderten* (MA, 4:1, 441), in which Goethe describes the friendship between two women in almost exactly the same terms in which he consistently describes desirous relationships between men. This incidence of female-female desire is briefly alluded to and then dropped. The second most explicit expression of female same-sex desire occurs in Goethe's play fragment *Prometheus*. In this early drama Prometheus's daughter Pandora describes the "nameless feelings" that she experiences first while watching her friend Mira embracing and kissing Arbar. Her own feelings are so aroused by this spectacle that she screams. Arbar retreats and Mira falls upon Pandora's breast. Pandora describes the racing desire she then feels: "Ihr Busen schlug/Als wollt er reißen / Ihre Wangen glühten / Es lechzt ihr Mund, und tausend Tränen stüerzten. / —Und ihre Küsse, ihre Glut / Hat solch ein neues unbekanntes Gefühl / Durch meine Adern durchgegossen, / —Sag / Was ist das alles was sie erschüttert / Und mich" ("her breast pounded as if it wanted to burst open, her cheeks glowed, her mouth panted, and a thousand tears fell. Her kisses, her passion shot a completely unknown feeling through my veins . . . do tell me, what all that is that has so moved [shattered] her and me," MA, I:I, 678–79). Prometheus's response to this highly charged expression of female-female desire is to tell his daughter that what she feels is "der Tod!"—that is, death itself. Other than these examples, Goethe's literary production is peopled with women who have almost no relationship to any other women. They typically sustain no friendships, are jealous of one another, and are isolated from others of their sex.

39. I quote the Weimar Edition here (by section, volume, and page), since the Münchner Edition does not include Goethe's *Farbenlehre*.

40. In more abstract terms Goethe refers to the poet's task in his essay *Einfache Nachahmung, Manier, Styl* as that of constructing a language of the self. He "macht sich selbst eine *Sprache*, um das, was er mit der Seele ergriffen, wieder nach seiner Art auszudrücken . . . Nun wird es eine Sprache, in welcher sich der Geist des Sprechenden unmittelbar ausdrückt und bezeichnet" ("made himself a language, in order to express what he had captured with his soul in his own manner . . . Now it becomes a language in which the spirit [soul] of the speaker is transparently expressed and signified," MA, 3:2, 187–88).

41. Here I am, of course, thinking of the impact of Freud's developmental model of sexual identity and desire as outlined in his *Three Essays on Sexuality*. There he suggests an anatomical basis for an "original predisposition to bisexuality" (7), an originary polymorphous perversity in childhood sexuality, and he illustrates how all

subjects ought to move through and beyond the Oedipal complex as they develop socially acceptable (read: heterosexual) identities and desires.

42. For this reason, I would disagree with Tobin's ("In and Against Nature," 109) analysis that Goethe's representations of "homosexuality" always leads to healthy "heterosexuality." Such an analysis does not accord with Goethe's paradigms of sexual identity and desire as they manifest themselves throughout his thought. MacLeod attempts similarly to identify a shift from a "polymorphous ideal of androgyny in Winckelmann to a model grounded in heterosexual complementarity, drained of sexuality, and central to the program of Wilhelm von Humboldt, Schiller, Goethe, and others" (MacLeod, "The Third Sex," 195–96). As we look at a broader spectrum of texts by Goethe and locate the reiterations of his metaphor of sexuality and desire, we will discover that Freudian models of sexual development do not adequately address the complexity of Goethe's conceptions.

43. I disagree with Tobin ("In and Against," 105), who views the shifts in desire in these passages in terms of developmental stages: "Homosexuality becomes a phase, albeit also a natural one, through which Werther grows." Like Eissler (374), Tobin assumes a Freudian notion of sexual development. And while it is true that Werther moves in this text from desire for a man to desire for a woman, it is not clear that his shifts in desire stop there. As we shall see in chapter three, in other works such as *Götz von Berlichingen, Tasso, Egmont,* and *Wilhelm Meister* the shifts in desire are just as likely to occur in the opposite direction—i.e., from desire for a woman to that for a man. And finally, the structure of Goethe's metaphor of desire/elective affinities clearly establishes the fluidity of desire throughout the subject's lifetime. The passages from the *Briefe* and from *Wilhelm Meister* that I am discussing in this chapter are only two examples of the trajectories of desire, and two scenarios of nascent desire are mapped out in them. The fluidity of desire they represent makes more sense if considered within the context of Goethe's recurrent paradigm of the structure of metaphoricity and/or the fluidity of desire.

44. This passage reads so uncannily like a short "coming out" narrative that I felt compelled to mention it, despite the fact that my comments constitute an anachronistic application of the notion to an early nineteenth-century text.

45. The homoerotic character of this passage has been, of course, noted before, see: Tobin ("In and Against,"106f); the notes to the Münchner Edition, vol. 4:1, 1100; Derks (260); and Eissler (374), who speculates that Goethe is abandoning himself to "his insatiable voyeuristic pleasures" here. In contrast, I am interested in the convergence of desire and metaphor in this text. Tobin (*Warm Brothers,* 108) hints at the significance of language here.

46. In this context we should remember Goethe's descriptions of the poet's "peopling" of the "literary world" with images of himself/beautiful people in his poem *Prometheus* (MA, 1:1, 675) and in his essay *Zum Schakespears Tag* (MA, 1:1, 414). For a discussion of "Prometheus," see Wellbery (*The Specular Moment,* 287–345).

47. This mirroring of the desiring self extends to the reading/writing self as well. In *Die Leiden des jungen Werthers,* Werther comments tellingly: " . . . dann lese ich einen Dichter der Vorzeit, und es ist mir als säh ich in mein eignes Herz" ("then I read a poet from the past and it is as if I am looking into my own heart," MA, 2:2, 429). See also Christoph Brecht (177), who alludes briefly to Werther's narcissistic self-identification with Ferdinand.

48. Brecht (164) asserts that the *Briefe* "make voyeurism their theme."

49. Derks (260) and Eissler (427–29) accentuate Werther's fear when confronted with the woman's naked body, but they associate it with fear of women or with a fear of sexual encounters with women rather than with a fear of losing himself and his own self-expression through metaphoricity. The male fear of the loss of articulation will become even clearer in the passages from *Wilhelm Meister's Travel Years*.

50. Compare Wellbery's description of the significance of the specular moment as it operates in Goethe's lyric production:

> In the lyric variant, specularity is a scene of desire and fulfillment. There
> is a female figure who, in presenting herself to the male subject, gives him
> simultaneously his identity and the truth of his desire. This gift passes down
> the wordless exchange of the reciprocal regard and, received into the subject
> (who thereby becomes a full and identical subject), grounds his creativity, his
> productivity as poet.(61)

Conversely, in the prose passages considered here it is not the woman who gives the male poet a sense of himself, but his male object of desire. Their verbal exchanges ground his creativity and assure the production of new poetic expressions of desire.

51. It should be noted that this passage was first added to the 1829 version of Goethe's novel. According to Mathias Mayer (151), the fisher story mirrors the structure of the entire novel. I would say it mirrors the larger structure of desire that organizes Goethe's literary production in general.

52. It is very intriguing that Wilhelm writes this letter to Natalie, for throughout this passage he insists upon his need to express his desire—specifically—to a male friend. One has the impression that in order to address this letter (about desire) to a woman (Natalie) it had to be done in the context of Wilhelm's expressions of desire for a man. That is, his descriptions of desire for men become the vehicle through which he is able to communicate something about his desire to Natalie. See also Mathias Mayer (152) who emphasizes Wilhelm's inability to express his feelings to Natalie in her presence. As he sees it, the letter becomes a distancing vehicle through which Wilhelm can first relate his feelings to her. Moreover, Mayer suggests that her absence indicates her function as a muse for Wilhelm (148). What Mayer does not realize is that it is not Natalie who functions as a muse, but the fisher boy. Her absence represents the fact that she is precisely *not* the source of Wilhelm's poetic creativity.

53. Eissler (1451–52) surmises that this scene is a description of a traumatic experience Goethe must have experienced in his youth.

54. In the notes to the Münchner Edition (MA, 17, 1164) this passage is said to lend "Wilhelm die Freude, die er [Goethe] selbst, wohl im Anschluß an Winckelmann's 'Beschreibung des Apollo im Belvedere' (1759), beim Anblick eines männlichen Körpers empfand, wenn er 'ganz nackt wie eine heidnische Gottheit erglänzte'" ("Wilhelm here the joy which he [Goethe] himself, in accord with Winckelmann's 'Description of Apollo of Belvedere' (1759), experienced while viewing a male body, when it shone 'completely naked like a pagan god.'"

55. Wellbery (*The Specular Moment*, 40) describes a similar structure of visual

reciprocity in Goethe's poem "Mir schlug das Herz" and points out that this figure of specular reciprocity recurs throughout Goethe's lyric poetry (51).

56. Compare again: Tobin ("In and Against," 108), who refers to the "fleeting nature of Wilhelm's homosexual desire," and Eissler (1452), who asserts that Wilhelm has taken flight "from homosexuality to heterosexuality."

57. Wellbery (*The Specular Moment*, 36) discusses a similar anxiety surrounding occluded vision (between a man and a woman, presumably) in Goethe's poem "Mir schlug das Herz." I say "presumably" because the poem does not reveal the sex of its addressee, or fictional author, for that matter.

58. Goethe's description here of the male subject's need for a male interlocutor who will draw him to a fuller understanding of his feelings is strikingly similar to Kleist's notion of the gradual fabrication of thought while speaking in his essay "Über die allmähliche Verfertigung der Gedanken beim Reden" (see Gustafson, "Die allmähliche"). In Goethe's conception, however, the interlocutor is not (as in Kleist's formulation) just any human object of address, but is specifically the man adulated and desired by the male subject coming to terms with his sentiments—and often, more precisely, his desire for another man.

59. Both Eissler (1453) and Tobin ("In and Against," 107–8) stress the fisher boy's death as evidence of the death of Wilhelm's homosexual desire. This interpretation only makes sense if you assume an underlying paradigm of sexual development leading from homosexuality to heterosexuality. This trajectory of desire is not in evidence here. In fact, the scene ends with a pretty erotic (albeit necrophilic) return on Wilhelm's part to his male lover. Tobin ("In and Against," 108) himself refers to the scene as "masturbatory." What I am interested in here is less the final trajectory of the desire represented here than the compulsion to a metaphorization of desire evoked throughout this story.

60. Here we should recall the opening passages of *Die Leiden des jungen Werther* in which Werther writes to his friend Wilhelm: "Wie froh bin ich, daß ich weg bin! Bester Freund, was ist das Herz des Menschen! Dich zu verlassen den ich so liebe, von dem ich unzertrennlich war und froh zu sein!" ("How happy I am that I am away! My best friend, what is the heart of man! To leave you whom I love so, from whom I was inseparable and to be happy!" MA, 2:2, 350). Like Wilhelm in the *Travel Years*, Werther insists on the inseparability of himself and his male partner (the same word "unzertrennlich" surfaces in each passage). And Werther continues his first addresses to his friend with references to his failed relationship with Leonore. So once again, the dual trajectory of the male protagonist's expressions of his desires and his need for a male interlocutor comes to the fore.

61. Tobin ("In and Against," 108–9) recognizes a link in Goethe's literary production between homosexual desire and writing and speculates on possible reasons for it. He suggests that Goethe is strengthening his heterosexual bonds (also Eissler's argument), constituting a sublimation of his homosexual sentiments and demonstrating a need on his part to provide a positive portrayal of homosexual desire, or reflecting Goethe's desire to be more urbane, cosmopolitan, and universal. I would argue that structurally, on a textual basis, it becomes clear that metaphors of desire and specifically of male-male desire incite the formulation of metaphors of male same-sex desire and the desire to talk about one's desire with another male

interlocutor. Writing and speaking and desire are inextricably connected because that is how desire flows. Without metaphoric mechanisms of expression, desire would simply well up in the subject, threatening to overflow his (or her) lips. We might also consider here the significance of the "kiss" for Goethe in general. As Gilman (41) reminds us, for Goethe the kiss figures as "a means of sexual release."

CHAPTER 3

1. Here we should recall Werther's sense of the loss of himself in the presence of the naked woman he views and desires. As in the Werther passages, here the visual experience of the desired woman results not in the discovery and expression of oneself as a desiring being, but in the impression on the part of the subject of having lost any sense of self—a stark contrast to the effect of male objects of desire/interlocutors throughout Goethe's literary production.

2. Here I am referring to Wellbery's (*The Specular Moment*) accentuation of moments of specular reciprocity in Goethe's poetry.

3. See Michelsen for an excellent analysis of Ottilie's later assertion of her free will in the face of her overwhelming desire for Eduard.

4. We might add that not all affinities lead to death. In the novella "Die Wunderlichen Nachbarskinder," the story of which is recounted by a visitor to Charlotte's and Eduard's estate, the two lovers who seemingly hate one another from childhood rediscover each other and their overwhelming affinity for one another just before the young woman is married to someone else. They then marry. In *Wilhelm Meisters Wanderjahre* another novella entitled "Wo steckt der Verräter?" relates the story of two couples destined to marry in accord with their parents' wishes. Lucidor is supposed to wed Julie, and Lucinde is required to marry Antoni. Once the four convene on the family estate, however, the elective affinities assert themselves, and Lucidor falls for Lucinde while Antoni is drawn to Julie. Eventually the parents are convinced to allow the switch of partners in accordance with the affinities. In these two cases the power of the affinities was recognized in time and the desiring couples were felicitously paired with one another. Neither of these novellas culminates in the death of the lovers.

5. We might note here that Goethe originally intended to include the *Wahlverwandtschaften* as a novella in *Wilhelm Meisters Lehrjahre*, so the fact that both works are constructed around his notion of the elective affinities is no surprise.

6. Compare Tobin (*Warm Brothers*, 111), who suggests: "An organization called the Tower Society, similar to the Masons and bearing the standard of Enlightened thinking (including medicine), attempts to socialize Wilhelm Meister to a heterosexual "healthiness."

7. One could, of course, argue that Werther and Eduard are deluded in their hopes for closer relationships with Lotte and Ottilie, but they are not confused about the direction and force of their desires in the way that Wilhelm is throughout the *Lehrjahre*.

8. Tobin also mentions this perfomative nature of sexual desire briefly (*Warm Brothers*, 109).

9. Tobin reminds us in *Warm Brothers* (42, 110) that Mignon was a signifier for a "male homosexual prostitute in the late eighteenth century."

10. Stephan (196–97) concurs while emphasizing that their desire is transformed into or ends up in a strengthened sense of father-daughter bonding. I suggest in opposition that the insistence on a father-daughter relationship indicates their attempt to mask their sexual desire for one another.

11. That Wilhelm's choice of Therese is a mistake is further underscored by his reaction to her acceptance of his proposal: "Wilhelm verstummte, und sah vor sich hin. Natalie sah ihn an, sie bemerkte, daß er blaß wird. Ihre Freude ist stark, fuhr sie fort, sie nimmt die Gestalt des Schreckens an, sie raubt Ihnen die Sprache" ("Wilhelm fell silent and gazed ahead. Natalie looked at him and noted that he was pale. Your joy is strong, she continued, it takes on the form of terror, and robs you of speech," MA, 5, 531). Of course, this is an effect opposite to that of male same-sex desire and obstructs the male subject's participation in the poetic project of metaphoric formation (whether of male-female or male-male desire).

12. For this reason, I disagree with Tobin's assertion ("Faust's Membership," 20) that Wilhelm's bonding with the men of the tower society is displaced through his graduation "to the love of Natalie." In fact, both desires coexist, and Wilhelm's male-male desire allows ultimately for his articulation and formulation of his desire for Natalie.

13. Schiller writes in his review of *Egmont* that the play does not accentuate any "vorwaltende Leidenschaft" (dominate passion) and is structured instead around action and the person of Egmont (Schiller, *Nationalausgabe*, vol. 22, 200).

14. W. Daniel Wilson (137–38) reads Egmont's reaction here as resisting Ferdinand's advances. He mentions the "homoerotic" character of Ferdinand's behavior in passing. As we read the entire scene, I think it will become apparent that Egmont is initially confused by Ferdinand's expression of love but is also drawn to him.

15. Here I am referring to the mirroring of male same-sex desire and identity in Werther's *Briefe aus der Schweiz* discussed in chapter two.

16. The motif of "living for one another" and loving one another arises as well in *Iphigenia* in an intimate discussion between Pylades and Orest. Pylades recounts to Orest that he does not know what would have happened to him if Orest had never lived: "Da ich auf dir und deinetwillen nur / Seit meiner Kindheit leb' und leben mag" ("For since my childhood I have only lived and may live for you and for your sake," MA, 3:1, 178). He continues with the assertion, "Da fing mein Leben an, als ich dich liebte" ("For my life began, when I loved you," MA, 3:1, 178).

17. This analysis of *Götz von Berlichingen* is from my article in *Outing Goethe*, edited by Alice Kuzniar.

18. Stephan (187) reminds us that Aristophanes's conception of the androgyne privileges the love relationships between men over those between men and women.

19. To this extent, the structures of homosocial exchange outlined by Sedgwick in her book *Between Men* appear subverted or at least critically challenged in Goethe's *Götz von Berlichingen*. See Hart (*Tragedy in Paradise*), who outlines further divergences from Sedgwick's model in eighteenth- and early nineteenth-century German drama. Of course, Sedgwick's brilliant analysis of eighteenth- and nineteenth-century English literature should not be assumed to apply automatically

to German drama of the late eighteenth and early nineteenth centuries. The usefulness of her study is rather underscored by the persistence of the structure of homosociality beyond eighteenth- and nineteenth-century English literature in its various permutations.

20. Tobin ("Faust's Membership," 20) maintains that Tasso's struggles with Antonio are part of his love for Leonore von Este. Again, it is clear that two equal desires are in question here. Tobin seems to have overlooked the dynamics of the relationship between Tasso and Antonio.

21. Here I think *Tasso* seems to operate as a counter-example to Wellbery's analysis (*The Specular Moment*, 130, 329) of lyric genius as the product of auto-origination. Tasso and Antonio work together and within a community of men (as we shall see in chapter four) to bring their expressions of male same-sex desire into poetic form.

CHAPTER 4

1. This analysis of *Götz von Berlichingen* is from my article "Male-Male Desire" in *Outing Goethe and His Age*, edited by Alice Kuzniar.

2. One might recall here the connection Boswell (*Same-Sex Unions*, 63–64) traces between military heroes and same-sex unions in the Greco-Roman world. Considering the eighteenth-century German fascination with "Greek love," it is not surprising that Goethe might evoke similar relationships between knights to signify male-male desire. Robert Smith (chapter two) outlines as well the connection between male bonding and military "adversativeness" in Shakespeare's plays. Indeed, he perceives of the myth of Combatants and Comrades as a fundamental pattern (76).

3. We might compare here, by way of contrast, the account in Schiller's *Don Carlos* of the boyhood relationship between Carlos and Posa. While the two men reminisce about their youth, Carlos admits to Posa that he loved him because he lacked the courage to emulate him: " . . . ich endlich / Mich entschloß, dich grenzenlos zu lieben, / Weil mich der Mut verließ, dir gleich zu sein" ("I finally decide to love you beyond all boundaries, because I lost the courage to be like you," 13). Posa, on the other hand, chides Carlos because his heart has died ("Dein Herz ist gestorben," 82–83). Indeed, he only loves himself: "Wie arm bist du, wie bettelarm geworden, / Seitdem du niemand liebst als dich!" ("How poor you are, how poor as a beggar you have become, / Ever since you have loved no one but yourself," 83). For Schiller, certainly, the boyhood trope of male-male desire does not signify the kind of same-sex desire and identification formation that it does throughout Goethe's literary production.

4. Later the novel notes that "Rittergeschichten" (stories of knights) were the new rage: "Rittergeschichten . . . waren damals eben neu, und hatten die Aufmerksamkeit und Neigung des Publikums an sich gezogen" ("Stories of knights . . . were new just at that time and had drawn the attention and inclination of the public," MA, 5, 123).

5. While the few allusions to Jonathan in the *Lehrjahre* might be significant, as Tobin points out ("In and Against Nature," 105), because of his love for David

and because Jonathan, like Ganymede, was a signifier for male-male desire in the eighteenth century, the passages mentioning Jonathan highlight Mariane's penchant for him and not Wilhelm's identification with him. There are, to my mind, much stronger, more telling, signifiers of male same-sex desire and identification in the *Lehrjahre* than these few references to Jonathan.

6. See Purdy (*Tyranny*), especially chapter 7.

7. Tobin (*Warm Brothers*, 39) reminds us as well that sodomites in the eighteenth century seemed to have specific clothing codes.

8. The only place Goethe mentions men cross-dressing as women is in his account of the Roman carnival in his essay "Women's Roles in Roman Theater Played by Men." Although he ostensibly reports on how male actors in Rome masquerading as women, Goethe says little about how these men looked like women. While he suggests in "Women's Roles" that the cross-dressed actor plays "eine dritte und eigentlich fremde Natur" ("a third and foreign nature" WA, I, 47, 272), i.e., not exactly his masculine self and not woman, Goethe focuses almost entirely on those sites in which the "true masculinity" of the performer bursts through the disguise. Goethe's analysis of Roman cross-dressing returns almost compulsively to those moments that underscore the male performers' masculinity. Throughout his account, he returns obsessively to the manner in which the male actor's "dress," "the costume itself," is subverted by his body and voice that refuse to be masked. Despite the Roman actors' attempts to portray women "so gut als möglich" ("as well as possible," WA, I, 47, 273) and to conceal "so viel als möglich" ("as much as possible," WA, I, 47, 271) any signs of their maleness and masculinity, their cross-dressing underscores relentlessly their inner masculinity as their deep voices and beards continually betray them. This is important in the context of the present analysis because it suggests the consistency of Goethe's representation of the function of cross-dressing, that is, that it allows a space for male-male desire.

9. Indeed, Purdy (*Tyranny*, XV) reminds us that in the eighteenth century "'desires' spoke as sartorial and material performances of personal identity."

10. Two recent studies focus on cross-dressing women in *Egmont*: W. Daniel Wilson ("Amazon, Agitator, Allegory") and David John ("Margarete von Parma"). Wilson and John both concentrate on Margarete von Parma's cross-dressing. Wilson dismisses Egmont's dressing (145), and John reiterates W. Daniel Wilson's position (126). Wilson further suggests that Egmont's cross-dressing reveals the "performativity of his masculinity." (145). I would agree, but I would suggest that the subtleties of the passage disclose the coding of the male same-sex identification Egmont's clothes signify.

11. W. Daniel Wilson (126) discusses Clare's song and the cross-dressing it represents for her but does not address the fact that Brackenburg is singing it as well.

12. This analysis of dressing up in *Wilhelm Meister* was first published in "From Werther to Amazons" in *Unwrapping Goethe's Weimar,* edited by Simon Richter, Suzanne Kord, and Burkhard Henke.

13. See also Stephan (195), who stresses Wilhelm's attraction to Mignon in terms of her "Mann-Weiblichkeit" and his inability to maintain a thoroughly heterosexual orientation.

14. I would agree with Tobin (*Warm Brothers,* 127), who suggests in passing that "when women in the novel (*Wilhelm Meister*) cross-dress, they generally seem to take on male characteristics that go beyond clothing."

15. Tobin ("In and Against," 105) has noted, "Mariane herself hints at Wilhelm's sexual ambiguity when she identifies him with the figure of Jonathan from his puppet theater. Jonathan, because of his love for David, was in the eighteenth century, like Ganymede, a signifier for homosexuality." I am convinced that Mariane's reference to Wilhelm as Jonathan is less a cipher for his sexual ambiguity than for his desire for men.

16. MacLeod ("Pedagogy," 397) writes: "Mariane herself almost occupies second place in the arms of her lover, after the male garments she is wearing." Within the context of Wilhelm's consistent fetishization of clothing and the significance of cross-dressing both in the story and in Weimar, I would suggest that Mariane definitely stands in second place to her uniform.

17. Given the manner in which Goethe describes how Wilhelm's childhood sexual experiences and feelings meld with his contemporary ones throughout the novel, it is clear that he is not indicating a structure of sexual development that begins with a homosexual or polymorphously perverse phase that is later replaced by "normal" heterosexual longings. Rather he is demonstrating how the primal same-sex desires experienced early in childhood by a man like Wilhelm persist into adulthood and are the present and driving forces underlying his sexual experiences as an adult. (See MacLeod and Tobin, who argue for a more Freudian explication of Wilhelm's phases of development.)

18. Intriguingly, Tobin (*Warm Brothers,* 80–81) outlines Moritz's same-sex desire for his friend Klischnig.

19. Tobin (*Warm Brothers,* 87) cites this passage as well in order to demonstrate Anton's same-sex desire. He does not, however, connect this passage to Moritz's quotations of Goethe's poetic formations of same-sex desire and identity.

EPILOGUE

1. Not only is Italy Tasso's homeland, but we recall that it was a site perceived in the eighteenth century as a source of the "Italian Menace," that is, same-sex activity and desire. See also Tobin ("Thomas Mann," 233), who points out that "For Mann and many upper-class Germans, Venice was the epitome of queer Italy." He refers as well to Winckelmann and Goethe as upper-class Germans intrigued by the "queer" character of Venice/Italy.

2. In this context we should also recall Mann's diaries and their revelation of his sentiments for men. One could also remember other highly suggestive passages in his literary work, such as in *Tonio Kröger* when Tonio offers Hans Hanssen Schiller's *Don Carlos,* intimating the intense attractions between the men in the play. This is, of course, also a gesture reminiscent of Moritz and Anton's compulsion to share literature with his male objects of desire. See Tobin, "Thomas Mann."

3. See Heilbut, x and 313.

WORKS CONSULTED

Ackroyd, Peter. *Dressing Up. Transvestism and Drag: The History of an Obsession.* New York: Simon and Schuster, 1979.

Adler, Jeremy. *"Eine fast magische Anziehungskraft." Goethes "Wahlverwandtschaften" und die Chemie seiner Zeit.* Munich: C. H. Beck, 1987.

————. "Goethe und Newton. Ansätze zu einer Neuorientierung am Beispiel der chemischen Verwandtschaft." In *Goethe im Kontext,* edited by Wolfgang Wittkowski, 300–12. Tübingen: Max Niemeyer Verlag, 1984.

Aldrich, Robert. *The Seduction of the Mediterranean: Writing, Art, and Homosexual Fantasy.* New York: Routledge, 1993.

Angermeier, John S. "Marienbad and Goethe as a Source of Motifs for Mann's *Der Tod in Venedig.*" *German Life and Letters* 48, No. 1 (1995): 12–24.

Armstrong, Nancy, and Leonard Tennenhouse. "A Novel Nation; or, How to Rethink Modern England as an Emergent Culture." In *Eighteenth-Century Literary History: An MLQ Reader,* edited by Marshall Brown, 9–26. Durham, N.C.: Duke University Press, 1999.

Baasner, Frank. *Der Befriff "sensibilite" im 18. Jahrhundert: Aufstieg und Niedergang eines Ideals/Frank Baasner.* Heidelberg: C. Winter, 1988.

Barner, Wilfried. "Gelehrte Freundschaft im 18 Jahrhundert. Zu ihren traditionellen Voraussetzungen." In *Frauenfreundschaft-Männerfreundschaft. Literarische Diskurse im 18. Jahrhundert,* edited by Barbara Becker-Cantarino and Wolfram Mauser, 23–45. Tübingen: Niemeyer Verlag, 1991.

Becker-Cantarino, Barbara. "Die 'Bekenntnisse einer schönen Seele': Zur Ausgrenzung und Vereinnahmung des Weiblichen in der patriarchalen Utopie von *Wilhelm Meisters Lehrjahren.*" In *Verantwortung und Utopie,* edited by Wolfgang Wittkowski, 70–90. Tübingen: Niemeyer Verlag, 1988.

————. "Zur Theorie der literarischen Freundschaft im 18. Jahrhundert am Beispiel der Sophie La Roche." In *Frauenfreundschaft-Männerfreundschaft. Literarische Diskurse im 18. Jahrhundert,* edited by Barbara Becker-Cantarino and Wolfram Mauser, 47–74. Tübingen: Niemeyer Verlag, 1991.

Beebee, Thomas O. "Kant, Goethe, Benjamin, and the Law of Marriage." In *Worldmaking,* edited by William Pencak, 193–210. New York: Peter Lang, 1996.

Begemann, Christian. "Poiesis des Körpers. Künstlerische Produktivität und Konstruktion des Leibes in der erotischen Dichtung des klassischen Goethes." *German Life and Letters* 52, No. 2 (April 1999): 211–37.

Bennett, Benjamin. *Modern Drama and German Classicism: Renaissance from Lessing to Brecht.* Ithaca: Cornell University Press, 1986.

————. "Prometheus and Saturn: Three Versions of Götz von Berlichingen." *German Quarterly* 58 (1985): 333–47.

Bielschowsky, Albert. *The Life of Goethe, 1749–1788.* Vol 1. New York: Putnam, 1909.

Blessin, Stefan. *Die Romane Goethes.* Königstein: Athenäum Verlag, 1979.

Boswell, John. *Same-Sex Unions in Premodern Europe.* 1994. Reprint, New York: Villard Books, 1995.

Boucé, Paul-Gabriel. "Imagination, Pregnant Women, and Monsters in Eighteenth Century England and France." In *Sexual Underworlds of the Enlightenment,* edited by G. S. Rousseau and Roy Porter, 86–100. Chapel Hill, N.C.: University of North Carolina Press, 1988.

Boyle, Nicholas. *Goethe: The Poet and the Age.* 2 vols. Oxford: Clarendon, 1991.

Bray, Alan. *Homosexuality in Renaissance England.* 1982. Reprint, New York: Columbia University Press, 1995.

Brecht, Christoph. "Werther als Voyeur: Ein Zwischenspiel zu Goethes Romanen." In *Von der Natur zur Kunst zurück,* edited by Moritz Baßler, Christoph Brecht, and Dirk Niefanger, 157–80. Tübingen: Max Niemeyer Verlag, 1997.

Burwick, Frederick. "Goethe's Classicism: The Paradox of Irrationality in *Torquato Tasso*." In *A Reassessment of Weimar Classicism,* edited by Gerhard Hoffmeister, 11–33. Lewiston: Edwin Mellen Press, 1996.

Buschendorf, Bernhard. *Goethes mytische Denkform. Zur Ikonographie der "Wahlverwandtschaften."* Frankfurt am Main: Suhrkamp Verlag, 1986.

Butler, Judith. *Gender Trouble. Feminism and the Subversion of Identity.* New York: Routledge, 1990.

Castle, Terry. "The Culture of Travesty: Sexuality and Masquerade in Eighteenth Century England. In *Sexual Underworlds of the Enlightenment,* edited by G. S. Rousseau and Roy Porter, 156–80. Chapel Hill, N.C.: University of North Carolina Press, 1988.

————. *Masquerade and Civilization. The Carnivalesque in Eighteenth-Century English Culture and Fiction.* Stanford, Calif.: Stanford University Press, 1986.

Coward, D. A. "Attitudes to Homosexuality in Eighteenth-Century France." *Journal of European Studies* 10 (1980): 231–55.

Craft-Fairchild, Catherine. "The Politics of 'Passing': The Scandalous Memoir and the Novel." In *Illicit Sex. Identity Politics in Early Modern Culture,* edited by Thomas DiPiero and Pat Gill, 45–67. Athens, Ga., and London: University of Georgia Press, 1997.

Denby, David J. *Sentimental Narrative and the Social Order in France, 1760–1820.* Cambridge: Cambridge University Press, 1994.

Derks, Paul. *Die Schande der heiligen Päderastie. Homosexualität und Öffentlichkeit in der deutschen Literatur, 1750–1850.* Berlin: Verlag Rosa Winkel, 1990.

Detering, Heinrich. *Das offene Geheimnis. Zur literarischen Produktivität eines Tabus von Winckelmann bis zu Thomas Mann.* Göttingen: Wallstein Verlag, 1994.

Diderot, Denis. *Diderot's Selected Writings,* edited by Lester G. Crocker, translated by Derek Coltman. New York and London: The Macmillan Company, 1966.

Dollimore, Jonathan. *Sexual Dissidence: Augustine to Wilde. Freud to Foucault.* Oxford: Clarendon Press, 1991.

Dye, Ellis. "Goethe's Die Wahlverwandtschaften: Romantic Metafiction." *Goethe Yearbook* 8 (1996): 66–92.

Edmiston, William F. "Shifting Ground: Sade, Same-Sex Desire, and the One-, Two-, and Three-Sex Models." In *Illicit Sex: Identity Politics in Early Modern Culture,* edited by Thomas DiPiero and Pat Gill, 143–60. Athens, Ga., and London: University of Georgia Press, 1997.

Eissler, K. R. *Goethe. A Psychoanalytic Study.* 2 Vols. Detroit: Wayne State University Press, 1963.

Ellis, Markman. *The Politics of Sensibility: Race, Gender and Commerce in the Sentimental Novel.* Cambridge: Cambridge University Press, 1996.

Epstein, Julia, and Kristina Straub, eds. *Body Guards: The Cultural Politics of Gender Ambiguity.* New York and London: Routledge, 1991.

Fahs, Wolfgang. "Zum Verhältnis Goethe-Schiller." In *Frauenfreundschaft-Männerfreundschaft. Literarische Diskurse im 18. Jahrhundert,* edited by Barbara Becker-Cantarino and Wolfram Mauser, 137–40. Tübingen: Niemeyer Verlag, 1991.

Falkner, Silke R. "Love Only Succors/Those Who Cannot Love": Mephisto's Desiring Gaze in Goethe's Faust." In *Queering the Canon. Defying Sights in German Literature and Culture,* edited by Christoph Lorey and John L. Plews, 142–58. Columbia, S.C.: Camden House, 1998.

Foucault, Michel. *The Order of Things. An Archaeology of the Human Sciences.* New York: Vintage Books, 1970.

———. *The Archaeology of Knowledge and the Discourse on Language.* New York: Pantheon, 1972.

———. *History of Sexuality.* New York: Random House, 1980.

———. *The Use of Pleasure.* New York: Random House, 1985.

———. *The Care of the Self.* New York: Random House, 1986.

———. "Technologies of the Self." In T*echnologies of the Self: A Seminar with Michel Foucault,* edited by Luther Martin, Huck Gutman, and Patrick Hutton, 16–49. Amherst, Mass.: University of Massachusetts Press, 1988.

Fout, John C., ed. *Forbidden History. The State, Society and the Regulation of Sexuality in Modern Europe.* Chicago and London: The University of Chicago Press, 1992.

Freud, Sigmund. *The Standard Edition of the Complete Psychological Works of Sigmund Freud,* translated by James Strachey. London: The Hogarth Press, 1986.

Friedel, Johann. *Briefe über die Galantieren von Berlin auf einer Reise gesammelt von einem österreichischen Offizier 1782.* Berlin: Eulenspiegel Verlag, 1987.

Friedell, Egon. *Kulturgeschichte der Neuzeit.* Vol. 2. Munich: C. H. Beck'sche Ver-lagsbuchhandlung, 1928.

Friedenthal, Richard. *Goethe, sein Leben und seine Zeit.* München: R. Piper, 1963.

Friedli, Lynne. "'Passing Women'—A Study of Gender Boundaries in the Eigh-teenth Century." In *Sexual Underworlds of the Enlightenment,* edited by G. S. Rousseau and Roy Porter, 234–60. Chapel Hill, N.C.: University of North Car-olina Press, 1988.

————. "Women Who Dressed as Men." *Trouble and Strife* 6 (Summer 1985): 25–29.

Fuss, Diana, ed. *Inside/Out: Lesbian Theories, Gay Theories.* New York: Routledge, 1991.

Gallagher, Catherine, and Thomas Lacquer, eds. *The Making of the Modern Body. Sexuality and Society in the Nineteenth Century.* Berkeley, Los Angeles, and London: University of California Press, 1987.

Garber, Majorie. *Vested Interests: Cross-Dressing and Cultural Anxiety.* New York: Routledge, 1992.

Gillis, John R. "Married but not Churched: Plebeian Sexual Relations and Marital Non-Conformity in 18th Century Britain." In *"Tis Nature's Fault": Unautho-rized Sexuality during the Enlightenment,* edited by Robert Purks Maccubbin, 31–42. Cambridge: Cambridge University Press, 1985.

Gilman, Sander. *Inscribing the Other.* Lincoln: University of Nebraska Press, 1991.

Gleim, Johann Wilhelm Ludwig. *Preussische Kriegslieder in den Feldzügen 1756 und 1757. Von Einem Grenadier. Mit neuen Melodien.* Berlin: Göritz, 1778.

Goethe, Johann Wolfgang von. *Sämtliche Werke nach Epochen seines Schaffens. Münchner Ausgabe,* edited by Karl Richter, Herbert G. Göpfert, Norbert Miller, and Gerhard Sauder. 24 vols. Munich: Carl Hanser, 1985.

————. *Werke. Herausgegeben im Auftrage der Großherzogin Sophie von Sachsen. Weimarer Ausgabe.* 143 vols. Weimar: Böhlau, 1887–1919.

Goldberg, Jonathan. *Sodometries: Renaissance Texts, Modern Sexualities.* Stanford, Calif.: Stanford University Press, 1992.

Graham, Ilse. *Goethe: Portrait of the Artist.* Berlin: Walter de Gruyter, 1977.

————. "Götz von Berlichingen's Right Hand." *German Life and Letters* 16 (1962–63): 212–28.

Gray, Ronald D. *Goethe the Alchemist. A Study of Alchemical Symbolism in Goethe Literary and Scientific Works.* Cambridge: Cambridge University Press, 1952.

Greenberg, David F. *The Construction of Homosexuality.* Chicago: University of Chicago Press, 1988.

Gustafson, Susan E. *Absent Mothers and Orphaned Fathers: Narcissism and Abjection in Lessing's Aesthetic and Dramatic Production.* Detroit: Wayne State University Press, 1995.

————. "Male Desire in Goethe's *Götz von Berlichingen.*" In *Outing Goethe and His Age,* edited by Alice Kuzniar, 111–24. Stanford, Calif.: Stanford University Press, 1996.

————. "From Werther to Amazons: Cross-Dressing and Male-Male Desire in 'Goethe's Weimar'." In *Unwrapping Goethe's Weimar,* edited by Burkhard Henke, Simon Richter, and Suzanne Kord, 178–99. Columbia, S.C.: Camden House, 1999.

————. "The Cadaverous Bodies of Vampiric Mothers and the Genealogy of Pathology in E. T. A. Hoffmann's Tales." *German Life and Letters* 52, No. 2 (April 1999): 238–54.

————. "'Die allmähliche Verfertigung der Gedanken beim Reden': The Linguistic Question in Kleist's Amphitryon." *Seminar* 25, No. 2 (May 1989): 104–26.

Härtl, Heinz. *Die Wahlverwandtschaften. Eine Dokumentation der Wirkung von Goethes Roman 1808–1832.* Berlin: Akademie Verlag, 1983.

Haggerty, George E. *Men in Love. Masculinity and Sexuality in the Eighteenth Century.* New York: Columbia University Press, 1999.

Halperin, David M. *One Hundred Years of Homosexuality, and Other Essays on Greek Love.* London and New York: Routledge, 1990.

Hamann, Johann Georg. *Hauptschriften*, edited by Otto Mann. Leipzig: In der Dieterich'schen Verlagsbuchhandlung, 1937.

Hart, Gail K. *Tragedy in Paradise. Family and Gender Politics in German Bourgeois Tragedy, 1750–1850.* Columbia, S.C.: Camden House, 1996.

Heilbut, Anthony. *Thomas Mann: Eros and Literature.* New York: Knopf, 1996.

Hekma, Gert, and Kent Gerard, eds. *The Pursuit of Sodomy: Male Homosexuality in Renaissance and Enlightenment Europe.* New York and London: Harrington Park Press, 1989.

Herder, Johann Gottfried. *Sämtliche Werke*, edited by Bernhard Suphan. Berlin: Weidmannsche Buchhandlung, 1887.

Hirschfeld, Magnus. *Die Transvestiten. Eine Untersuchung über den erotischen Verkleidungstrieb.* Leipzig: Verlag "Wahrheit" Ferdinand Spohr, 1925.

Hull, Isabel V. *Sexuality, State and Civil Society in Germany, 1700–1815.* Ithaca: Cornell University Press, 1996.

Huussen, Arend. H., Jr. "Sodomy in the Dutch Republic in the Eighteenth Century." In *Hidden from History: Reclaiming the Gay and Lesbian Past,* edited by Martin Dubermann, Martha Vincinus, and George Chauncey, Jr., 141–52. Middlesex, England: Penguin Books, 1989.

Huyssen, Andreas. "Das leidende Weib in der dramatischen Literatur von Empfindsamkeit und Sturm und Drang: Eine Studie zur bürgerlichen Emanzipation in Deutschland." *Monatshefte* 69 (Summer 1977): 159–73.

John, David G. "Margarete von Parma in Goethe's *Egmont*: Text and Performance." In *Queering the Canon. Defying Sights in German Literature and Culture,* edited by Christoph Lorey and John L. Plews, 126–41. Columbia, S.C.: Camden House, 1998.

Kant, Immanuel. *Eine Vorlesung über Ethik*, edited by Gerd Gerhardt. Frankfurt am Main: Fischer Taschenbuch Verlag, 1990.

Kates, Gary. "D'Eon Returns to France: Gender and Power in 1777." In *Body Guards: The Cultural Politics of Gender Ambiguity,* edited by Julia Epstein and Kristina Straub, 112–41. New York and London: Routledge, 1992.

Kelly, Veronica, and Dorothea von Muecke. *Body and Text in the Eighteenth Century.* Stanford, Calif.: Stanford University Press, 1994.

Kittler, Friedrich. "Ottilie Hauptmann." In *Goethes Wahlverwandtschaften. Kritische Modelle und Diskursanalysen zum Mythos Literatur,* edited by Norbert W. Bolz, 260–75. Hildesheim: Gerstenberg Verlag, 1981.

Kittler, Wolf. "Goethes Wahlverwandtschaften: Soziale Verhältnisse symbolisch dargestellt." In *Goethes Wahlverwandtschaften. Kritische Modelle und Diskurs-analysen zum Mythos Literatur,* edited by Norbert W. Bolz, 230–59. Hildesheim: Gerstenberg Verlag, 1981.

Klauss, Jochen. *Alltag im 'klassischen' Weimar, 1750–1850.* Weimar: Nationale For-schungs- und Gedenkstätte der klassischen deutschen Literatur, 1990.

Kord, Susanne T. "Eternal Love or Sentimental Discourse? Gender Dissonance and Women's Passionate 'Friendships.'" In *Outing Goethe and His Age,* edited by Alice Kuzniar, 228–49. Stanford, Calif.: Stanford University Press, 1996.

Kristeva, Julia. *The Powers of Horror. An Essay on Abjection.* New York: Columbia University Press, 1982.

———. *Desire in Language.* Translated by T. Gora, A. Jardine, and L. S. Roudiez. New York: Columbia University Press, 1980.

Kuzniar, Alice A., ed. *Outing Goethe and His Age.* Stanford, Calif.: Stanford Uni-versity Press, 1996.

Lacan, Jacques. *Ecrits,* translated by Alan Sheridan. New York: Norton, 1977.

Lämmert, Eberhard. "Die Chemie der *Wahlverwandtschaften.*" *Zeitschrift für Sozial-wissenschaft* (1986): 19–37.

Laqueur, Thomas. *Making Sex. Body and Gender from the Greeks to Freud.* Cam-bridge and London: Harvard University Press, 1990.

Larrett, William. "Wilhelm Meister and the Amazons." *PEGS* 34 (1968–69): 31–56.

Lindner, Burkhardt. "Goethes *Wahlverwandtschaften* und die Kritik der mythischen Verfassung der bürgerlichen Gesellschaft." In *Goethes Wahlverwandtschaften. Kritische Modelle und Diskuranalysen zum Mythos Literatur,* edited by Norbert W. Bolz, 23–44. Hildesheim: Gerstenberg Verlag, 1981.

Ludwig, Emil. *Goethe, Geschichte eines Menschen.* Stuttgart and Berlin: Cotta, 1920.

Luhmann, Niklas. *Love as Passion: The Codification of Intimacy.* Cambridge and London: Harvard University Press, 1956.

Maccubbin, Robert Purks, ed. *"Tis Nature's Fault." Unauthorized Sexuality during the Enlightenment.* Cambridge and New York: Cambridge University Press, 1985.

MacLeod, Catriona. "Pedagogy and Androgyny in *Wilhelm Meisters Lehrjahre.*" *MLN* 108 (April 1993): 389–426.

———. "The Third Sex in an Age of Difference." In *Outing Goethe and His Age,* edited by Alice Kuzniar, 194–214. Stanford, Calif.: Stanford University Press, 1996.

Mann, Thomas. *Briefe 1889–1936,* Vol. 1, edited by Erika Mann. Frankfurt am Main: S. Fischer Verlag, 1961.

———. *Der Tod in Venedig.* Frankfurt am Main: Fischer Taschenbuch Verlag, 1978.

———. "Zu Goethes *Wahlverwandtschaften.*" In *Aufsätze, Reden, Essays.* Vol. 3.: 1919–1925. Berlin: Aufbau Verlag, 1986.

Martin, Biddy. "Sexualities without Genders and Other Queer Utopias." *Diacritics* 24, Nos. 2–3 (Summer-Fall 1994): 104–21.

Mauser, Wolfram. "Freundschaft und Verführung. Zur inneren Widersprüchlichkeit von Glücksphantasien im 18. Jahrhundert. Ein Versuch." In *Frauenfreundschaft-Männerfreundschaft. Literarische Diskurse im 18. Jahrhundert,* edited by Barbara Becker-Cantarino and Wolfram Mauser, 213–35. Tübingen: Niemeyer Verlag, 1991.

Mayer, Hans. *Outsiders.* Cambridge and London: MIT Press, 1982.

Mayer, Mathias. *Selbstbewußte Illusion.* Heidelberg: Carl Winter Verlag, 1989.

McCormick, Ian. *Secret Sexualities: A Sourcebook of 17th and 18th Century Writing.* New York: Routledge, 1997.

McIntosh, Mary. "The Homosexual Role." *Social Problems* 16, No. 2 (Fall 1968): 182–92.

McFarlane, Cameron. *The Sodomite in Fiction and Satire, 1660–1750.* New York: Columbia University Press, 1997.

Merrick, Jeffrey. "Sexual Politics and Public Order in Late Eighteenth Century France: The *Memoires secrets* and the *Correspondence secrete.*" In *Forbidden History. The State, Society and the Regulation of Sexuality in Modern Europe,* edited by John C. Fout, 171–87. Chicago and London: The University of Chicago Press, 1992.

Metzger, Lore. "Spatial Relations and Subject Formation in *Wahlverwandtschaften* and *Mansfield Park.*" *Proceedings of the XIIth Congress of the International Comparative Literature Association.* Vol. 3, 474–79. Munich: iudicum verlag, 1990.

Meyer-Krentler, Eckhard. "Freundschaft im 18. Jahrhundert. Zur Einführung in die Forschungsdiskussion." In *Frauenfreundschaft-Männerfreundschaft. Literarische Diskurse im 18. Jahrhundert,* edited by Barbara Becker-Cantarino and Wolfram Mauser, 1–22. Tübingen: Niemeyer Verlag, 1991.

Michelsen, Peter. "Wie frei ist der Mensch? Über Notwendigkeit und Freiheit in Goethes *Wahlverwandtschaften.*" *Goethe Jahrbuch* 113 (1996): 139–60.

Miller, J. Hillis. *Ariadne's Thread.* New Haven and London: Yale University Press, 1992.

Moritz, Karl Philipp, and Salomon Maimon, eds. *Magazin zur Erfahrungsseelenkunde.* Berlin, 1783–93.

———. *Anton Reiser,* edited by Horst Günther. Frankfurt am Main: Insel Verlag, 1981.

Morrison, Jeff. "The Discreet Charm of the Belvedere: Submerged Homosexuality in Eighteenth-Century Writing on Art." *German Life and Letters,* 52, No. 2 (April 1999) 123–35.

Nägele, Rainer. "Götz von Berlichingen." In *Goethes Dramen. Neue Interpretationen,* edited by Walter Hinderer, 65–77. Stuttgart: Reclam, 1980.

Neumann, Gerhard. "Bild und Schrift." *Freiburger Universitätsblätter* 103 (1989): 119–31.

Noyes, John. "Die blinde Wahl. Symbol, Wahl und Verwandtschaft in Goethes *Wahlverwandtschaften.*" *Dvjs* 65 (1991): 132–51.

Oliver, Kelly. *Reading Kristeva: Unraveling the Double-Bind.* Bloomington and Indianapolis: Indiana University Press, 1993.

Patterson, Craig. "The Rage of Caliban: Eighteenth-Century Molly Houses and the Twentieth-Century Search for Sexual Identity." In *Illicit Sex. Identity Politics in Early Modern Culture,* edited by Thomas DiPiero and Pat Gill, 256–69. Athens, Ga., and London: University of Georgia Press, 1997.

Pfeiffer, Joachim. "Friendship and Gender: The Aesthetic Construction of Subjectivity in Kleist." In *Outing Goethe and His Age,* edited by Alice Kuzniar, 215–27. Stanford, Calif.: Stanford University Press, 1996.

Pruys, Karl Hugo. *Die Liebkosungen des Tigers. Eine Erotische Goethe Biographie.* Berlin: edition q, 1997.

Purdy, Daniel L. *The Tyranny of Elegance. Consumer Cosmopolitanism in the Era of Goethe.* Baltimore: Johns Hopkins University Press, 1998.

Puszkar, Norbert. "Verwandtschaft und Wahlverwandtschaft." *Goethe Yearbook* 4 (1988): 161–83.

Reh, Albert M. "Wunschbild und Wirklichkeit: Die Frau als Leserin und als Heldin des Romans und des Dramas der Aufklärung." In *Die Frau als Heldin und Autorin: Neue kritische Ansätze zur deutschen Literatur,* edited by Wolfgang Paulsen, 82–95. Munich: Franke, 1979.

Rey, Michel. "Police and Sodomy in Eighteenth-Century Paris: From Sin to Disorder." *Journal of Homosexuality* 16 (1988): 129–46.

Ribbat, Ernst. "Sprechen, Schreiben, Lesen, Schweigen. Zu Goethes Roman Die Wahlverwandtschaften." In *Critica Poeticae,* edited by Andreas Gößling and Stefan Nienhaus, 171–86. Würzburg: Königshausen & Neumann, 1992.

Richter, Simon. *Laocoon's Body and the Aesthetics of Pain.* Detroit: Wayne State University Press, 1992.

———. "Winckelmann's Progeny: Homosocial Networking in the Eighteenth Century." In *Outing Goethe and His Age,* edited by Alice Kuzniar, 33–46. Stanford, Calif.: Stanford University Press, 1996.

———. "Wieland and the Homoerotics of Reading." In *Outing Goethe and His Age,* edited by Alice Kuzniar, 47–60. Stanford, Calif.: Stanford University Press, 1996.

Rickels, Laurence A. "Psi Fi Explorations of Out Space: On Werther's Special Effects." In *Outing Goethe and His Age,* edited by Alice Kuzniar, 147–73. Stanford, Calif.: Stanford University Press 1996.

Rousseau, G. S., and Roy Porter, eds. *Sexual Underworlds of the Enlightenment.* Chapel Hill, N.C.: University of North Carolina Press, 1988.

———. "The Pursuit of Homosexuality in the Eighteenth Century: 'Utterly Confused Category' and/or Rich Repository?" In *"Tis Nature's Fault." Unauthorized Sexuality during the Enlightenment,* edited by Robert Purks Maccubbin, 132–68. Cambridge and New York: Cambridge University Press, 1985.

Rousseau, Jean-Jacques. *Emile, or On Education.* Translated by Allan Bloom. New York: Basic Books, Inc., 1979.

Ryder, Frank. "Toward a Revaluation of Goethe's *Götz*: Features of Recurrence." *PMLA* 79 (1964): 58–66.

Sauder, Gerhard, ed. *Der junge Goethe,* Vol. 1.1. Munich: Hanser, 1985.

———. *Empfindsamkeit. I: Voraussetzungen und Elemente.* Stuttgart: Metzler Stuttgart, 1974.

Schehr, Lawrence. *The Shock of Men. Homosexual Hermeneutics in French Writing.* Stanford, Calif.: Stanford University Press, 1995.

Schiller, Johann Christoph Friedrich von. *Schillers Werke. Nationalausgabe.* Vol. 22. Edited by Herbert Meyer. Weimar: Hermann Böhlaus Nachfolger, 1958.

Schindler, Stephan. "Homosocial Necrophilia: The Making of Man in Jung-Stilling's Idyllic Patriarchy" In *Outing Goethe and His Age,* edited by Alice Kuzniar, 61–76. Stanford, Calif.: Stanford University Press, 1996.

Schlaffer, Heinz. "Namen und Buchstaben in Goethes *Wahlverwandtschaften.*" In *Goethes Wahlverwandtschaften. Kritische Modelle und Diskursanalysen zum Mythos Literatur,* edited by Norbert W. Bolz, 211–29. Hildesheim: Gerstenberg Verlag, 1981.

———. "Exoterik und Esoterik in Goethes Romanen." *Goethe Jahrbuch* 95 (1978): 212–26.

Schlegel, Friedrich. *Lucinde.* Paris: Aubier-Flammarion, 1971.

Schneider, Sabine M. "Kunstautonomie als Semiotik des Todes? Digressionen im klassischen Diskurs der schönen Menschengestalt bei Karl Phillip Moritz." *German Life and Letters* 52, No. 2 (April 1999): 166–83.

Schreiber, Jens. "Die Zeichen der Liebe." In *Goethes Wahlverwandtschaften. Kritische Modelle und Diskursanalysen zum Mythos Literatur,* edited by Norbert W. Bolz, 276–307. Hildesheim: Gerstenberg Verlag, 1981.

Schwan, Werner. *Goethes "Wahlverwandtschaften." Das nicht erreichte Soziale.* Munich: Wilhelm Fink Verlag, 1983.

Sedgwick, Eve Kosofsky. *Between Men: English Literature and Male Homosocial Desire.* New York: Columbia University Press, 1985.

———. *Epistemology of the Closet.* Berkeley and Los Angeles: University of California Press, 1990.

Smith, Bruce. *Homosexual Desire in Shakespeare's England: A Cultural Poetics.* Chicago: University of Chicago Press, 1991.

Sørensen, Bengt Algot. "Freundschaft und Patriarchat im 18. Jahrhundert." In *Frauenfreundschaft-Männerfreundschaft. Literarische Diskurse im 18. Jahrhundert,* edited by Barbara Becker-Cantarino and Wolfram Mauser, 279–92. Tübingen: Niemeyer Verlag, 1991.

Steakley, James D. "Sodomy in Enlightenment Prussia: From Execution to Suicide." In *The Pursuit of Sodomy: Male Homosexuality in Renaissance and Enlightenment Europe,* edited by Kent Gerard and Gert Hekma, 163–76. New York and London: Harrington Park Press, 1988.

Stephan, Inge. "Mignon und Penthesilea. Androgynie und erotischer Diskurs bei Goethe und Kleist." In *Annäherungsversuche,* edited by Albert Horst Glaser, 183–208. Stuttgart: Verlag Paul Haupt, 1993.

Stone, Lawrence. *The Family, Sex and Marriage in England, 1500–1800.* London: Weidenfeld and Nicolson, 1977.

Sweet, Denis M. "The Personal, the Political, and the Aesthetic. Johann Joachim Winckelmann's German Enlightenment Life." In *The Pursuit of Sodomy: Male Homosexuality in Renaissance and Enlightenment Europe,* edited by Kent Gerard and Gert Hekma, 147–62. New York and London: Harrington Press, 1987.

Tasso, Torquato. *Jerusalem Delivered,* edited and translated by Ralph Nash. Detroit: Wayne State University Press, 1987.

Tobin, Robert D. "In and Against Nature: Goethe on Homosexuality and Heterotextuality." In *Outing Goethe and His Age,* edited by Alice Kuzniar, 94–110. Stanford, Calif.: Stanford University Press, 1996.

———. "Faust's Membership in Male Society: Prometheus and Ganymede as Models." In *Interpreting Goethe's Faust Today,* edited by Jane Brown, Meredith Lee, and Thomas Saine, 17–28. Columbia, S.C.: Camden House, 1994.

————. "The Life and Work of Thomas Mann: A Gay Perspective." *Death in Venice: A Case Study in Contemporary Criticism,* edited by Naomi Ritter. New York: St. Martin's Press, 1998, 225–244.

————. *Warm Brothers. Queer Theory and the Age of Goethe.* Philadelphia: University of Pennsylvania Press, 2000.

Todd, Janet. "Jane Austen, Politics and Sensibility." In *Feminist Criticism: Theory and Practice,* edited by Susan Sellers, Linda Hutcheon, and Paul Perron, 71–87. Toronto: University of Toronto Press, 1991.

Trumbach, Randolph. "Modern Prostitution and Gender in *Fanny Hill:* Libertine and Domesticated Fantasy." In *Sexual Underworlds of the Enlightenment,* edited by G. S. Rousseau and Roy Porter, 69–85. Chapel Hill, N.C.: University of North Carolina Press, 1988.

————. "Sodomitical Subcultures." In *"Tis Nature's Fault": Unauthorized Sexuality during the Enlightenment,* edited by Robert Maccubbin, Cambridge and New York: Cambridge University Press, 1985.

————. "London Sapphists: From Three Sexes to Four Genders in the Making of Modern Culture." In *Body Guards: The Cultural Politics of Gender Ambiguity,* edited by Julia Epstein and Kristina Straub, 112–41. New York and London: Routledge, 1991.

————. "The Birth of the Queen: Sodomy and the Emergence of Gender Equality in Modern Culture, 1600–1750." In *Hidden from History: Reclaiming the Gay and Lesbian Past,* edited by Martin Dubermann, Martha Vincinus, and George Chauncey, Jr., 129–40. Middlesex, England: Penguin Books, 1989.

————. "Sex, Gender, and Sexual Identity in Modern Culture: Male Sodomy and Female Prostitution in Enlightenment London." In *Forbidden History. The State, Society and the Regulation of Sexuality in Modern Europe,* edited by John C. Fout, 89–106. Chicago and London: The University of Chicago Press, 1992.

————. "London's Sodomites: Homosexual Behavior and Western Culture in the Early 18th Century." *Journal of Social History* 11, No. 1 (1977): 1–33.

Vaget, Hans Rudolf. *Goethe. Der Mann von 60 Jahren.* Königstein: Athenäum Verlag, 1982.

Van der Meer, Theo. "Tribades on Trial: Female Same-Sex Offenders in Late Eighteenth Century Amsterdam." In *Forbidden History. The State, Society and the Regulation of Sexuality in Modern Europe,* edited by John C. Fout, 189–210. Chicago and London: The University of Chicago Press, 1992.

Vila, Anne C. *Enlightenment and Pathology. Sensibility in the Literature and Medicine of Eighteenth Century France.* Baltimore and London: The Johns Hopkins University Press, 1998.

Vincent-Buffault, Anne. *The History of Tears: Sensibility and Sentimentality in France.* New York: St. Martin's Press, 1991.

Von Muecke, Dorothea. *Virtue and the Veil of Illusion. Generic Innovation and the Pedagogical Project in Eighteenth-Century Literature.* Stanford, Calif.: Stanford University Press, 1991.

Von Thadden, Elisabeth. *Erzählen als Naturverhältnis. "Die Wahlverwandtschaften."* Munich: Wilhelm Fink Verlag, 1993.

Wagner, Irmgard. *Critical Approaches to Goethe's Classical Dramas.* Columbia, S.C.: Camden House, 1995.

Wagner, Peter. "The Discourse on Sex or Sex as Discourse: Eighteenth Century Medical and Paramedical Erotica." In *Sexual Underworlds of the Enlightenment*, edited by G. S. Rousseau and Roy Porter, 46–68. Chapel Hill: University of North Carolina Press, 1988.

Weeks, Jeffrey. *Against Nature. Essays on History, Sexuality and Nature.* London: Rivers Oram Press, 1991.

———. "Inverts, Perverts, and Mary-Annes. Male Prostitution and the Regulation of Homosexuality in England in the Nineteenth and Early Twentieth Centuries." *Journal of Homosexuality* 6 (1980–81): 113–34.

———. "Discourse, Desire, and Sexual Deviance: Some Problems in a History of Sexuality." In *The Making of the Modern Homosexual*, edited by Kenneth Plummer, 76–111. London: Hutchinson, 1981.

———. *Sex, Politics and Society. The Regulation of Sexuality Since 1800.* London and New York: Longman, 1981.

Wegmann, Nikolaus. *Diskurse der Empfindsamkeit. Zur Geschichte eines Gefühls in der Literatur des 18. Jahrhunderts.* Stuttgart: J. B. Metzlar, 1988.

Wellbery, David. *The Specular Moment.* Stanford, Calif.: Stanford University Press, 1996.

———. "*Die Wahlverwandtschaften*," in *Goethes Erzählwerk. Interpretationen*, edited by Paul Michael Lützeler and James E. McLeod, 291–318. Stuttgart: Philipp Reclam, 1985.

Wells, G. A. "*Götz von Berlichingen*: History, Drama, and Dramatic Effectiveness." *Publications of the English Goethe Society* 56 (1985–86): 74–96.

Wertheim, Ursula. "Goethe-Motive im Wandel oder Ein Goethe Motif bei Thomas Mann." *Goethe Jahrbuch* 106 (1989): 160–68.

Wheelwright, Julie. "Amazons and Military Maids: An Examination of Female Military Heroines in British Literature and the Changing Construction of Gender." *Women's Studies International Forum* 10:5 (1987): 489–502.

Wilkinson, Elizabeth. "Sexual Attitudes in Goethe's Life and Works." In *Goethe Revisited*, edited by E. Wilkinson, 171–84. London: John Calder, 1984.

Wilson, W. Daniel. "Amazon, Agitator, Allegory: Political and Gender Crossing(-Dress)ing in Goethe's *Egmont*." In *Outing Goethe and His Age*, edited by Alice A. Kuzniar, 125–46. Stanford, Calif.: Stanford University Press, 1996.

Wilson, Jean. *The Challenge of Belatedness. Goethe, Kleist, Hoffmannsthal.* New York: University Press of America, 1991.

Winckelmann, Johann Joachim. *Geschichte der Kunst des Altertums*, edited by Victor Fleischer. Berlin and Wien: Meyer, 1913.

———. *Briefe.* 4 Vols. Edited by Walther Rehm und Hans Diepolder. Berlin: Walter de Gruyter and Co., 1952.

Winnett, Susan. *Terrible Sociability. The Text of Manners in Laclos, Goethe, and James.* Stanford, Calif.: Stanford University Press, 1993.

Zmegac, Viktor. "Zu einem Thema Goethe's und Thomas Manns: Wege der Erotik in der modernen Gesellschaft." *Goethe Jahrbuch* 103 (1986): 152–67.

Zons, Raimer Stefan. "Ein Denkmal voriger Zeiten über die *Wahlverwandtschaften*." In *Goethes Wahlverwandtschaften. Kritische Modelle und Diskursanalysen zum Mythos Literatur*, edited by Norbert W. Bolz, 323–52. Hildesheim: Gerstenberg Verlag, 1981.

INDEX

Books in the Kritik: German Literary Theory and Cultural Studies series

Walter Benjamin: An Intellectual Biography, by Bernd Witte, trans. by James Rolleston, 1991

The Violent Eye: Ernst Jünger's Visions and Revisions on the European Right, by Marcus Paul Bullock, 1991

Fatherland: Novalis, Freud, and the Discipline of Romance, by Kenneth S. Calhoon, 1992

Metaphors of Knowledge: Language and Thought in Mauthner's Critique, by Elizabeth Bredeck, 1992

Laocoon's Body and the Aesthetics of Pain: Winckelmann, Lessing, Herder, Moritz, Goethe, by Simon Richter, 1992

The Critical Turn: Studies in Kant, Herder, Wittgenstein, and Contemporary Theory, by Michael Morton, 1993

Reading After Foucault: Institutions, Disciplines, and Technologies of Self in Germany, 1750–1830, edited by Robert S. Leventhal, 1994

Bettina Brentano-von Arnim: Gender and Politics, edited by Elke P. Frederiksen and Katherine R. Goodman, 1995

Absent Mothers and Orphaned Fathers: Narcissism and Abjection in Lessing's Aesthetic and Dramatic Production, by Susan E. Gustafson, 1995

Identity or History? Marcus Herz and the End of the Enlightenment, by Martin L. Davies, 1995

Languages of Visuality: Crossings between Science, Art, Politics, and Literature, edited by Beate Allert, 1996

Resisting Bodies: The Negotiation of Female Agency in Twentieth-Century Women's Fiction, by Helga Druxes, 1996

Locating the Romantic Subject: Novalis with Winnicott, by Gail M. Newman, 1997

Embodying Ambiguity: Androgyny and Aesthetics from Winckelmann to Keller, by Catriona MacLeod, 1997

The Freudian Calling: Early Viennese Psychoanalysis and the Pursuit of Cultural Science, by Louis Rose, 1998

By the Rivers of Babylon: Heinrich Heine's Late Songs and Reflections, by Roger F. Cook, 1998

Reconstituting the Body Politic: Enlightenment, Public Culture, and the Invention of Aesthetic Autonomy, by Jonathan M. Hess, 1999

The School of Days: Heinrich von Kleist and the Traumas of Education, by Nancy Nobile, 1999

Walter Benjamin and the Corpus of Autobiography, by Gerhard Richter, 2000

Heads or Tails: The Poetics of Money, by Jochen Hörisch, trans. by Amy Horning Marschall, 2000

Dialectics of the Will: Freedom, Power, and Understanding in Modern French and German Thought, by John H. Smith, 2000

The Bonds of Labor: German Journeys to the Working World, 1890–1990, by Carol Poore, 2000

Schiller's Wound: The Theater of Trauma from Crisis to Commodity, by Stephanie Hammer, 2001

Goethe as Woman: The Undoing of Literature, by Benjamin Bennett, 2001

Peripheral Visions: The Hidden Stages of Weimar Cinema, edited by Kenneth S. Calhoon, 2001

Narrating Community after Kant: Schiller, Goethe, and Hölderlin, by Karin Schutjer, 2001

The Survival of Images: Art Historians, Psychoanalysts, and the Ancients, by Louis Rose, 2001

The Myth of Power and the Self: Essays on Franz Kafka, by Walter Sokel, 2002

Men Desiring Men: The Poetry of Same-Sex Identity and Desire in German Classicism, by Susan E. Gustafson, 2002